P9-CLF-756

Presidential Elections

Presidential Elections

Strategies of American Electoral Politics

FOURTH EDITION

Nelson W. Polsby

Aaron Wildavsky

CHARLES SCRIBNER'S SONS, NEW YORK

CARNEGIE LIBRARY
LIVINGSTONE COLLEGE
SALISBURY, N. C. 28144

Copyright © 1976, 1971, 1968, 1964 Aaron Wildavsky
and The Polsby Daughters' Trust

Library of Congress Cataloging in Publication Data

Polsby, Nelson W.
    Presidential elections.

    Includes index.
    1. Presidents—United States—Election.
I. Wildavsky, Aaron B., joint author. II. Title.
JK528.P63 1976   329'.00973   75-33907
ISBN 0-684-14459-X
ISBN 0-684-14458-1 (paper)

This book published simultaneously in the
United States of America and in Canada—
Copyright under the Berne Convention

All rights reserved. No part of this book
may be reproduced in any form without the
permission of Charles Scribner's Sons.

1 3 5 7 9 11 13 15 17 19 C/C 20 18 16 14 12 10 8 6 4 2
3 5 7 9 11 13 15 17 19 C/P 20 18 16 14 12 10 8 6 4 2

Printed in the United States of America

329.00973
P778

To the Memory of
Alexander Mordecai Bickel

160784

PREFACE TO THE FOURTH EDITION

The central purpose of this book is to provide what for want of a better name might be called civic education. Our notion is that people are entitled to information about the choices they make—not merely the alternatives presented, but also the processes that produce alternatives. Since, in the United States, presidential elections entail significant choices for millions of Americans and in one way or another affect nearly everyone else, it has seemed to us worthwhile to offer a discussion of the entire presidential election process that is unsentimental, nonpartisan, and explicit about how and why things happen as they do. Ideally, this should help people follow, and participate in, events in ways that make sense to them, minimize the production of false hopes, and supply an antidote to the unrealistic and cynical views of politics that tend to develop when people do not understand why things turn out contrary to their fondest desires.

We suggest that civic education has an important part to play in the chancey business of self-government. It alerts people to changes that are likely to affect their lives. Changes in the nominating process such as we describe here, changes that are not incremental but radical, may well have such effects. The probability of a prospective nominee of the party out of office commanding a majority before the convention has decreased because of rules fragmenting large state delegations, while the probability of convention delegates being unable to bargain with one another has increased because the same rules increase the numbers of delegates who are likely to be against compromise. When we described these changes to a colleague outside our field, he responded by saying that what we were discussing was the breakup of the major political parties. Perhaps; no one can tell yet. But it is now clear, at least, that the changes in the nominating process of the last few years add up to a fundamentally different rationale and role for political parties, a rationale that should be debated before the changes accumulate into an inexorable and inevitable pattern.

The question is whether our parties will remain agencies seeking office through maintaining consensus or will become organizations purely of policy advocacy. Every party must do—and does—some of each: reconcile conflicting interests and advocate policies. But how much of each? The balance has been altered in favor of advocacy to the detriment of consensus. There would be no drastic difficulty in this if it were not that the policy positions advocated by party activists tend to be popular with party activists but unpopular with most other people. Thus, the nominating process threatens to produce candidates who appeal to delegates but not to voters. This happened to the Democrats in 1972 and the Republicans in 1964. If our national parties no longer aspire to perform the integrative function of keeping the country together, what agencies will? This is the question that we must keep in mind while pondering the seeming technicalities of formulas for financing elections and of calculations for allocating delegates on the basis of votes in primaries.

We have tried not merely to catalog changes in the rules governing candidate selection, political campaign contributions, party delegate participation, voting eligibility, and the like, but in addition to organize and synthesize these into the general view of political resources and political strategies that has informed our approach to presidential elections from the beginning. As always, we are confident that our understanding of these matters is imperfect, as the unfolding of events will make only too clear. We have, however, as in earlier editions, attempted to stay abreast of political life in America and to shift our gaze toward those elements of the system that seem most important in shaping the strategies and the outcomes of politics in the 1970s, just as earlier editions attempted the same tasks for the 1960s. We only hope that what we say in this edition is sufficiently interesting so that in another edition, four years hence, it will still seem worthwhile for us to try again to come nearer to the mark.

When we wrote the first edition of *Presidential Elections*, in the early 1960s, the rules and practices of the presidential nomination and election process had not changed for thirty years. Since then, they have done nothing but change. Anyone who claims that there is no such thing as real or fundamental change in American politics need only glance at our account of what has happened—procedures for making nominating decisions, the kinds of people who are influential in making them, the characteristics of the delegates, and their basic dispositions toward politics have all undergone drastic alterations over the years.

This is not to say that Rip Van Delegate, who has been sleeping for the last thirty years, would find presidential elections totally unrecognizable. He would, and he wouldn't. For as so often happens in the history of reform, the new does not necessarily entirely displace the old but rather coexists side by side with it. The professional party stalwarts of our first edition, who wanted party unity in order to win the presidential election, are still here and active, although increasingly they are outnumbered by the amateur purists of the second and third editions, who would rather be right and remain a minority than wrong and maintain a majority. State primaries and state conventions are still around but the proportions have changed to give delegates selected in primaries a dominant voice. Money is still, as Jess Unruh once said, the mother's milk of politics, but it is now needed earlier and in different and more dispersed feedings. State caucuses and candidate organizations still matter a great deal at the conventions but so do organized caucuses of youth, women, black people, Mexican-Americans, and other demographic groups. Working people and business people are notable by their relative absence, though they survive in diminished numbers. All this explains why so much of what we say has to be qualified by saying that this is how things once were, or that our remarks apply to some actors sometimes but not to all actors most of the time or to any of them all of the time. Squaring the old with the new seems to cube the complexity.

We are happy to acknowledge that for this edition, as for its predecessors, we have been able to call on the knowledge and the goodwill of colleagues and friends who have, without necessarily sharing all our opinions, kept us from at least some mistakes that we otherwise would have made. Bruce Wallin undertook the heroic task of running down footnotes and keeping the paper flowing between us. Gerry McQueen typed our manuscript with the patience and forbearance that is the hallmark of all those who work for either of us. Her services, and much effort in duplicating and circulating our manuscript, were supplied by the Center for Advanced Study in the Behavioral Sciences, where Aaron Wildavsky was a Fellow in 1974–75. We are grateful to the center as well for its atmosphere of hospitality to scholarship.

Much of the help that Byron Shafer and Bill Cavala gave us on our last edition has stood the test of time, and their influence appears once again in these pages. In addition a number of colleagues read and commented on a draft of our manuscript. These include Joel Fleischman, Jeane Kirkpatrick, Allan P. Sindler, William Lunch, Jeffrey L. Pressman, and Austin Ranney. Since the original publication of this book, bits and pieces of information, advice, comment, and encouragement have flowed in from so many sources it is impossible for us to list them all, but we would like, in particular, to remember our good friend Richard Brody, Harvey Zeidenstein, Robert Putnam, Lawrence Longley, Tom Roback, Susan King, Herb Alexander, David Broder, Fred Wertheimer, and the other participants at the Tiburon conference on reform of campaign finance sponsored by the American Bar Association in early 1975.

This edition carries a dedication to the memory of a friend and colleague who in our view set a high standard in his devotion to the idea and practice of civic education in America. Alexander M. Bickel's sparkling presence and the developing contours of his thought about politics and the Constitution gave us stimulation and sustenance as we struggled our way through many of the problems discussed in this book. When he was carried off in November of 1974, at the tragically early age of forty-nine, amidst the unfinished business on our agenda was the hope that we could resume the conversations about the foundations of the American political system that we three began a few years ago and temporarily had set aside. Life in any civilized society is diminished without people who can speak to central problems of politics with clarity, learning, and moral force, as Alex did, and we very much desire to think that we are carrying on in the spirit of his splendid example.

Berkeley, California   N. W. P.

August 8, 1974   A. W.

CONTENTS

INTRODUCTION

Political Strategies and Presidential Elections

This book is about the winning of presidential office. Although many writers have alleged that the president occupies a great and lonely eminence, the presidential office exists within a cultural and political tradition that guides and shapes the ways in which it is won and, later, the ways in which presidential power is exercised. We will, however, not speak further here about the exercise of executive power. Rather, the task before us is to make plain the context within which the battle for presidential office is waged, to discuss the strategies of contending parties, and, if possible, to explain why some strategies are used by some contestants and other strategies by others. In this way we hope to elucidate a significant area of our common political life.

Our thesis is a simple one: the strategies of participants in a presidential election make sense once we understand the web of circumstances in which they operate. This principle applies to candidates and their managers, to delegates at nominating conventions, to party workers, and to voters. Strategies are courses of action consciously pursued toward well-understood goals. Watching strategies helps us to learn how political leaders use the constraints and opportunities of their environment to achieve their goals.

Both the political strategies of participants in presidential elections and the circumstances that give rise to them are relatively stable, persistent features of our political system. We have had a two-party political system with the same two major parties for a little over a hundred years. Presidential nominees have been picked by national party conventions for an even longer period.[1] Presidential candidates have always been faced with such problems as deciding whether more or less emphasis on their party affiliation will help them gain votes. Contemporary evidence that party preferences are not distributed evenly among the electorate helps explain, for example, why the strategy of recent Democratic candidates has been to place great stress on their party label, while Republicans have been more inclined to minimize their connection with their party.

Political strategies that persist over a period of time are reasonably easy to identify, even when they are colored by the distinctive styles and personalities of particular candidates. We hope, therefore, to achieve a level of discussion that goes beyond the special circumstances of 1976, or any other year, and say something about American presidential elections in general. This task is not made easier by the undeniable fact that the rules of the game themselves have undergone changes over time; but it has not been made impossible either. Our intention is to show how changes in the rules affect changes in the way politicians behave in presidential election politics. In fact, the very rapidity with which the rules have recently changed makes clearer than ever the importance politicians ascribe to them. Their disagreements over the rules reveal that real differences in outcomes are at stake when the game is played by one set of rules or another.

In large measure, a description and analysis such as ours is possible because of the efforts of dozens of scholars who have reported upon and investigated, with ever increasing detail and accuracy, the component parts of the American political system. The purpose of this book is to synthesize these reports for the enlightenment and use of interested citizens. But we cannot forecast the outcome of any particular election, and we have no desire (at least, not here) to advise people how to vote.

In the first two chapters we identify characteristics of the American political system that make up the strategic environment within which the pursuit of the presidency takes place. The would-be president must come to terms with voters, who enter each election period as complex bundles of already formed habits, attitudes, and loyalties. The ways in which interest groups and parties activate these habits are largely out of the hands of any single participant in the process. Another element, the rules by which votes are counted, is also beyond any participant's control. In the second chapter, we discuss the comparative availability to candidates of certain key resources, such as money and control over information.

These two chapters lay out a framework for much that follows in the third, fourth, and fifth chapters. These deal, successively, with the various steps of the nomination and election processes. At this point in the book, we discuss a variety of classic strategic "moves," such as entering or not entering primaries, the manipulation of interpretations of primary results, the starting and stopping of bandwagons at national party conventions, the selection of areas of the country in which to campaign, and the choice of issues to emphasize. In Chapters 3, 4, and 5, we try to relate those moves to their necessary preconditions in terms of resources and also to relate them to their probable consequences.

In the sixth chapter, we discuss significant reforms that have altered the strategic framework of presidential elections—as well as proposals for reform that would in some respects reconstitute the party system and redistribute resources among contestants for the presidency. Reforms and reform proposals are often debated rather abstractly on their presumed merits, without being related to any concrete consequences. We hope to provoke fresh insight into the subject by looking at these reforms in the light of the new distribution of benefits and handicaps which we believe they allocate to various participants in presidential elections.

Finally, in Chapter 7, we attempt to state in general terms the properties of political parties as they are beginning to emerge in the framework provided by contemporary presidential elections. In particular we juxtapose the emerging parties of advocacy with the persisting fact that in our system public officials receive few specific and meaningful policy directives from the electorate. We try to show that while our political system discourages both strict application of majority rule and mandates on specific policies, it is still meaningful to speak of our form of government as democratic, open, and responsive—as well as flexible, tough, stable, and resourceful.

Whether these qualities will persist, however, depends on the maintenance of major political parties that will continue to reconcile divergent interests. The capacity of parties to mediate between citizen and government and among sectors of society is now under severe strain. Government by party consensus is giving way to government by partisan advocacy. Purists are replacing politicians in the presidential nominating process. The final chapter calls attention to this trend and asks what the gains and costs are of moving in this direction.

Presidential elections are important to us as citizens. They constitute a major (though, of course, not the only) means of guiding our future. They also remind us of our heritage of political responsibility and freedom, a heritage that in a troubled world seems to us increasingly precious.

Note

1. See Paul T. David, Ralph M. Goldman, and Richard C. Bain, *The Politics of National Party Conventions* (New York, 1964), for a lengthy treatment of the history of the national party conventions. For further information, including accounts of more recent conventions, see Herbert Eaton, *Presidential Timber: A History of Nominating Conventions, 1868–1960* (Glencoe, Ill., 1964); Gerald Pomper, *Nominating the President* (New York, 1966); James W. Davis, *Springboard to the White House: Presidential Primaries; How They Are Fought and Won* (New York, 1967); Richard C. Bain and Judith H. Parris, *Convention Decisions and Voting Records* (Washington, D.C., 1973); and Dennis G. Sullivan, Jeffrey L. Pressman, Benjamin I. Page, and John J. Lyons, *The Politics of Representation: The Democratic Convention, 1972* (New York, 1974).

Presidential
Elections

CHAPTER ONE

The Strategic Environment: Participants

All political strategies are worked out within a framework of circumstances which are in part subject to manipulation but to even a greater degree are "given." Needless to say, this fact of life also applies to the strategies of aspirants to the presidency, who must construct extremely complex plans of action within a context of hundreds of relevant circumstances, most of which lie beyond their control. Some of these circumstances are contingent and relate to the strategies being pursued by other active participants in the election process and to the resources at their command. Other circumstances are more stable and have to do with features of the American political system that are in place before the contest starts. These features provide advantages and handicaps differently to Democrats and Republicans, to incumbent presidents and challengers, to household names and newcomers. In this chapter and the next, we shall deal with these "givens" of the political system to show how they shape the decisions of presidential election strategists.

Voters

Precisely what part does the voter play in American politics? This depends entirely on his interest and activity. Most people, however, are not interested in most public issues most of the time.[1] In a society like ours, it is apparently quite possible to live comfortably without being politically concerned. Political activity is costly. It eats up time and energy at an astounding rate. To be informed on strategic problems in nuclear politics or on the operations of a municipal electric plant is not a matter of a few moments of reflection; many hours must be spent. One must ordinarily attend meetings, listen to or participate in discussion, write letters, attempt to persuade or be persuaded by others, and engage in other time-consuming labor. This means foregoing other activities, like devoting extra time to the job, playing with the children, and watching TV. So far as we can tell it is these other activities rather than public affairs that are the primary concerns of most people, and the costs of participation in public affairs appear, for most people, to be greater than the returns. Only a few people receive financial rewards or hold jobs or are acclaimed in the public arena—considerations that might lead them to devote the time and effort required to participate. It is only in regard to a few issues, such as prolonged unemployment or rapid inflation, that most citizens find it worthwhile to attend to politics rather than do other things.

Even so, there are a few people who are continuously interested in a wide variety of issues. These are usually public officials, interest group leaders, newspaper editors, and academics—all people whose occupations require political interest. There is a larger number who have specialized interests in specific policy areas. These may include public officials, officers and members of civic organizations and interest groups, citizens who are directly affected, and a sprinkling of others who make a hobby of being interested, including seekers after causes and people who like to get their names on letterheads. These political activists, who may or may not themselves be leaders, are different from ordinary voters, as we shall see.

The fact that individuals do vary enormously in their degree of interest has profound implications for political life. For ordinary citizens, interest is a necessary condition of influence. The interested tend to go to meetings where public affairs are discussed and decided. They tend to belong to political parties and to work in various ways to help the party of their choice. They cultivate their access to public officials. They tend to care more about the outcomes of public policies and to communicate their concerns to decision-makers. And so they become more influential.

Differences in interest also influence voting behavior: people who are interested in politics tend to vote and those who are uninterested tend not to vote.[2] Who are included in these two groups? In general, the better-educated people are more active and interested in public affairs. They also tend to be better off financially.[3] This is, of course, also the population from which the Republican party draws dispro-portionate support, which consequently gives a substantial advan-tage to that party among voters who tend to turn out most reliably for presidential elections. On the other hand, the low-turnout groups (normally Democratic) tend to be numerically greater than the high-turnout groups. Furthermore, traditionally Democratic groups may be clustered in a way that maximizes their strength in presidential elections by being located in areas that are favored by the Electoral College system of vote-counting. We shall return to this topic later.

How do voters make up their minds whom to support? By far the majority of people vote according to their habitual party affiliation.[4] In other words, most people will have made up their minds how to vote in 1976 before the candidates are chosen because they always support a particular party. These party regulars are likely to be more interested and active in politics and have more political knowledge than the "independents." [5] But they rarely change their minds. They tend to listen to their own side of political arguments and to agree with the policies espoused by their party. They even go so far as to ignore information which they perceive to be unfavorable to the party of their choice.[6]

If party is so important in giving a structure to a voter's picture of reality and in helping him choose a presidential candidate to vote for before the candidate is even nominated, we had best inquire where people get their party affiliations. There seems to be no simple answer to this. The party affiliations of most voters seem to be governed by a number of forces. An individual lives in a social context and inherits a social identity from his parents that contains a political component. People are Democrats or Republicans, in part, because their families and the other people with whom they interact are Democrats or Republicans.[7] Most individuals come into close contact only with people who are predominantly one or the other.[8] And just as people tend to share characteristics with their friends and families such as income and educational level, religious affiliation, area of residence, and so on, so they also tend to share party loyalties with them.[9]

Of course, we all know of instances when people do not share various status-giving characteristics with their parents and at least some of their friends, and so it should come as no surprise that sometimes children do not share the politics of their parents. In fact, political differences tend to run together with the other kinds of differences as well. But, by and large, voters retain the party loyalties of the primary groups of which they are a part.

The result of this process is to give each of the major political parties reservoirs of voting strength they can count on from year to year. Republicans traditionally do well in the small towns and rural areas of New England, the Middle Atlantic states, and the Middle West. They draw their support from people who are richer and better educated, occupy managerial or professional positions or run small businesses, tend to live in or to move into the well-to-do suburban areas, and are predominantly Protestant. Democrats draw great support from the large cities outside of the South. Wage earners, union members, Catholics, black voters, and many of the descendants of the great waves of immigrants who entered this country in the latter half of the nineteenth century—Jews, Irish, Polish people—all contribute disproportionately to the Democratic vote.[10]

One may ask, How did these particular groups come to have these particular loyalties? We must turn to history to find answers to this question. Enough is known about a few groups to make it possible to speculate about what kinds of historical events tend to align groups with a political party.

Let us take a few examples. We all know about the "Solid South," which from the Civil War until the era of George Wallace and Barry Goldwater was predominantly Democratic in its presidential voting. For all those years, resentment against the harsh Reconstruction period under the leadership of the Republican party was reflected in the election returns. Less well known is the fact that the South was not unanimous in its enthusiasm for the Civil War or in its resentment of Reconstruction. In many states of the Old South, there were two kinds of farms: plantations on the flat land that grew cash crops, used slaves, and, in general, before the Civil War, prospered; and subsistence farms in the uplands that had a few or no slaves and, in general, were run by poorer white people. This latter group formed the historical core of mountain areas that year after year, well into the latter half of the twentieth century, voted Republican in presidential elections in western Virginia and North Carolina, eastern Tennessee and Kentucky, and southeastern West Virginia.[11]

The voting habits of black citizens, where they have voted, have been shaped by several traumas. The Civil War freed them and made them Republicans. The Counter-Reconstruction disenfranchised them, and the industrial revolution brought them North, where a crushing burden of economic destitution was added to racial discrimination. The differing effects of the Great Depression of 1929 on black voters in the North brought them into the New Deal coalition, and the northern black voter has remained Democratic ever since.[12] And, as black voters have observed Democratic politicians espousing causes in which they believe, they have increased their already high levels of support.

If, for some people, the historical events of the Civil War and the depression shaped their political heritage, for others the critical forces seem less dramatic and more diffuse. It is possible perhaps to see why the poor become Democrats, since the Democratic party has in recent years been so welfare-minded; but why do the rich lean toward the Republicans? Perhaps, in part, this is a reaction to the redistributive aspirations of some New Deal programs and the inclination of Democratic presidents to expand the role of government in the economy. But in all probability it is also a response to the record of the congressional wing of the Republican party which so thoroughly dominated the post–Civil War era of industrial expansion. In this era, Republican policies vigorously encouraged risk-taking by private businessmen, granted them federal aid in a variety of forms, and withheld federal regulation from private enterprise.

Sometimes party affiliation coincides with ethnic identification because of the political and social circumstances surrounding the entry of ethnic groups into the country. In southern New England, politics was dominated by the Republican party and by "Yankees" of substance and high status during the decades following the Civil War. During these decades, thousands of Irish people streamed into this area. The Democratic party welcomed them; the Republicans

Vote by Groups in Presidential Elections since 1952

	1952 (percent)		1956 (percent)		1960 (percent)		1964 (percent)		1968 (percent)			1972 (percent)	
	Stev.	Ike	Stev.	Ike	JFK	Nixon	LBJ	Gold.	HHH	Nixon	Wallace	McG.	Nixon
	44.6	55.4	42.2	57.8	50.1	49.9	61.3	38.7	43.0	43.4	13.6	38	62
NATIONAL													
SEX													
Men	47	53	45	55	52	48	60	40	41	43	16	37	63
Women	42	58	39	61	49	51	62	38	45	43	12	38	62
RACE													
White	43	57	41	59	49	51	59	41	38	47	15	32	68
Non-White	79	21	61	39	68	32	94	6	85	12	3	87	13
EDUCATION													
College	34	66	31	69	39	61	52	48	37	54	9	37	63
High School	45	55	42	58	52	48	62	38	42	43	15	34	66
Grade School	52	48	50	50	55	45	66	34	52	33	15	49	51
OCCUPATION													
Professional and Business	36	64	32	68	42	58	54	46	34	56	10	31	69
White Collar	40	60	37	63	48	52	57	43	41	47	12	36	64
Manual	55	45	50	50	60	40	71	29	50	35	15	43	57
Members of Labor Union Families	61	39	57	43	65	35	73	27	56	29	15	46	54
AGE													
Under 30 years	51	49	43	57	54	46	64	36	47	38	15	48	52
30–49 years	47	53	45	55	54	46	63	37	44	41	15	33	67
50 years and older	39	61	39	61	46	54	59	41	41	47	12	36	64

RELIGION													
Protestants	37	63	37	63	38	62	55	45	35	49	16	30	70
Catholics	56	44	51	49	78	22	76	24	59	33	8	48	52
POLITICS													
Republicans	8	92	4	96	5	95	20	80	9	86	5	5	95
Democrats	77	23	85	15	84	16	87	13	74	12	14	67	33
Independents	35	65	30	70	43	57	56	44	31	44	25	31	69
REGION													
East	45	55	40	60	53	47	68	32	50	43	7	42	58
Midwest	42	58	41	59	48	52	61	39	44	47	9	40	60
South	51	49	49	51	51	49	52	48	31	36	33	29	71
West	42	58	43	57	49	51	60	40	44	49	7	41	59

SOURCE: *Gallup Monthly Opinion Index*, May 1975.

7

did not. Soon the Democratic percentage of the two-party vote began to increase, and Irish politicians took over the Democratic party.[13]

In the Middle West, events such as American involvement in two wars against Germany under Democratic auspices seem to have shaped the political preferences of Americans of German descent.[14]

Specific candidates of special attractiveness—or unattractiveness—may under certain circumstances sway voters to leave the party of their choice. The extraordinary elections of President Eisenhower are one example of this. His appeal to Democrats was quite amazing. But this was possible partially because these Democrats did not perceive President Eisenhower as a partisan figure, and so it is not surprising that his personal popularity did not greatly aid other Republicans who ran with him, or the Republican party, once he no longer headed the ticket. The candidacy of George McGovern had the opposite effect; it propelled Democrats out of their party.[15]

Most of the time issues have much the same sporadic and peripheral effect as candidates. Let us see why. We can say to begin with that at least three preconditions must be satisfied for a voter's opinion about an issue to change his vote.[16] First, a voter must know about the issue; second, he must care about it at least a little; and third, he must be able to distinguish the positions of the parties and their candidates on the issue. Data from public opinion polls tell us that most people are not well informed about the content of issues most of the time.[17] All but major public issues are thus eliminated for most people. And even these major issues may enter the consciousness of most people in only the most rudimentary way.

It makes a difference whether a person has a weak preference on an issue or breathes fire when the subject is mentioned. The number who care, even a little, is substantially less than those who know about issues, although caring is often a prerequisite of knowledge rather than the other way around.

Once a voter has some grasp of the content of a public policy and learns to prefer one outcome rather than another, he must also find public leaders to espouse his point of view. Finding differences on policy issues between parties is not always easy. Party statements on policy may be vague because leaders have not decided what to do. They may deliberately obfuscate an issue for fear of alienating interested publics. They may try to hold divergent factions in their parties together by glossing over, as best they can, disagreements on many specific issues. Even when real party differences on policy exist, many voters may not be aware of them. The subject may be rather esoteric to the common understanding, or the time required to master the subject may be more than most people are willing to spend. By the time we get down to those who know and care and can discriminate between party positions on issues, we usually have a small proportion of the electorate, rarely larger than 30 percent.[18] What can we say about these people?

Their most obvious characteristic is interest in and concern about issues and party positions. But these are precisely the people who are most likely to be strong party identifiers, men and women who are characterized by a deep devotion to party, which makes it most unlikely that they will shift allegiance just because of a disagreement on one or two issues.[19] The number of issue-oriented "independents" who are left must be very small. And it is not unlikely that these people are distributed about equally on both sides of major policy questions so that the total number of votes changed by the impact of any specific issue is bound to be minute.

We still have some preconditions to satisfy, however, before even these changes can be accepted as certain. One is that there must not be other issues that are also highly salient to voters and that work the other way. For if voters were willing to change their votes on one particular issue, why should they not switch their support back because of another? There are usually many issues in a campaign; only if all or most of the issues pointed voters in the same direction would they be likely to switch their votes. But what is the likelihood that parties will arrange their policies along a broad front, forcing large numbers of "independent" voters from or into the fold? It is low—but not impossible. In 1964 the Republicans may have done so. And in 1972 the Democratic candidate, George McGovern, "was perceived as so far left on issue after issue that Nixon was closer to the total electorate issue position across 11 out of 14 separate issues." Republican candidate Nixon was not only far closer to his own party and to independents but slightly closer to Democratic voters than was his opponent.[20]

Although it is true that the less knowledge a person has about public affairs, the more likely he is to vote for a candidate of the opposite party, it is important to distinguish between those who only have a little knowledge and those who have none at all. For the voter utterly without any contact with the political world, except at the polls, has no reason whatsoever to change his customary party vote. Thus changes in vote from one party to another are likely to be concentrated among those who receive a little but not a great deal of information about parties, issues, and candidates.[21]

Recent studies have penetrated more thoroughly into the problem of issue voting. One seeks to demonstrate that there is considerable issue content in the citizen's behavior at the polls by showing that those who change party from one election to the next are generally sympathetic to some key policies of their new party. The standpatters, on the other hand, generally are in sympathy with major policies of their party.[22] Whether the citizen is taught what to believe by his party or finds a party in accordance with his beliefs cannot be determined from evidence presently available.

We can now see that a strong issue orientation is likely to guide voting decisions under some circumstances. One set of circumstances occurs when an issue becomes so intensely important that the voter is willing to lay aside his party preferences and his preferences on other issues. An unpopular war, severe economic deprivation (whether or not it is related to governmental policies), a fixation on a subject like keeping water free of fluoride, have at times led to the required intense feeling. The pocketbook nerve seems especially sensitive.[23] Another possibility occurs when a party is seen to change across the spectrum of policies, as the Democrats appeared to do in 1972, or when the voter himself undergoes such a broad-scale change of heart. Finally, in a historical sense we can say that issues may have a lasting impact on voting behavior through the ways in which they shape the party affiliations of whole generations of voters. But if parties and their leaders make the issues and give them meaning for most people, then fundamental changes in party allegiance among large numbers of people are not likely to arise from their own reasoned look at issues. A depression, a civil war, events felt immediately and personally by millions, have precipitated the great changes in party allegiances, not debates on the merits of this or that comparatively minor matter. The sheer, brute impact of great events does more to change votes over the long run than any single policy problem.

This picture of the relation between voters and issues is somewhat unreal in any case. For as far as we are able to tell, voters adopt most of their issue orientations at the instigation of the parties: strong party identifiers are more likely to learn more about issues and to care more about them, in part, precisely because it reinforces their party identification.[24] This means that there are few issues that are not made by parties and political leaders, and hence few party identifiers are lost as a result of the policies adopted by the party of their choice.

The complex relationship between issues and electoral outcomes was illustrated by two issues in the 1968 election: the war in Vietnam and what was delicately called the "social issue"—racial conflict, crime, and law and order. Both issues had enormous public exposure and excited the passions of the politically aware. Yet the most sensitive and sophisticated analysis we have of these issues and their relation to public opinion shows that party identification had "fifty times the net impact of the Vietnam issue" [25] in determining the relative favorability of voters toward presidential candidates Nixon and Humphrey. Party was so powerful that it cannot be considered on the same scale with other forces. The figure, which summarizes the impact of various issues on the 1968 presidential vote, shows that domestic policy issues (the bread-and-butter matters of social welfare, employment, and prosperity) were considerably more important than the Vietnam and social issues combined. Like other Democrats before him, Humphrey gained on domestic policy because voters saw themselves as closer to him than to his Republican opponent. Richard Nixon gained on the foreign policy side because of the Democratic image as the party of war.

Why was the Vietnam issue so unimportant? Most voters found Senators Robert Kennedy and Eugene McCarthy too "dovish" for their taste and Governor George Wallace much too "hawkish." The candidates of the major parties were rather close to the voters' preferences, with Nixon coming in a little ahead. It is difficult for an issue to have a major impact on an election outcome when the voters do not differentiate greatly among the candidates with respect to that issue. So, once again, we come back to party as the great organizer of voters' ideas and sentiments.

When voters perceive a vast chasm separating them from one of the candidates, as they did with George McGovern in 1972, the importance of issues relative to party is bound to grow. The research group at the Michigan Center for Political Studies (successor organization to the Survey Research Center) estimates that in 1972, party identification and issue differences each accounted for approx-

Domestic Policy More Important Than Vietnam and Urban Issues
Combined: Issue Forces and the Presidential Vote, 1968

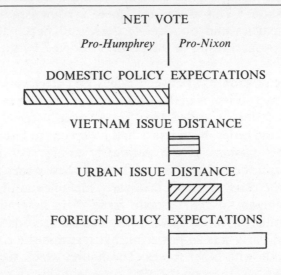

NET VOTE

Pro-Humphrey | *Pro-Nixon*

DOMESTIC POLICY EXPECTATIONS

VIETNAM ISSUE DISTANCE

URBAN ISSUE DISTANCE

FOREIGN POLICY EXPECTATIONS

SOURCE: Richard A. Brody, Benjamin I. Page, et al., "Vietnam, the Urban Crisis and the 1968 Presidential Election: A Preliminary Analysis," prepared for delivery at the 1969 meeting of the American Sociological Association, September 1969.

imately one-third of the total vote. This was an election in which Nixon received almost all (94 percent) Republican votes, two-thirds of independents' votes (66 percent), and nearly half (42 percent) the votes of people calling themselves Democrats. This was a better showing among Democrats than Dwight D. Eisenhower managed in his landslide year of 1956, when he got 28 percent of the Democratic vote. Why did this happen? Because "McGovern was seen as quite distant from the population's policy preferences and Nixon was relatively much closer to the issue positions preferred by Americans on the average." The Michigan group concludes that "a candidate such as McGovern who may represent only one segment of the national policy preference spectrum may capture control of a political party that shares his preferences but cannot go on to win an electoral victory under contemporary conditions of polarization." [26] This suggests that if most voters disagree with a candidate, and know they disagree with him, they are likely to vote against him.

Merely to list the functions that party identification performs for the voter—reducing his costs of acquiring political information, telling him what side he is on, organizing his information, ordering his preferences, letting him know what is of prime importance—is to suggest the profound significance of parties for voting behavior. Politics is amazingly complex; there are scores of possible issues, a myriad of relevant political personalities, and often many choices to be made on Election Day. The voter who follows his party identification, however, can vastly simplify the choices he must make and thus reduce to manageable proportions the amount of time he spends on public affairs. He need only follow his party's nomination to arrive at a voting decision. When issues arise, the voter with strong party identification need not puzzle over each and every one. He can, instead, listen to the pronouncements of his party leaders who inform him what issues are important, what information is most relevant to those issues, and what position he ought to take. Of course, the citizen with greater interest in public affairs will want to investigate matters for himself. Even so, his party identification provides him with important guides for the many matters on which he cannot possibly be well informed. Indeed, all of us, including full-time participants like the president, have to find ways to cut information costs on some issues.[27] For most people who vote, most of the time, identification with one of the two major political parties performs that indispensable function. And, despite growing criticism of parties, they will continue to perform that function unless and until organizations arise to take their place.

Interest Groups and Voting Blocs

Interest groups are collections of people who are similarly situated with respect to one or more policies of government and who organize to do something about it. The interest groups most significant for elections in our society are those having the following characteristics:

1. They have a mass base, that is, are composed of many members.
2. They are concentrated geographically, rather than dispersed thinly over the entire map.
3. They represent major resource investments of members—such as in the case of the *producers* of bicycles, whose entire livelihoods are tied up in the group involved, as against the *consumers* of bicycles, for whom investment in a bicycle is not anywhere near as important.

4. They involve those characteristics of people that give them status in society—such as their race or ethnicity.

5. Finally, and this is a new characteristic of effectiveness in interest groups, resulting from recent changes in the rules of presidential election politics, an effective interest group is composed of people who are able to participate actively in politics; that is, of people who have time and money to spare.

Interest groups may be more or less organized and more or less vigilant and alert on policy matters that concern, or ought to concern, them. They are not necessarily organized in ways that make them politically effective; very often the paid lobbyists of interest groups spend more time trying unsuccessfully to alert their own members to the implications of government policies than they spend lobbying with politicians.[28]

In American politics, interest group activity is lively and ubiquitous, even when it is not particularly effective or meaningful in terms of policy outcomes. We shall be concerned with interest groups in three ways. First, we must recognize that membership in these groups may be quite important in giving voters a sense of affiliation and political position. In this respect, interest groups act much the way parties do, helping to fill in the voter's map of the world with preferences, priorities, and facts.

Second, interest groups are important because of their partisan political activities; they may actively recruit supporters for candidates and aid materially in campaigns. Third, interest groups may influence party policy by making demands with respect to issues in return for their own mobilized support. The extent to which interest groups can "deliver" the votes of their members, however, is always problematic; to a great extent interest group leaders are the prisoners of past alliances their group has made. Even so, the black vote, the farm vote, the labor vote, the youth vote, the consumer vote, and many other "votes" are bandied about as though they were political commodities that can be manipulated easily in behalf of one or another candidate for public office. While the use of election statistics and opinion polls was in its infancy, claims to guarantee support or threats to withdraw it could be accepted or rejected on intuitive grounds and no person could claim much greater competence than another. The appearance of voting studies and the development of the arts of statistical manipulation have created new opportunities for the purveyors of bloc votes and new difficulties for the interested but necessarily amateur citizen and public official. How are they to evaluate these important political claims backed up by impressive and complicated arrays of data?

The usual argument is that if one or another candidate captures the allegiance of a particular bloc, that bloc's pivotal position in a state or large population will enable the fortunate aspirant to capture all of the electoral votes and thus win the election. It is incorrect to speak of any one combination of states totaling more than a majority of electoral votes as in any sense more critical, valuable, or pivotal than any other such combination. In a fairly close election the defection of any number of combinations of states to the other side would spell the difference between victory and defeat.

An important point to remember is that appeals to various groups arc necessarily conditioned by time, place, and circumstance. There is little doubt that under *some* conditions during *some* elections *some* social characteristics of voters and candidates may have *some* relevance to the polling results. Finding the conditions under which specified social characteristics become relevant to voter choice is most difficult. We know that in a competitive political system various participants (parties, interest groups, leaders) put forward candidates and issues designed to capture the allegiance of various groups of people. Rarely is it possible to appeal to one group and one group alone, not only because there are so many different groups, with all sorts of conceptions of policy, but also because each individual may have many social characteristics that are potentially relevant to his voting decision. While some people may be so single-minded that they have only one interest that is important in determining their vote—color, religion, ethnic background, income —most of us have multiple interests which sometimes conflict. Ecological interest groups, for example, may have less success in 1976, if environmental concerns conflict with employment, than they did when jobs were of less concern. And the concern with unemployment may mitigate the feelings of some voters about governmental support of people who are not working. Much depends on the movement of events which may bring one or another interest to the forefront of the voter's consciousness and incline him toward the candidate he believes best represents his preferences on that matter.[29] For voters in many categories, the more directly pecuniary appeals which may have been relevant at the turn of the century slowly lost their effectiveness in the 1960s and gave way to a period when more symbolic issues or matters of national economic and foreign policy assumed primary importance. Today, in the mid-1970s, the enormous increase in governmental transfer payments in money, like Social Security, and in goods, like food stamps, may lead recipients and providers alike to see a close cash connection between public policy and their individual welfare. Long-term social trends, as well as the strategies of candidates, have much to do with the impact of appeals to bloc votes.

In each election members of the various groups that make up the American voting population turn out to vote, dividing their loyalties in varying ways between the major parties. To determine the contribution that a particular group makes to a party, it is necessary to know three things: how big the group is, how many of its members actually vote, and how devoted they are to one party or another.

For example, let us look at the contribution of poor people—defined as those whose incomes are $3,000 a year or less—to the Democratic party. Basing his analysis on Survey Research Center polls, Robert Axelrod has shown that the contribution of the poor to the total Democratic vote has fallen from 28 percent in 1952 to only 10 percent in 1972.[30] This trend can be accounted for in any—or all—of three ways: (1) more of the non-poor are voting Democratic these days, diluting the contribution of the poor; (2) fewer poor people are voting Democratic these days; (3) there are simply fewer poor people, by the standard definition, and this dilutes their vote. This last is certainly true: in 1952, poor people made up 35 percent of the U.S. adult population; the proportion defined by the standard measure as poor had sunk to 16 percent in 1969 and 12 percent in 1972, partly (but not entirely) because of inflation.

While the poor have not been an important part of the Democratic coalition in recent years, black people have established themselves as a substantial component. "Their contribution has grown substantially from 5% to 7% in 1952–1960 to 12% in 1964, and 19% in 1968." In 1972 the percentage rose again, to 22 percent. Since the black population has remained a relatively constant 11 percent of the total population, their vastly increased contribution is the result of a near doubling of their turnout throughout the nation and of their high loyalty to the Democratic party.

While union members and their families made up a third of all Democratic votes in the 1950s, their contribution fell slightly to 28 percent in 1968 and rose again to 32 percent in 1972. They are important to the party because a quarter of all adults are in union families, their turnout is reasonably good, and they vote more Democratic than other people. Although less than half of union members voted Democratic in 1972, the overall defection among other Democrats was so great that union members still voted 8 percent more Democratic than others. Whereas union families contributed four times as many votes as black people to the Democratic party in 1960, unionists contributed only one and a half times as many Democratic votes as black voters in 1968 and 1972.

Although Catholics are just a quarter of the population, they still provide a third of all Democratic votes. In 1952 and 1956, southerners still voted about 10 percent more Democratic than voters in the rest of the country, but in recent elections they have been slightly more Republican than other people. They gave a quarter of their votes to the third-party movement of George Wallace in 1968. Black southerners stayed with the Democrats, but white southerners split their presidential vote among all three parties.

The major change (and perhaps the only positive one from the Democratic point of view) has been the increase in the votes of young people, that is, those under thirty years of age. Until 1972, they were not part of any party coalition and their low turnout reduced any impact that their 18 percent of the population might have had. Now things may be different. Because the voting age has been lowered to eighteen and because of the baby boom after the Second World War, their proportion of the population has increased to 28 percent, more than half again what it was a few years ago. Their turnout in 1972 was only 9 percent less than the overall average compared to 15 percent less in 1968. Their loyalty to the Democratic party, moreover, never exceeding 3 percent since 1952, had increased fourfold to 12 percent in 1972.[31] Whether youth was so important to the Democrats in 1972 mainly because older citizens deserted George McGovern's candidacy in droves or whether age will emerge as a permanent divider of the parties remains to be seen.

The Republican coalition appears to be as follows: white people who comprise approximately 90 percent of the U.S. population vote anywhere from 3 to 5 percent more Republican than Democratic. The comparatively small size of the black population means that even in 1960, when Nixon got about a quarter of the black vote, 97 percent of his total came from whites; 99 percent of his vote came from whites in 1968, 98 percent in 1972. If one can conceive of nonunion families and Protestants as "groups" in the usual sense, they make up about 75 percent of the population and vote 3 percent more Republican than the nation as a whole. The Republican party gets its vote, then, from white people, nonunion members, and Protestants outside the central cities.

We can also say a word about the coalition that in 1968 supported George Wallace. The only "group" in the country that gave him substantially more support than his 14 percent national total was the South, including the border states, which provided 28 percent of his votes. The poor, youth, and union families gave him on the average a few more percentage points than he got from the nation as a whole.

As the table on pp. 20–21 indicates, *turnout* varies enormously among different groups in the population, rising with income, occupational status, education, and, in general, with age. Since Republicans are disproportionately located in the high-turnout groups and Democrats in the low, this tends to give Republicans electoral advantages that in some measure—varying from election to election—make up for the preponderance of Democrats in the potential electorate.

It is possible, then, to analyze party coalitions in terms of the group memberships of the people who vote regularly for one party or another. Likewise, it is possible to consider the differential impact of different candidates on these various groups.

The picture of voters and interest groups we have drawn thus far can be generalized. Presidential elections and election campaigns are events that activate the personal loyalties of voters. The amount of new information about candidates or issues that citizens ordinarily need in order to participate at the minimal level of voting, or in order to hold casual conversations about the election, is slight, because the political component of their personal identities is reasonably stable and familiar to them. So long as their main reference groups do not swiftly shift their stance, party loyalty and membership in interest groups provides a shortcut to voter preferences and minimizes the costs of getting information about the specifics of the issues and candidates in any particular election year.

Interest groups act as intermediary agencies that help voters to identify their political preferences quickly—by actively soliciting their members' interest in behalf of specific candidates and parties and, more importantly, by providing still another anchor to the voter's identity. This helps the voter fix his own position quickly and economically in what otherwise would be a confusing and contradictory political environment.

Although interest groups in the past have differed with one another over policy, they have not (at least since the acceptance of industrial unions in the 1930s) denied the rights of opponents to advocate their policy preferences. But, in one significant respect, that is no longer true. The rising "public interest" lobbies such as Common Cause have attacked the legitimacy of "private interest" groups. If we think of intermediary organizations as those that stand between citizens and their government—political parties, labor unions, trade associations, that is, "special interest" groups—then the essential mission of the so-called public interest groups is to reduce the power of private interests that attempt to mediate between the people and their government. In pursuit of this aim, laws have been passed and consitutional amendments proposed that restrict the amounts of money unions and corporations can contribute to campaigns and use in lobbying. At another level, public interest lobbies have sought to weaken the power of party leaders and strong party identifiers as compared with citizens who are weakly identified with parties and who emerge during a particular election campaign or in response to a fashionable issue. The stress on internal party democracy—more primaries, more conferences, more frequent and more open elections to party bodies—leads, given the self-appointing definition of membership, to party domination by activists who have time and training and are able to take the trouble to go to meetings.

What kinds of people evidence these characteristics? Among others, the middle- and upper-middle-class professionals who predominate in supporting Common Cause, Nader's Raiders, and other public interest lobbies. Thus, among interest groups, if money matters less as a resource, business matters less; if time and talk matter more, ordinary workers matter less. As leaders of labor, business, and the parties lose power, organizers of public interest lobbies gain.

Parties

A third aspect of the social framework that will help us to account for the strategies of participants in presidential elections is the nature of political parties in this country. These can best be defined as

Participation in National Elections, by Population Characteristics: 1968 and 1972

Persons in thousands. As of November. Covers civilian noninstitutional population. For 1968, persons 18 years old and over in Georgia and Kentucky, 19 and over in Alaska, 20 and over in Hawaii, and 21 and over elsewhere; for 1972, persons 18 years old and over in all states. Includes aliens. Figures are based on a population sample. Differences in percentages may also be due to overreporting of voting by persons in the sample. Excludes persons who did not report whether or not they had voted.

Characteristic	1968				1972			
	Persons of voting age	Persons reporting they voted		Percent reporting they did not vote	Persons of voting age	Persons reporting they voted		Percent reporting they did not vote
		Total	Percent			Total	Percent	
Total	116,535	78,964	67.8	30.0	136,203	85,766	63.0	37.0
Male	54,464	38,014	69.8	27.6	63,833	40,908	64.1	35.9
Female	62,071	40,951	66.0	32.1	72,370	44,858	62.0	38.0
White	104,521	72,213	69.1	28.9	121,243	78,166	64.5	35.5
Negro	10,935	6,300	57.6	38.5	13,493	7,032	52.1	47.9
18–20 years old	432	144	33.3	64.1	11,022	5,318	48.3	51.7
21–24 years old	11,170	5,707	51.1	45.6	13,590	6,896	50.7	49.3
25–34 years old	23,198	14,501	62.5	35.8	26,933	16,072	59.7	40.3
35–44 years old	22,905	16,223	70.8	27.1	22,240	14,747	66.3	33.7
45–64 years old	40,362	30,238	74.9	22.8	42,344	29,991	70.8	29.2
65 years and over	18,468	12,150	65.8	31.9	20,074	12,741	63.5	36.5
Median age (years)	45.2	46.7	(x)	(x)	42.4	44.9	(x)	(x)
Metropolitan residence	75,756	51,503	68.0	32.0	99,248	63,799	64.3	35.7
Nonmetropolitan residence	40,778	27,461	67.3	32.7	36,855	21,967	59.4	40.6
North and West residence	81,594	57,970	71.0	29.0	93,653	62,193	66.4	33.6
South residence	34,941	20,994	60.1	39.9	42,550	23,573	55.4	44.6

Years of school completed:

8 years or less	30,430	16,592	54.4	45.5	28,065	13,311	47.4	52.6
9–11 years	20,429	12,519	61.3	38.7	22,277	11,587	52.0	48.0
12 years	39,704	28,768	72.5	27.5	50,749	33,193	65.4	34.6
More than 12 years	25,971	21,086	81.2	18.8	35,113	27,675	78.8	21.2
Employed	70,002	49,772	71.1	28.9	80,164	52,899	66.0	34.0
Unemployed	1,875	977	52.1	47.9	3,735	1,863	49.9	50.1
Not in labor force	44,657	28,215	63.2	36.8	52,305	31,004	59.3	40.7

x Not applicable.
SOURCE: U.S. Bureau of the Census, *Current Population Reports*, series P-20, Nos. 192 and 253. From *Statistical Abstract*, 1974, p. 437.

organizations devoted to maintaining or increasing their own opportunities to exercise political power.

By "political power" we mean the ability to make decisions or to influence decision-making by governments. Instrumental to this goal is access to those offices and officials legally entitled to make such decisions.[32] Access, in turn, depends in part upon one's participation in staffing the government, either by selecting officials to fill appointive offices (patronage) or by significantly influencing the nomination and election of elected officials. Since elected officials are usually empowered to select appointed officials, access to them is often instrumental to the dispensation of patronage. There are, of course, numerous ways of gaining access to public officials, but their original selection is the primary avenue of access used by political parties.[33]

An additional goal that political parties may from time to time seek to promote is the expression of the political views of their most active and influential members. People vary in their ability to make their views known to and accepted by the party organization. When party activists seek power primarily over the party, and only secondarily over the government, we refer to them as "purists." Purists wish their views to be put forth by the parties without equivocation or compromise and although they otherwise seek to win elections, they do not care to do this at the expense of self-expression.[34] Where a party politician might promote his own views up to the point where it would cost his party's candidate the election, the purist pursues electoral victory but not past the point where it would impede the expression of his views. In the purist conception of things, instead of a party convention being a place where a party meets to choose candidates who can win elections by pleasing voters, it becomes a site for finding a candidate who will embody the message delegates seek to express.

At each level of government, the elected chief executive (mayor, governor, president) generally has the most political power, and as a result the party organizations depend more upon controlling these offices than on any other source for their political power. In addition, parties are accountable for the activities of chief executives elected under their endorsement. Accountability means that when the party endorses a candidate, it designates him as its agent before the electorate. The fortunes of the party depend on the success of party candidates. Candidates come and go, but parties and electorates remain. The party organizations, therefore, are quite concerned about selecting suitable officeholders since it is assumed that the actions and identities of these men and women will in the long run marginally determine the extent and location of the party's appeal within the electorate and its record of success at the polls.

Just as the party is greatly dependent, at any moment, upon its incumbent officeholders for its political power, these officeholders in turn often have great discretion in the distribution of rewards to the party, and it is expected that they will seek to strengthen themselves within the party organization by the judicious dispensation of favors and patronage. As people who have won office at the head of party tickets, elected chief executives will probably come closer than other individuals to possessing the kinds of control over the party organization that will make it possible for them to impose their own preferences on party organizations. Indeed, where parties are weak, they may become mere appendages of the major officeholders who use the label and manipulate the machinery until the next ad hoc collection of activists mobilizes around a new leader.

State party organizations are not simple in their internal workings. Sometimes elected chief executives run them; sometimes they are run by coalitions of party chieftains representing the local organizations of several large cities or counties. Sometimes party officials and elected officials work cooperatively; sometimes they work at cross-purposes. A strong national committeeman in a state party organization whose party, nationally, occupies the presidency may find his position amplified as *the* avenue of access in the distribution of federal largess if there are few elected officeholders in the state with whom he might have to share power. On the other hand, there are instances of governors who have felt that their chances of continuing personal victory would improve if they thoroughly disassociated themselves from the party whose label they nominally bore, causing the party organization in the state to shrivel on the vine. A strong party organization, well led, can force on an executive choices suitable for the party's purposes that conflict with alternative choices more likely to enhance the executive's position regardless of its effect on the party. A weak party organization may have the actual conduct of election campaigns torn entirely from its grasp as happened to the Republicans in 1972. Leaders of party organizations are frequently at odds with the party's elected officeholders for a variety of reasons. Many elected officials see their party leaders as potential threats to their positions; many party leaders see the officeholders as ungrateful louts with whom the organization is unfortunately saddled.

Even so, what party leaders ordinarily care about most is getting their candidates into office and keeping them there. Other considerations are usually secondary. Party leaders are neither for nor against policies in the abstract; they are concerned with policies as means to the end of officeholding. If new policies help win elections, they are for them; if they help lose elections, they are against them. If officeholders are popular, party leaders have to accept them; if they are unpopular, threatening to bring the party into disrepute, party leaders will turn against them as former President Nixon eventually discovered. That it took so long for Republican party leaders to demand that the president tell the truth or leave office may be due to the fact that now there are so few acknowledged party leaders. Where parties are purist, however, activists control candidates. Their purpose is to remain pure. If they can do that and win, so much the better for them; if the price of purism is prohibitive—defeat—so much the worse for the candidate. If a choice has to be made by purist activists, purism outside office is better than power in government.

Though political party leaders try to espouse policies which they believe will enhance their political power and try to avoid very unpopular points of view, this does not mean that they are necessarily indifferent to the substance of policy questions. Because they are more interested and active than most citizens, they also tend to care more about the policies with which they have to deal. In fact, some politicians who hold public office make a specialty of being policy oriented. At times they may deliberately incur some unpopularity in order to serve their policy preferences, although they are unlikely to go so far as purposely to lose the election for which they are a candidate. The heavy losses of the Republicans in the 1964 election and the presidential landslide against the Democrats in 1972 are extreme cases, and they are instructive in this connection. For in general, political party leaders regard policy to a certain extent as a result of an interaction among legitimate political demands—as a bargainable product—and not as purists regard it—as an inflexible set of logical or ideological imperatives.[35]

In spite of some efforts being made in the other direction by the national Democratic party, political parties in America are not yet organizations with elaborate procedures of membership, dues, and formal organizational structure. They are constituted differently in different localities and exist primarily to make nominations for and elect candidates to a variety of state and local elective offices. They are regulated by state law and are often quite cohesive up to the state level. But the state parties are joined together nationally only in loose federations. The most obvious indicator of this decentralization is the way the national parties are organized on a geographical basis with the state units as the constituent elements. The state party organizations meet formally by sending delegates to national committee meetings, and most importantly, by coming together at national conventions to nominate a president. Subject to guidelines set out at the national level, they choose their representatives to national party bodies; the national committees and conventions do not choose officers of state parties.[36] In a negative sense, the permanent national party organizations are not in a position to help the state parties; they have neither the funds, nor the personnel, nor the contacts to contribute substantially to the nomination or election of candidates for Congress or local offices who must run within state boundaries.[37]

In this respect, the operation of the so-called presidential coattail is problematic: It does not help state parties and candidates who must try to win every year in numerous elections at the state and local level. At best, coattails operate every four years and then only if there happens to be a strong presidential candidate on the ballot.[38]

The state parties, however, have substantial powers enabling them to share in the making of national policy. Their representatives and senators in Washington compete for the distribution of federal resources and for assignments to advantageous positions on congressional committees. The states have their own sources of patronage and, through their congressmen and senators, a share in federal patronage. The very circumstance that the states are separate constitutional entities engenders a drive for autonomy as those who hold places of prestige and profit in the state governments and parties seek to protect their jurisdictions, much as the framers of the Constitution hoped they would. Federalism, however, is much more than a legal fact. The states have great vitality because there are distinct, numerous, and vigorous ethnic, religious, racial, and economic groups that are disproportionately located in specific geographic areas and that demand separate recognition. State organizations, therefore, become infused with the purposes of groups of citizens who use their state parties for the recognition and enhancement of their separate identities and needs. Italians in Rhode Island, Jews and black people in New York, dairy farmers in Wisconsin, wheat growers in Kansas, and many others make the idea of a decentralized party system a living reality.[39] Each of the state parties is composed of different personnel, with somewhat different interests to protect and demands to make. Control over these organizations must be exercised from within each state, since the various states do not control one another and the national party exercises only partial control. This, we take it, is the essence of what is meant by a decentralized party system in which power is dispersed among many independent state bodies. Efforts to control the criteria for delegate selection to national conventions from the center may lead state parties that consider themselves disadvantaged to adopt two sets of rules—one for state and local nomination, and another for federal—leading to even greater fragmentation of the party system.

Thus, despite changes in their rules which have tended to nationalize the parties, they largely remain coalitions of state parties which meet every four years for the purpose of finding a candidate and forging a coalition of interests sufficiently broad to win a majority of electoral votes. This means making a coalition of state parties and party factions—southern and northern Democrats, coastal and midwestern Republicans—who disagree on some major policy issues. As a result, it is necessary to compromise and, sometimes, to evade issues that would split the parties and lead to drastic losses of support. A candidate and a set of policies, however loosely joined, must be found that can blend disparate party elements for the purpose of securing electoral victory. Parties and national conventions that, for one reason or another, forget this simple lesson or, being purist, think it an immoral lesson, as the Republicans did in 1964 and the Democrats did in 1972, doom themselves to spectacular failure in the general election.

The major parties, as we have seen, cull their electoral support from somewhat different groups in the population, *but,* no party has a monopoly of support from any of these groups; each party draws significant, and often indispensable, support from almost all the categories.[40] How could Republicans hope to win without some support from wage earners, or Democrats without some votes from

business and professional people? The parties are sufficiently varie-
gated to draw support from many quarters. In a close election the
ability of a party to increase its support within one group from, say,
20 to 30 percent may be crucial, even though that group still votes
overwhelmingly for the opposition. The strategic implications of
these remarks color all of national campaign politics: when they are
trying to win, the parties do things that will keep happy the groups
consistently allied to them without alienating other groups unduly.

Thus the temptation for political parties to avoid specific policy
commitments in many areas is very great. The American population
is so extraordinarily varied—crisscrossed by numerous economic,
religious, ethnic, racial, sectional, and occupational ties—that it is
exceedingly difficult to guess at the total distribution of policy
preferences in the population at any one time, except for questions
that have already been settled between the parties like Social
Security and unemployment compensation. They may haggle over
the amount but they do not dispute the principle. It is even more
difficult to predict how these aggregations of actual and potential
interest groups might react to shifts in party policy positions, and
still more hazardous to prophesy what different policy commitments
might do to the margin of votes required for victory. This pervasive
problem of uncertainty makes the calculation of gain from policy
positions both difficult and risky and suggests that the self-interests
of the parties and candidates in seeking office might best be served
by vague, ambiguous, or contradictory policy statements which will
be least likely to offend anyone. The advantages of vagueness about
policy are strengthened by the facts that the vast majority of citizens
are not interested in policy or are narrowly focused on a few things,
and that only a few groups in the population demand many specific
policy commitments from their parties and candidates.

Yet, despite all this, political leaders and parties do make policy
commitments that are often surprisingly precise, specific, and
logically consistent. Thus, we must consider not only why the parties
sometimes blur and avoid commitments on issues, but also why they
often commit themselves to policies more than their interest in
acquiring or retaining office would appear to require.

Part of the answer may arise from the fact that the parties serve
slightly different functions for their own activists than for people
who vote but are otherwise largely disengaged from politics. Party
activists are people who are much more interested in politics and

attentive to political issues than the general population is. The interest and attentiveness of political activists leads them to formulate and elaborate political opinions and preferences. Their desires to make these preferences internally consistent and consistent with the preferences of the party of their choice and the mutual reinforcement of activist opinions when activists interact with one another would certainly lead to demands upon the party leadership for policy positions that are reasonably clear and forthright.[41]

There are some differences between the parties in the social identities of party activists. Activists in both parties have disproportionately high social and economic status, but activist Democrats are more likely to come from working-class backgrounds; activist Republicans, on the other hand, are more middle-class. These differences may be reflected in the noticeable tendencies for the two parties to support policies intended to benefit the members of the social strata from which their active members are drawn.[42]

The interest groups most closely allied with each party also make policy demands upon them which must be met to some extent. While it is true that voters are generally uninterested in specific policies, interest group leaders and their paid bureaucracies are manifestly concerned. If they feel that the interests they represent are being harmed, they may inform their members or even go so far as to attempt to withdraw support from the party at a particular election. Should voters find that groups with which they identify are opposed to the party with which they identify, they may temporarily support the opposition party, or they may withdraw from participation and not vote at all. Consequently, the party finds that it risks losing elections by ignoring the demands of interest groups. The demands of many of these groups conflict, however. If unions object to antipollution devices because they increase costs and decrease car sales, for example, labor and ecology groups cannot both be equally satisfied. Thus, the parties have no choice but to mediate among interest groups, hoping to strike compromises which, though they give no one group everything, give something to as many groups as they can.

Finally, throughout the years the opposing political parties have become identified with somewhat different policies. When new candidates arise they may bring with them somewhat new policy preferences. But there are bound to be many areas of policy on which they are not informed or do not have strong preferences. In such cases the existing set of policies traditionally associated with the parties provides the candidates with a useful economizing device. They can accept the going positions and concentrate on the policies that they may wish to revise, supplant, or present anew. This tack is bound to be popular with the party faithful who have been brought up on the rallying cries of the past, who have learned to prefer what their party prefers, and who respond with vigor and enthusiasm to the cues provided by mention of their party's chief stocks-in-trade. Just as voters commonly use parties as a means of cutting their information costs on issues and candidates, and activists use them as reference groups, so may candidates use the parties' traditional policy positions to ease their burden of calculation.

Political parties today, however, are not as reliable as guideposts for the faithful as they once were. For the past forty years the New Deal structured the nature of political conflict in the United States. Those who were for or against a greater role for the federal government, for or against public or private power, for or against medical care for the aged and a host of other issues, knew immediately where they stood. When the Republicans nominated Barry Goldwater, however, huge Democratic majorities were elected to both houses of Congress, and the 89th Congress effectively enacted the agenda of the New Deal. These episodes sharply altered the content of partisan conflict at the national level. Since then new issues have arisen in bewildering profusion and new groups have come to public attention, clamoring to determine the shape of public policy. It is no longer clear that Republicans stand for local control and Democrats for central direction. Issues from pollution of the environment to law and order have not yet taken on firm identification with either of the major political parties. Hence there is more fluidity in political life, more leeway for the presidential nominees to set their party's course, and less opportunity for them to rely on the past policy positions associated with their respective parties.

New Party Activists:
Purists versus Professionals

Through the efforts of journalists like Theodore H. White and Jules Witcover, more and more is known with each passing election about the goals and maneuvers of political leaders. Correspondingly impressive work has been done—mostly by academic survey researchers—on the attitudes and political views of the voting masses. Much less, however, is known about the people in between who have played such important roles in the last two or three presidential elections. What motivates these people to become politically active? We have noted some of the things that are important to regular party workers, and some of the traditional appeals that are made by and to them; doubtless there is a great variety of reasons that drew them into political activity originally and continues to draw them year after year. But hundreds of new recruits to political activity seem to have been made by the candidacies of Barry Goldwater in 1964, Eugene McCarthy in 1968, and George McGovern in 1972. Were these new activists likely to remain in the years to come, joining the ranks of party workers? Or would they fade like the "morning glories" that Plunkitt of Tammany Hall long ago observed in the New York reform movement? Because the requisite work has never been done, it is impossible to do more than guess at the staying power of new activists in national politics, but their influence over the short run is quite impressive. The presence of a large number of activists with intense personal loyalties is an important resource which a candidate can to some degree substitute for money, incumbency, or years of party service.

Obviously, Goldwater, McGovern, and McCarthy recruits are not similar in every way. They certainly do not agree about the substance of governmental policy, at least on most issues. McGovern's and Goldwater's supporters captured their party machinery and then lost roundly in the general election, while McCarthy supporters were at their strongest in the various state primaries, but had little luck in their party convention. But the similarities among these groups are also striking. The same concerns, the same perceptions of their man and his opponents, recur again and again, arguing that what we have in the presence of these new activists is a phenomenon that is not best seen as a matter of right versus left, or organization versus antiorganization, but rather in terms of political purists (found among the Goldwater, McCarthy, and McGovern people) versus professional politicians.

Whatever their disagreements on specific policies, left- and right-wing activists both excoriate the immorality of men in office. These political purists consider the stock-in-trade of the politician— compromise and bargaining, conciliating the opposition, bending a little to capture public support—to be hypocritical; they prefer a style that relies on the announcement of principles and on moral crusades. Since it is difficult to make public policy or to win elections without compromising oneself in some way, there is an understandable tendency for purist political leaders to adopt a highly critical view of the main activities of American politics. Politicians have been accused of many things; until recently, it has not been usual to accuse them of wishing to lose elections. But perhaps in specifying only the paramount goal of winning, we have been taking a narrow view of the matter. Interviews held with Goldwater delegates to the Republican convention of 1964 and with McCarthy delegates to the Democratic convention of 1968 illustrate this problem.[43]

One Goldwater delegate said: "The delegates are for Goldwater because they agree with his philosophy of government. That's what you people will never understand—we're committed to his whole approach." He was undoubtedly correct. There was a remarkable fit between Goldwater and a substantial majority of his followers. What they liked about Goldwater, however, was not merely or even primarily his policy positions but rather his "approach," his style of operation. When we asked Goldwater delegates to tell us what they most liked about their candidate only a few mentioned his position on the issues, and those who did were content with brief references to constitutional principles like state's rights.

By far the most frequent delegate characterization of Goldwater referred to his consistency, honesty, integrity, and willingness to stick by principles.[44] It was not so much his principles (though these were undoubtedly important) but the belief that he would stick to them that counted most with his supporters. "He can be trusted." "He is straightforward." "He does not compromise." "He doesn't pander to the public; he's against expediency." "He is frank." "He has courage." "He stands up for what he believes." "He won't play footsie with the people." "He votes his convictions when he knows he's right." "He doesn't go along with the crowd." "He meets issues head-on." "Goldwater speaks about things others avoid. Most politicians like to avoid issues." "He keeps promises." "He doesn't change his mind." "He is not confused." As one of Goldwater's supporters perceptively observed, "He's different from most politicians." And so were most of Goldwater's followers.

Many Goldwater delegates held attitudes quite different from those characteristic of American politicians. They were "purists" in the sense we have already described—political activists whose attitudes about politics have strongly moralistic overtones. Here is an example. This Goldwater purist was a delegate from a rural area in Pennsylvania attending his first convention.

> INTERVIEWER: What qualities should a presidential candidate have?
> DELEGATE: Moral integrity.
> I: Should he be able to win the election?
> D: No; principles are more important. I would rather be one against 20,000 and believe I was right. That's what I admire about Goldwater. He's like that.
> I: Are most politicians like that?
> D: No, unfortunately.
> I: What do you like about Goldwater?
> D: I am in sympathy with many of his philosophies of government, but I like him personally for his moral integrity. I always believed that a candidate should carry out his promises. Scranton didn't do that. But now, for the first time in my life, we have a candidate who acts as he believes. He doesn't change his position when it is expedient.
> I: Do you think that if the party loses badly in November it ought to change its principles?
> D: No. I'm willing to fight for these principles for ten years if we don't win.
> I: For fifty years?
> D: Even fifty years.
> I: Do you think it's better to compromise a little to win than to lose and not compromise?
> D: I had this problem in my district. After we fighters had won [the nomination for] the congressional seat the local [Republican] machine offered to make a deal: they wouldn't oppose our candidate if we didn't oppose theirs. I refused, because I didn't see how I could make a deal with the men I'd been opposing two years ago for the things they did. So I lost, and I could have won easily. I've thought about it many times, because if I had agreed I could have done some good at least. But I don't believe that I should compromise one inch from what I believe deep down inside.

At this same convention an observer remarked, "I've talked to some of the California delegates, and I don't understand them at all; they talk like they don't care if we win." In a sense he was wrong, because the delegates desperately wanted Goldwater to win. But our informant was essentially correct in the sense that these delegates cared more about maintaining their purity—"I would rather lose and be right"—than about winning. The essential element of this style is a devotion to principles, especially the principle that men in politics should have, maintain, and cherish their principles.

Here we begin to see the distinguishing characteristics of the purists: their emphasis on internal criteria for decision, on what they believe "deep down inside"; their rejection of compromise; their lack of orientation toward winning; their stress on the style and purity of decision—integrity, consistency, adherence to internal norms.

The professionals looked at politics quite differently. Here is a California delegate strongly for Goldwater, with more than fifteen years in party work, attending his third Republican convention.

> INTERVIEWER: You seem different from many of the Goldwater supporters. How would you characterize your position in comparison with them?
>
> DELEGATE: Yes, I'm more practical. I realize you have to live together. For example, I'm going up now to a meeting of the California Republican committee and we've got to handle a liberal candidate and an ultraconservative. I'm going to urge them to accept the liberal because we've got to work together. We [the Republicans] are a minority party in California and we can't afford to squabble amongst ourselves. The art of politics is the art of compromise. If I can get a whole loaf, I'll take it. If not, I'll take half rather than lose it all.
>
> I: What would Goldwater do about . . . Social Security?
>
> D: We've had it for a long time. It's part of our system. That's something some of these Goldwater people don't realize. They're a new breed and sort of naive on things like this. They think you can suddenly shift the whole range of government to the right. What they don't realize is that you can only bend a little back away from the left.
>
> I: What if Goldwater loses by a landslide?
>
> D: Well, I don't think that will happen.
>
> I: Suppose it does?
>
> D: Well, then, maybe the people aren't ready for a change. . . . Yes, we'll have to try to change, maybe a little more toward the liberal side.

One great difference between the purists and the professionals lay in what they considered valid grounds for preferring not to win. The professionals emphasized specific unfortunate consequences, such as race riots and war. The purists emphasized departures from internal principles—such as consistency, integrity, and standing firm—held by their party leaders. The professionals were oriented toward what might happen to other people; the purists, toward their own consciences.

McCarthy's great attraction was his political style. From the comments of his supporters he emerges as the antithesis of the unscrupulous politician who changes his views on public policy in order to curry favor with the electorate. He opposed the Vietnam war before it was politically popular to do so. He is pictured as a man outside the ordinary political framework who holds the morally bankrupt politicians to account. Since McCarthy's integrity was his stock-in-trade, his supporters were concerned that he remain pure at all times. Many of his supporters eagerly assured us that "McCarthy wouldn't sell out. He wouldn't compromise." The same emphasis on internal criteria for decision, the same rejection of compromise, the same absence of an orientation toward winning, the same stress on style and purity—all are there.

Democratic professionals, not surprisingly, looked askance at this whole development. To the regular delegates with long years of service the McCarthy supporters were like spoiled children, an analogy party regulars themselves used several times: "The McWhinnies [McCarthy supporters] are like little boys with marbles: you don't play by their rules—they want to break up the game."

The predominant focus of the McCarthy forces on the issue of the war in Vietnam was widely seen as preventing the normal give and take through which internal party differences could be resolved. When many issues are at stake, support for one can be traded for help on another. When issues are strung out over a period of time, early losses may be accepted as the price for later gains. According to exponents of party unity, McCarthy's men "pursue the single issue so hard that they become intolerant." A single issue of overriding importance at a specific moment in time breaks party solidarity.

The belief in compromise and bargaining; the sense that public policy is made in small steps rather than big leaps; the concern with conciliating the opposition and broadening public appeal; and the willingness to bend a little to capture public support are all characteristic of the traditional American politician.

Emphasizing Differences

An important component of the Goldwater style was the guiding principle that the parties ought to be different. The ideal party of the

Goldwater purists was not merely a conservative party; it was a distinct and separate community of cobelievers who differ with the opposition party all down the line. To this extent their style merges with that of the liberal Democratic reformers who wish to see the parties represent clear and opposing alternatives and to gain votes only through appeals based on policy differences rather than on such "irrational" criteria as personality, party identification, or ethnic status.[45] But the Goldwater purists went even further in their willingness to cast aside whole groups of voters who did not agree with them. "We won't get Negro votes anyway, so there's no point in trying." "They can vote for the other party for all I care." "We won't change our principles just to get a few votes from Negroes." In the same spirit, Barry Goldwater suggested that people who favored the kind of government the United States has had since 1932 should not vote for him.

For the professionals, the desire to win is intimately connected with the belief that a political party should try to get as much support from as many diverse groups as possible. Hence the professionals were concerned with the possible loss of a substantial part of the small black vote they had received in the past. "You just can't go around throwing away votes. The object of a party is to draw voters together to the party, not to push them away." A delegate from Philadelphia was more specific. He had "nothing personal against Goldwater" but feared that if Goldwater were to run "we'll get the hell kicked out of us. We've been out of [state] power for ten or twelve years. Now we're getting some of the Polish vote and the Italians don't treat us too bad. The Jews and the Negroes go about 75 percent against us, but at least we get part of the Negro vote and that helps us hold the line in the state generally."

To their dichotomous view of political parties and their belief that issue preferences are the only moral way to choose between the parties, the Goldwater purists added a strong desire to simplify political choice: a party for the growth of government and a party against; a party that believes in standing up to the enemy and one that believes in appeasement; a party that believes in private initiative and one that wishes to stifle it; a party of free enterprise and a party of socialism.

The Privatization of Politics:
Semipermanent Opposition

We may sum up the purist style by saying that it represents a virtually complete privatization of politics. The private conscience of the leader—rather than his public responsibilities—becomes the focal point of politics. Internal criteria—possession of, devotion to, and standing up for private principles—become the standards of political judgment. Constituents disappear, and we are left with a political leader determining policy on the basis of compatibility with his private principles.

A central part of McCarthy's appeal to his style-oriented followers was that he did not act like a politician. He wrote poems, he was too reflective, he was too frank, he refused to bargain. He would not make the traditional gesture of supporting the party's nominee after he had lost. He attracted the political innocents rather than the worldly. His followers took all this as a sign that he was, like themselves, an outsider to the party who refused to become just another politician. Where Goldwater sought to save a fundamentally sound political system by bearing witness to its potential purity, however, McCarthy took the position of an outsider who was in semipermanent opposition to it. He apparently sensed the impatience of his followers with normal politics and yet knew that he must at times take an active position within existing political institutions. So he talked of basic changes in political processes but moved into action only when this consisted of a form of opposition.

This style of what we have called "semipermanent opposition" springs from the privatization of politics, for to such an opposition, coalition-building in order to win ceases to be important. The parties must prove themselves each time on every issue or they and their candidates are not worthy of support. Thus the legitimacy of the American political system comes under attack. Such attacks change the incentives for public activity and political leadership. If a politician fails in the difficult task of organizing disparate coalitions to support sound legislation, he has little to show for his labors. If he succeeds, he may be told that he has not accomplished anything worth doing. This suggests a situation where whatever the "Establishment" does is by definition small and inconsequential; in that case the only way of knowing whether a policy is significant is that it does not gather support.

The greater the attack on the legitimacy of the political system, the less the willingness to accept responsibility for it. The greater the rejection of modest improvements in favor of wholesale changes, the less the ability of the political system to make changes of any kind. Indeed, the more requirements are stated in stylistic terms, the less it is possible to know whether they have been met at all. What are party leaders to make of the simultaneous demands that they reduce the impact of money and increase internal participation when this participation—more primaries, more conferences, more meetings—costs more money? As demands for governmental performance become ever larger and more contradictory, the likelihood of any action receiving widespread approval decreases. Under these conditions, the temptation to engage in semipermanent opposition is bound to increase. No doubt there will still be a preponderance of governmental officials who will concentrate on the substance of public policy, but we can expect increasing numbers of them to seek what the French call "the cure of opposition." Those who are deep-dyed conservatives in the Goldwater mold have in fact been in near total opposition since New Deal days. Should a significant number of politicians on the left also choose "semipermanent opposition," the room for constructive coalition-building could be severely curtailed.

There is, of course, one fundamental difference between Goldwater purists and McCarthy purists. Goldwaterites were and are party insiders; McCarthyites, with rare exceptions, are not. The Goldwaterite sentiments of Republican activists sharply differentiate Republican activists from the bulk of the American population and make winning difficult for the Republican party. If Democratic activists become more purist in their orientations, they too would part company with most Americans on at least some issues. If Democratic leaders became more purist and less concerned with winning, we believe they would win less often, elections would be more bitterly contested than they now are, the costs of losing would rise, and the complex tasks of governing would become even more difficult.

What does the 1972 "McGovern" Democratic convention suggest about this trend? Apparently purism evidenced a rapid rise in 1972 and party identification showed a dramatic decrease. Using the same measures of purism (they call it "amateurism") employed in 1968, John W. Soule and Wilma E. McGrath (see table on p. 38) found that the population of purists at the Democratic convention grew from just under a quarter to just over half of the delegates, an increase of over 100 percent. On the basis of this evidence, Soule and McGrath say that they "are forced to reconsider the basic assumption that party leaders meet in conventions for the explicit purpose of nominating a candidate who will win in November."[46]

Amateurism-Professionalism among Delegates
1968–1972 Democratic National Conventions

Year	Amateur	Semiprofessional	Professional	Total
	(percent)	(percent)	(percent)	(percent)
1968 (N = 188)	23	61	16	100
1972 (N = 314)*	51	22	27	100

* Delegates do not total 326 because of failure to respond to all of the items composing the amateurism-professionalism scale.

Questionnaire items used to test for amateurism or professionalism in 1968 and 1972:

1. Party organization and unity is more important than permitting free and total discussion which may divide the party.
2. A good party worker must support any candidate nominated by the convention even if he disagrees with him.
3. Controversial positions should be avoided in the party platform in order to insure party unity.
4. As a convention delegate, basically my only job is to choose a candidate who will win in November.
5. Would you characterize yourself as someone who:
    a. works for the party year after year, win or lose, whether or not you like the candidate or issues; or
    b. works for the party only when there is a particularly worthwhile candidate or issue?

SOURCE: John W. Soule and Wilma E. McGrath, "A Comparative Study of Presidential Nominating Conventions: The Democrats 1968 and 1972," *American Journal of Political Science* 19 (August 1975), pp. 510, 511.

Utilizing different but related measures of purism, a group from Dartmouth found even higher levels at the 1972 Democratic convention with the 83 percent for McGovern delegates outstripping the 65 percent for adherents of George Wallace.[47] Nor did McGovern delegates become more programmatic as it became clear their man was going to win. While they were willing to accept some discipline to see McGovern nominated, they were unwilling to follow his lead in attempting to unify the party. After the nomination, they thought of themselves even more than before as representatives of special constituencies—youth, black people, women—than they did as representatives of the Democratic rank and file.

Strength of Party Identification by Party Affiliation
of Delegates to the 1972 Presidential Nominating Conventions

Party Identification	Democratic	Republican
	(percent)	*(percent)*
Strong Democratic	47.7	0.0
Democratic	20.8	0.0
Independent Democratic	30.4	0.0
Independent	0.7	0.0
Independent Republican	0.4	12.0
Republican	0.0	14.9
Strong Republican	0.0	73.1
N =	283	242

X^2 = 521.10961 with 6 d.f.
Kendall's Tau B = 0.78526
Kendall's Tau C = 0.97325
Significance = 0.0000
Sample: 285 Democrats, 244 Republicans out of 750 of each party.
SOURCE: Joseph H. Boyett, "Background Characteristics of Delegates to the 1972 Conventions: A Summary Report of Findings from a National Sample,"*Western Political Quarterly*, September 1974.

As one might expect, the strength of Democratic party identification among delegates to the 1972 Democratic National Convention was compatible with purism. A survey by Joseph H. Boyett (see table above) reveals that almost a third of Democratic delegates were weak party identifiers. In contrast, far fewer Republicans were weak party identifiers. Almost three-quarters of the Republicans thought of themselves as strong partisans, but less than half of the Democratic delegates questioned considered themselves strong party loyalists.[48]

There is striking confirmation from the Dartmouth study. Of those delegates who preferred McGovern, only 10 percent identified themselves as strong Democrats and had prior convention experience compared to 3 percent of the Wallacites and 29 percent of Humphrey, Muskie, or Jackson supporters. These party professionals began to show some disinterest in party unity after Senator McGovern was actually nominated, while McGovern delegates began to respond more like professionals, perhaps because at that point 72 percent of the McGovern delegates thought their nominee would win the election, a premise that regular party politicians found hard to accept.[49] This suggests that the differences between party purists and party professionals include important matters of cognition, that is, beliefs about what it takes and what it costs in terms of compromise and conciliation to win elections in this country.

The Electoral College

Another element of the strategic environment within which the drama of a presidential election is played is that peculiarly American institution, the Electoral College. American presidential elections are not decided by popular vote, but rather popular votes are collected within each state, and each state casts all of its electoral votes for the candidate receiving the most popular votes within the state. This "winner take all, loser take nothing" approach is called a "unit rule." [50] We will explain some consequences of this rule presently.

Each state is allowed as many electoral votes as it has senators and representatives in Congress. Thus, all states, no matter how small, have at least three electoral votes. This means that mathematically, sparsely populated states are overrepresented by the Electoral College. In 1972, 95,000 Alaskans influenced the disposition of three electoral votes, which gives a ratio of one electoral vote for every 31,666 voters. In New York, on the other hand, 7,166,000 voters went to the polls and voted for 41 electors, a ratio of one electoral vote for every 174,780 voters. In California, 8,368,000 voters for 45 electors produced a ratio of one electoral vote for every 185,955 voters. One might conclude, therefore, that each Alaskan had about six times as much influence on the final outcome as each Californian. But this is not entirely valid.

Why not? Because the unit rule of the Electoral College provides that the candidate having the most votes in a state receives the entire electoral vote of the state. This means that each Alaskan was influencing the disposition of all three of Alaska's electoral votes, and each Californian was helping to decide the fate of all forty-five of California's votes. Ask any politician whether he would rather have three votes or forty-five—the answer is immediately apparent. In fact, the present method of electing the president tends to give greater power to the large urban states, not the small rural states, because the large states can deliver to the winner large blocks of the votes he needs to win. Consequently, presidential nominees tend to come from big states and tend to run on platforms likely to appeal to big-city interest groups. They concentrate their campaigns in the big centers of population, and, as politicians know, they stand or fall on the big state votes.[51]

As politicians develop their strategies for winning nomination and election to the presidency, they will have to keep in mind numerous facts about participation that are given in their political environment and probably not subject to change by anything they may do. Among these are the following facts:

1. Most voters are not sufficiently concerned with specific policies to change their votes in response to policy appeals.
2. Rather, they vote the way they do out of party habit.
3. They may or may not *turn out* in great numbers, however, and therefore it is necessary to activate intermediary organizations and party activists in order to help turn out one's own voters.
4. Parties usually seek to win elections but may occasionally prefer to express the views of their activists as their major goal.
5. Either party has a reasonably good chance to win the election: the Democrats because they are in the majority; the Republicans because they are much more likely to turn out.
6. Intermediary organizations such as interest groups and party organizations can be activated by policy commitments and reaffirmations and promises of access to governmental decision-making.
7. Each of the parties consists of a loose coalition of interest groups and state and local parties.
8. The Electoral College puts a premium on votes from large two-party states.

Most or all of these basic facts about participants are well understood by presidential candidates and their managers. In addition, they must consider certain basic facts about the other resources available to them, to which we now turn.

Notes

1. In his major work on public opinion, V. O. Key, Jr., states, "For most Americans issues of politics are not of central concern. . . ." At another point Key summarizes the literature as follows: "In analysis after analysis of opinions on specific issues, sizable proportions of persons have been shown to lack an opinion." *Public Opinion and American Democracy* (New York, 1961), pp. 47, 185. When asked, "What things are you most concerned with these days?" two out of three people in a

representative sample of registered voters in New Haven, Connecticut, spoke of personal matters like jobs, health, and children. Only one out of five cited local, state, national, or international affairs. Robert A. Dahl, *Who Governs?* (New Haven, 1961), p. 279. A similar survey conducted in Oberlin, Ohio, showed that only 17 percent of a random (but representative) sample said that they were concerned with public affairs. Aaron B. Wildavsky, *Leadership in a Small Town* (Totowa, N.J., 1964). Further supporting evidence may be found in Julian L. Woodward and Elmo Roper, "Political Activity of American Citizens," *American Political Science Review* 44 (December 1950), pp. 872–75, and Samuel Stouffer, *Communism, Conformity and Civil Liberties* (Garden City, N.Y., 1955), Chapter 3. Using data from the Survey Research Center, Philip E. Converse estimates that those who are strongly ideological number about 3.5 percent of the voting population, and those who have some ideological capacities number no more than 12 percent. He finds that 17.5 percent of the population have attitudes with no issue content whatsoever. See his article "The Nature of Belief Systems in Mass Politics," in *Ideology and Discontent*, ed. David E. Apter (New York, 1964), pp. 206–61, especially the table and commentary on p. 218.

2. See Angus Campbell, Philip E. Converse, Warren E. Miller, and Donald E. Stokes, *The American Voter* (New York, 1960), pp. 89–115. Writing of the 1956 presidential election, for example, the authors say that "the rate of turnout among persons of high interest exceeded that among persons of low interest by nearly 30 per cent . . ." (p. 102). See also Gordon M. Connelly and Harry M. Field, "The Non-Voter—Who He Is, What He Thinks," *Public Opinion Quarterly* 8 (Summer 1944), pp. 175–87. The work of Angus Campbell and his associates at the University of Michigan's Survey Research Center, to which we will refer frequently, is based on numerous sample surveys of the entire American voting population. These studies, which have been going on since 1948, have through the years increased in breadth and sophistication and at the moment represent the largest pool of data we have on the political habits of Americans. The work of Paul Lazarsfeld, Bernard Berelson, and their associates at the Columbia Bureau of Applied Social Research has been going on since 1940. Rather than national sample surveys, the BASR group has collected data of a more focused kind, often limited to a single community. The BASR group pioneered in the use of panel surveys, which consist of series of reinterviews with a sample of respondents. For a description and critique of these and other materials we shall be using, see Peter H. Rossi, "Four Landmarks in Voting Research," in *American Voting Behavior*, eds. Eugene Burdick and Arthur J. Brodbeck (Glencoe, Ill., 1959), Chapter 1, and Peter B. Natchez, "Images of Voting: The Social Psychologists," *Public Policy* 17 (Summer 1970), pp. 553–88.

3. Bernard Berelson, Paul F. Lazarsfeld, and William N. McPhee, *Voting* (Chicago, 1954), p. 25; Campbell, Converse, Miller, and Stokes, *The American Voter*, pp. 475–83; Key, *Public Opinion and American Democracy*, pp. 195–99. For a detailed discussion of socioeconomic status and political participation, see Sidney Verba and Norman H. Nie, *Participation in America: Political Democracy and Social Equality* (New York, 1972), especially Chapter 8.

4. Campbell, Converse, Miller, and Stokes, *The American Voter*, pp. 120–45. Robert E. Lane concludes, "Over the long run party identification has more influence over a

person's vote decision than any other single factor. . . ." *Political Life* (Glencoe, Ill., 1959), p. 300.

5. It is likely that there is more than one kind of "independent." Research published to date does not differentiate among independents, however, and characterizes the entire population of independents as follows: The authors of *The American Voter* write that in comparison to habitual party identifiers, "independents tend as a group to be somewhat less involved in politics. They have somewhat poorer knowledge of the issues, their image of the candidates is fainter, their interest in the campaign is less, their concern over the outcome is relatively slight, and their choice between competing candidates . . . seems much less to spring from discoverable evaluations of the elements of national politics." Campbell, Converse, Miller, and Stokes, p. 143. See also Berelson, Lazarsfeld, and McPhee, *Voting*, pp. 25–27, and, for a somewhat different treatment, Robert Agger, "Independents and Party Identifiers," in *American Voting Behavior*, eds. Burdick and Brodbeck, Chapter 17. William H. Flanigan uses Survey Research Center data to conclude, "In all recent elections the independents and weak partisans were more likely to make up their minds during the campaign, while the strong partisans characteristically make their decisions by the end of the conventions." *Political Behavior of the American Electorate*, 2nd ed. (Boston, 1972), p. 111.

6. Berelson, Lazarsfeld, and McPhee, *Voting*, pp. 215–33. George Belknap and Angus Campbell state that "for many people Democratic or Republican attitudes regarding foreign policy result from conscious or unconscious adherence to a perceived party line rather than from influences independent of party identification." "Political Party Identification and Attitudes Toward Foreign Policy," *Public Opinion Quarterly* 15 (Winter 1951–52), p. 623. Campbell and his associates speak of "the electorate's profound loyalty to the existing parties. Our [Survey Research Center] studies regularly have shown that three-quarters of the adult population grants outright its allegiance to the Republican or Democratic Party and that most of those who call themselves Independents acknowledge some degree of attachment to one of the parties. These partisan identifications . . . appear highly resistant to change." Campbell, Converse, Miller, and Stokes, *The American Voter*, pp. 552–53. Although no comparable study exists for the American experience, a forthcoming dissertation by Richard Johnston of Stanford gives strong evidence that in Canada, shifts in party allegiance are less a result of changes in party identification by existing party members than they are the product of the replacement of old voters with new. Arthur S. Goldberg's study of American data finds that children tend to defect from the party identification of their parents when the parents' party identification is atypical for their status and the children are relatively well educated. "Social Determinism and Rationality as Bases of Party Identification," *American Political Science Review* 63 (March 1969), pp. 5–25.

7. The various voting studies previously cited all contain substantial discussions of this subject. See Robert E. Lane, "Fathers and Sons: Foundations of Political Belief," *American Sociological Review* 24 (August 1959), pp. 502–11; Campbell, Converse, Miller, and Stokes, *The American Voter*, pp. 146–47; H. H. Remmers, "Early Socialization of Attitudes," in *American Voting Behavior*, eds. Burdick and Brodbeck, pp. 55–67. Key, *Public Opinion and American Democracy*, pp. 293–314,

sums up in these words: "Children acquire early in life a feeling of party identification; they have sensitive antennae and since they are imitative animals, soon take on the political color of their family . . ." (p. 294); see, especially, Fred I. Greenstein, *Children and Politics* (New Haven, 1965), Chapter 4. In a more recent work, Paul R. Abramson presents an interesting discussion of this familiar link and the forces that later play against it. See *Generational Change in American Politics* (Lexington, Ky., 1975), especially Chapters 3 and 4.

8. ". . . People are more likely to associate with people like themselves—alike in political complexion as well as social position." Berelson, Lazarsfeld, and McPhee, *Voting*, p. 83. See also Robert D. Putnam, "Political Attitudes and the Local Community," *American Political Science Review* 60 (September 1966), pp. 640–54, and more recently, Ada W. Finifter, "The Friendship Group as a Protective Environment for Political Deviants," *American Political Science Review* 68 (June 1974), pp. 607–26.

9. Paul Lazarsfeld, Bernard Berelson, and Hazel Gaudet, *The People's Choice* (New York, 1944), pp. 16–28.

10. Ibid.; Angus Campbell and Homer C. Cooper, *Group Differences in Attitudes and Votes* (Ann Arbor, 1956); Woodward and Roper, "Political Activity of American Citizens," pp. 872–75; Key, *Public Opinion and American Democracy*, pp. 99–120, 121–81; Berelson, Lazarsfeld, and McPhee, *Voting*, pp. 54–76; Robert Axelrod, "Where the Votes Come From: An Analysis of Electoral Coalitions, 1952–1968," *American Political Science Review* 66 (March 1972), and "Communication," *American Political Science Review* 68 (June 1974), pp. 717–20.

11. V. O. Key, Jr., *Southern Politics* (New York, 1950), pp. 75–81, 223–28, 280–85. The South is becoming more evenly divided in its political loyalties because two trends have outweighed the effects of a third: the migration of Republicans into the South and the conversion of conservative southerners to Republicanism have not been made up by the increasingly heavy turnout of black people who vote overwhelmingly Democratic in presidential elections.

12. V. O. Key, Jr., "A Theory of Critical Elections," *The Journal of Politics* 17 (February 1955), pp. 3–18; Campbell, Converse, Miller, and Stokes, *The American Voter*, p. 160. See, more generally, James Q. Wilson, *Negro Politics* (Glencoe, Ill., 1960). Barry Goldwater's 1964 candidacy intensified the Democratic loyalties of black voters.

13. See Duane Lockard, *New England State Politics* (Princeton, 1959); Dahl, *Who Governs?* pp. 33–51, 216–17; Elmer E. Cornwell, "Party Absorption of Ethnic Groups: The Case of Providence, R.I.," *Social Forces* 38 (March 1960), pp. 205–10; J. Joseph Huthmacher, *Massachusetts People and Politics* (Cambridge, Mass., 1959), pp. 118–26.

14. Samuel Lubell, *The Future of American Politics* (New York, 1951), pp. 129–57.

15. On Eisenhower see Campbell, Converse, Miller, and Stokes, *The American Voter*, pp. 55–57, 525–28, 537, and Herbert H. Hyman and Paul B. Sheatsley, "The Political Appeal of President Eisenhower," *Public Opinion Quarterly* 19 (Winter 1955–56), pp. 26–39. On McGovern, see Samuel L. Popkin, John W. Gorman, Charles Phillips, and Jeffrey A. Smith, "Comment: What Have You Done for Me

Lately? Toward an Investment Theory of Voting," *American Political Science Review* 70 (June 1976).

16. The portions of this analysis that deal with voters and issues are taken from Chapter 8, "Public Policy and Political Preference," in Campbell, Converse, Miller, and Stokes, *The American Voter*, pp. 168–87.

17. In a methodologically excellent national sample survey conducted in 1954 which was designed to discover the concerns of the American people on subjects then agitating American political elites relating to communism and civil liberties, Samuel Stouffer found: "The number of people who said that they were worried either about the threat of Communists in the U.S. or about civil liberties was, even by the most generous interpretation of occasionally ambiguous responses, *less than 1 per cent*. Even world problems, including the shadow of war, did not evoke a spontaneous answer from more than 8 per cent." Stouffer, *Communism, Conformity and Civil Liberties*, p. 59. See Hazel Gaudet Erskine, "The Polls: The Informed Public," *Public Opinion Quarterly* 26 (Winter 1962), pp. 669–77. This article summarizes questions asked since 1947 of national samples of Americans designed to ascertain their information on current news topics. Similar data for 1935–46 are contained in Hadley Cantril and Mildred Strunk, *Public Opinion, 1935–1946* (Princeton, 1951).

18. The data on which this conclusion is based refer to issues in rather general categories such as "economic aid to foreign countries," "influence of big business in government," and "aid to education." Campbell, Converse, Miller, and Stokes, *The American Voter*, p. 182. It is highly probable that the proportion of people meeting the three requirements would be substantially reduced if precise and specific policies within these general issue categories formed the basis of questions in a survey.

19. The authors of *The American Voter* tentatively conclude that in the Eisenhower years, covered by their study, "people who paid little attention to politics were contributing very disproportionately to partisan change." Campbell, Converse, Miller, and Stokes, p. 264.

20. Arthur H. Miller, Warren E. Miller, Alden S. Raine, and Thad A. Brown, "A Majority Party in Disarray: Policy Polarization in the 1972 Election," unpublished paper, delivered at the American Political Science Association annual meeting, September 1974, p. 17. The issues studied include: Vietnam withdrawal, amnesty for draft dodgers, reducing military spending, government health insurance, guaranteed standard of living, urban unrest, campus unrest, protecting the rights of those accused of crime, government aid to minorities, equal rights for women, abortion, legalization of marijuana, busing, and a "liberal-conservative philosophic position." See also Jeane J. Kirkpatrick, "Representation in National Political Conventions: The Case of 1972," paper delivered at the American Political Science Association annual meeting, September 1974.

21. Philip E. Converse, "Information Flow and the Stability of Partisan Attitudes," *Public Opinion Quarterly* 26 (Winter 1962), pp. 578–99.

22. V. O. Key, Jr., with the assistance of Milton C. Cummings, Jr., *The Responsible Electorate: Rationality in Presidential Voting, 1936–1960* (Cambridge, Mass., 1966).

23. Campbell, Converse, Miller, and Stokes, *The American Voter*, pp. 153–60; Key,

"A Theory of Critical Elections," pp. 3–18. Stouffer, *Communism, Conformity and Civil Liberties*, p. 87, says that Americans are concerned not with world problems, but with personal problems. He adds, "A 'business recession' finds a path into almost every home—whether it is that of a factory worker or that of a butcher who finds his sales of meat declining. It becomes a threat that is immediate and personal."

24. Key asserts that "as has been demonstrated, the citizen's identification with party tends to produce a tie consistent with his policy preferences." *Public Opinion and American Democracy*, p. 460. See also Lazarsfeld, Berelson, and Gaudet, *The People's Choice*, Chapter 9.

25. Richard A. Brody, Benjamin I. Page, et al., "Vietnam, the Urban Crisis and the 1968 Presidential Election: A Preliminary Analysis," paper prepared for delivery at the 1969 meeting of the American Sociological Association, September 1969. The authors polled four national samples of the electorate during the campaign and asked numerous questions (rather than only a few) about each issue. For a more recent interpretation of their findings, see Page and Brody, "Policy Voting and the Electoral Process: The Vietnam War Issue," *American Political Science Review* 66 (September 1972), p. 979.

26. Miller, Miller, Raines, and Brown, "A Majority Party in Disarray," pp. 18, 19, 38.

27. This notion is developed by Anthony Downs, *An Economic Theory of Democracy* (New York, 1957).

28. See Raymond A. Bauer, Ithiel de Sola Pool, and Lewis Anthony Dexter, *American Business and Public Policy* (New York, 1963), pp. 323–99, especially p. 373.

29. See Seymour M. Lipset, Paul F. Lazarsfeld, Allen H. Barton, and Juan Linz, "The Psychology of Voting: An Analysis of Political Behavior," in *Handbook of Social Psychology*, ed. Gardner Lindzey (Cambridge, Mass., 1954).

30. Axelrod, "Where the Votes Come From: An Analysis of Electoral Coalitions, 1952–1968."

31. Axelrod, "Communication," p. 720.

32. "Access" is the opportunity to press claims upon decision-makers. This does not imply that those who have more access are more successful in pressing their claims, but it is generally supposed that claims have a better chance of realization when they are presented repeatedly and auspiciously to decision-makers, and by "known" rather than "unknown" claimants. See David B. Truman, *The Governmental Process* (New York, 1951), pp. 264–70.

33. Our interpretation of parties is based largely on Pendelton Herring, *The Politics of Democracy* (New York, 1940); V. O. Key, Jr., *Politics, Parties and Pressure Groups*, 4th ed. (New York, 1958); David B. Truman, "Federalism and the Party System," in *Federalism Mature and Emergent*, ed. Arthur Macmahon (New York, 1955), Chapter 8; Anthony Downs, *An Economic Theory of Democracy* (New York, 1957); and a burgeoning literature (some of it already cited) on state and local political party organizations. See especially Truman, *The Governmental Process*, pp. 262–87.

34. An acutely self-satiric evaluation of the purist mentality is contained in P. M.

Koster's "Surprise Party," *Harper's*, March 1975, p. 31: "Alan Baron, the sharpest of the young pros, who had coached the liberals brilliantly on the Mikulski and charter commissions, declared that, whatever happened, the conference was a success: we might lose organized labor, but we'd brought in God."

35. Herring, *The Politics of Democracy*, especially pp. 272–87. See also Edward C. Banfield, *Political Influence* (New York, 1961).

36. The structure of American political parties is treated, among other places, in Key, *Politics, Parties and Pressure Groups.* A recent decision of the Supreme Court gives the national convention the right to regulate standards for admission to it, and in this important respect national standards can be imposed on state party organizations. See *Cousins* v. *Wigoda*, 419 U.S. 477 (1975).

37. If the federal government ends up subsidizing the national committees instead of individual candidates, the next phase of party reform could give the national parties much greater leverage.

38. See Warren E. Miller, "Presidential Coattails: A Study in Political Myth and Methodology," *Public Opinion Quarterly* 19 (Winter 1955–56), pp. 26–39.

39. William S. Livingston, "A Note on the Nature of Federalism," *Political Science Quarterly* 67 (March 1952), pp. 81–95.

40. See Robert R. Alford, *Party and Society* (Chicago, 1963), Chapter 6, "The Politics of Diversity." This reanalysis of a variety of surveys suggests that class-oriented voting in the United States, while it exists, does not polarize voters to the extent that can be found in Great Britain or Australia. See also Axelrod, "Where the Votes Come From" and "Communication."

41. Herbert McClosky, Paul J. Hoffman, and Rosemary O'Hara, "Issue Conflict and Consensus Among Party Leaders and Followers," *American Political Science Review* 54 (June 1960), pp. 406–27. The authors, who compared large samples of Democratic and Republican leaders on twenty-four major public issues, conclude that "the belief that the two American parties are identical in principle and doctrine has little foundation in fact. Examination of the opinions of Democratic and Republican leaders shows them to be distinct communities of co-believers who diverge sharply on many important issues." They add, "Little support was found for the belief that deep cleavages exist among the electorate but are ignored by the leaders. One might, indeed, more accurately assert the contrary, to wit: that the natural cleavages between the leaders are largely ignored by the voters" (pp. 425–26).

42. Key, *Public Opinion and American Democracy*, p. 439, observes, "Of Democratic high participators . . . only 34 per cent fall into white-collar occupations; of the Republican group comparable in political activity, 48 per cent are from white-collar occupations. Substantially more Democratic than Republican high participators are blue-collar workers. Occupational differences between the party identifiers become more marked as level of political participation increases." See also Verba and Nie, *Participation in America*, especially Chapter 16.

43. The 1964 interviews were conducted in the lobby of the Fairmont Hotel in San Francisco—where the California, Illinois, and New Jersey delegations were

housed—by Aaron Wildavsky, Judy Gordon, Maralyn Millman, James Payne, and Joseph Paff. While these unstructured interviews in no way represent a systematic sample of the delegates, they were undertaken because they have one great advantage over the usual mail questionnaire: they can elicit spontaneous information about respondents' attitudes that a more structured method might well miss. The 1968 interviews were conducted at the Democratic convention in Chicago by Aaron Wildavsky and associates, including Frank Levy, Andrew McFarland, Bill Cavala, Robert Nakamura, Jeffrey Pressman, Philip Auerbach, Jo Freeman, Laura Martin, Wallet Rogers, and Theodore Totman. We wish to thank Dean Sanford Elberg of the Graduate Division of the University of California for providing the funds that made this research possible. It consists of approximately five hundred interviews lasting from a few minutes to an hour. All the major delegations—California, New York, Illinois, Texas, Ohio, Pennsylvania—were covered, as were smaller delegations from each section of the nation. We placed ourselves in the hotels where the delegates stayed and were able to interview them easily from early in the morning until the late afternoon when the buses left for the convention hall. The violence that marked the convention week took place largely outside the hotels and did not inhibit our activities. We were never denied access to any hotel. Aaron Wildavsky, Frank Levy, William Lunch, and Jesse McCorry also conducted interviews to check on past findings at the 1972 Democratic convention in Miami. A sample survey conducted at the 1968 convention by John W. Soule and James Clark of Florida State University ("Amateurs and Professionals: A Study of Delegates to the 1968 Democratic Convention," *American Political Science Review* 64 [September 1970], pp. 888–99) agrees with our main contention that the major difference among the delegates was stylistic rather than substantive. The material that follows is adapted from Aaron Wildavsky, "The Goldwater Phenomenon: Purists, Politicians, and the Two-Party System," *The Review of Politics* 27, no. 3 (July 1965), pp. 386–413, and "The Meaning of 'Youth' in the Struggle for Control of the Democratic Party," *The Revolt Against the Masses and Other Essays on Politics and Public Policy* (New York, 1971).

44. This is borne out by findings of the Michigan Survey Research Center. Integrity was the personal quality most admired in him by his supporters. See Angus Campbell, "Interpreting the Presidential Victory," in *The National Election of 1964*, ed. Milton C. Cummings, Jr. (Washington, D.C., 1966), p. 261.

45. See James Q. Wilson, *The Amateur Democrat* (Chicago, 1962).

46. John W. Soule and Wilma E. McGrath, "A Comparative Study of Presidential Nominating Conventions: The Democrats, 1968 and 1972," *American Journal of Political Science* 19 (August 1975), pp. 501–17. For additional evidence see E. Gene DeFelice, "Pre-Convention Politics: The Surge of Amateur Delegates from Illinois, 1972," paper delivered at the annual meeting of the American Political Science Association, 1974.

47. "Not only does the McGovern organization display a high level of purism but it has all the other characteristics associated with purism." Sullivan, Pressman, Page, and Lyons, *The Politics of Representation*, pp. 122–24.

48. Joseph H. Boyett, "Background Characteristics of Delegates to the 1972

Conventions: A Summary Report of Findings from a National Sample," *Western Political Quarterly*, September 1974, p. 477.

49. Sullivan, Pressman, Page, and Lyons, *The Politics of Representation*, pp. 125–29.

50. The unit rule is not prescribed in the Constitution or by federal law. Rather, it is the result of individual state action which provides, in all states, that electors for party nominees are grouped together and elected *en bloc,* on a "general ticket" such that a vote for one elector is a vote for all the electors on that ticket, with the majority vote electing all electors for the state. Senator Thomas Hart Benton said in 1824, "The general ticket system . . . was the offspring of policy. . . . It was adopted by the leading men of [ten states] to enable them to consolidate the vote of the state. . . ."

Thomas Jefferson had earlier pointed out that ". . . while ten states choose either by legislatures or by a general ticket it is folly and worse than folly for the other states not to do it." In short, once a few states maximized their impact by using the unit rule, the others followed suit. See *Motion for Leave to File Complaint, Complaint and Brief, Delaware* v. *New York*, No. 28 Original, U.S. Supreme Court, October term, 1966; and Neal R. Peirce, "The Electoral College Goes to Court," *The Reporter*, October 6, 1966.

51. Further confirmation of this view is provided by Steven J. Brams and Morton D. Davis, "The 3/2's Rule in Presidential Campaigning," *American Political Science Review* 68 (March 1974), pp. 113–34; Claude S. Colatoni, Terrence J. Levesque, and Peter C. Ordeshook, "Campaign Resource Allocations Under the Electoral College," *American Political Science Review* 69 (March 1975), pp. 141–52; and John A. Yunker and Lawrence D. Longley, "The Biases of the Electoral College: Who Is Really Advantaged?" in *Perspectives on Presidential Selection*, ed. Donald R. Matthews (Washington, D.C., 1973), pp. 172–203.

CHAPTER TWO

The Strategic Environment: Resources

The Distribution of Resources

Certain resources which, at any given time, are disproportionately available to Democrats and Republicans play a significant part in the strategic environment of presidential elections. For example, possession of the presidential office, skill in organization, knowledge of substantive policies, a reputation for integrity, facility in speech-making, ability to devise appealing campaign issues, wealth, stamina—all can be drawn upon to good advantage in a presidential campaign. There are, it is clear, more resources available to the parties than any one book could deal with exhaustively. But some resources are obviously going to be more important than others, and the importance of different resources varies from occasion to occasion. It would be sensible to regard as especially important those resources that one side effectively monopolizes—such as the presidential office—and those resources that can be easily converted into other resources, or directly into public office—such as money, which can be used to buy competent staff, newspaper space, and so on.

Although political resources are distributed unequally between the parties, in a competitive two-party system such as ours the inequalities do not all run in the same direction. Sometimes the Republicans reap the benefits; sometimes the Democrats do. One result of these inequalities of access to different resources, however, is that different strategies are more advantageous to each of the two parties. Let us examine three resources commonly held to be extremely important in the strategic environment of the presidential election—money, control over information, and the presidential office—in order to see what effects they have on election strategies.

Money[1]

Presidential campaigns are terribly expensive. Radio and television appearances, newspaper advertising, travel for the candidate and his entourage, mailings of campaign material, buttons and placards, maintaining a network of offices to run the campaign, taking polls, and raising money itself—all cost a great deal of money. It is estimated that the various committees (the Republican and Democratic national committees, the House and Senate campaign committees of both parties, and various ad hoc volunteer committees that spring up in each campaign) at the national level spent approximately $20 million in 1960, $25 million in 1964, over $44 million in 1968, and roughly $100 million in 1972.[2] There is no sign that costs are decreasing. And substantial sums were also spent by state and local organizations in behalf of the presidential candidates. Total political costs for all candidates at all levels of government amounted to something like $140 million in 1952, $155 million in 1956, an estimated $175 million in 1960, $200 million in 1964, approximately $300 million in 1968, and $425 million in 1972.[3] The huge costs involved inevitably raise serious questions about the relationship between wealth and decisions in a democracy. Are presidential nominating and electoral contests determined by those who have the most money? Do those who make large contributions exercise substantial or undue influence as a result of their largess? Is the victorious candidate under obligation to "pay off" his major financial contributors? Do those who pay the piper call the tune?

First, let us establish some basic facts. In the general election—that is, after the primaries—Republicans do spend more than Democrats in most places, but the difference is not as overwhelming

CARNEGIE LIBRARY
LIVINGSTONE COLLEGE
SALISBURY, N. C. 28144

as some would suppose. The Democratic percentage of major party postnomination expenditures from 1932 to 1972 has varied from a low of 33 percent in 1972 (when McGovern lost) to a high of 51 percent in 1960 (when Kennedy won).[4] Although the Johnson forces spent more money in 1964 than Kennedy's had in 1960 (the Democrats in 1964 managed to spend $12 million), Goldwater's forces spent $17.2 million, significantly more than Johnson's.[5] Thus, total expenditures of both parties are high in absolute terms, but outlays per voter per party are quite modest, running in the 1972 election to about $1.31 for each of the 76.02 million voters.[6] "Contrary to frequent assertion," says an author who has made a comprehensive study of party finance, "American campaign monies are *not* supplied solely by a small handful of fat cats. Many millions of people now give to politics. Even those who give several hundred dollars each number in the tens of thousands." [7]

Since 1956, roughly 10 percent of the population has been contributing in presidential election years. Data from the Survey Research Center show that 10 percent of a national population sample said they had contributed in 1956, 12 percent in 1960, and 11 percent in 1964. Translating these numbers into individuals, we find that 8 million people in 1956, 10 million in 1960, and 12 million in 1964 contributed to political campaigns.[8] It remains true, however, that the bulk of the money to run campaigns comes from people who contribute over $100. For the years before 1956, two-thirds of the campaign war chests at the national level were made up of contributions of over $500, and an additional one-fifth came from contributions of over $100. At the local level, where approximately six-sevenths of election expenses are met, the proportion of gifts over $500 declines to one-half or one-third. The figures on contributors for 1952 will perhaps give some idea of the numbers. Around 3 million people made some contribution. At least one gift of $100 was made by 150,000 contributors, $500 by 20,000 of these people, and $10,000 or more was given by 200 of these individuals.[9]

The most obvious and most important conclusion in our view is that money does not buy election victories. The candidates and party with the most money do not always win. Otherwise, Republicans would have won every election in the last forty years, and we know, in fact, that the Democrats have won seven of the eleven presidential contests from 1932 to 1972. Nor does there seem to be a correlation between the amount of money spent and the extent of electoral victory in national elections.[10] In 1968, for example, the Republican party outspent the Democrats by more than two to one, yet they won the election by a mere half-million votes out of the 72 million votes cast. One would expect that money would flow into the coffers of the party that is believed to have the best chance of victory. Yet with the possible exception of 1968, there does not seem to be a single presidential election in this century that any competent observer believes would have turned out differently if the losing candidate had spent more money than the winner. We can at once eliminate all the Democratic victories because the Democrats spent less than the Republican losers. Dwight Eisenhower was so popular that his two elections now seem to have been certain, whether he had a substantial campaign surplus or not. No doubt part of the reason he had as much money to run with as he did was his personal appeal to the people who contribute to campaigns, and they might well have given to him even if he had run as a Democrat. Nixon in 1968 had a great deal of money—indeed, probably a surplus—and Humphrey had less than he needed to make an effective race. Because the final outcome of the election was so close and the financial situations of the two major parties so disparate, 1968, it may be argued, is the single exception to the rule, even though it seems more plausible to argue that it was not lack of money but rather the deep divisions within the Democratic party (only trivially reflected in a diminution of contributions) that hurt even more. In 1972, the Committee to Reelect the President raised a colossal amount of money—and, judging from the revelations of Watergate, spent much of it foolishly. The Democrats, meanwhile, had to make do with much less (though more than in 1968), but nobody believes that more money would have helped Senator McGovern's hapless candidacy. The Republicans who won in the period from 1900 to 1928 did so with substantial majorities as befits the party that then enjoyed the allegiance of a preponderant part of the voting citizenry. The problem, then, is not to explain why money is crucial but, on the contrary, to explain why it is not.

No one doubts that money is important; parties and candidates, not to speak of ordinary mortals, can hardly function without it. If a candidate could not raise any money, or only a pitifully small amount, he would be dreadfully handicapped and might not be able to run at all. But this situation has never arisen—Humphrey in 1968 came close—after the national convention has made its choice. The crucial question is not the total spent by the candidates but the difference in the amounts they spend. The first part of our explanation, therefore, is that the differences in spending have ordinarily not been so great as to give any candidate an overwhelming advantage. So long as the poorer candidate can raise the minimum amount necessary to mount a campaign—that is, to hire employees, distribute literature, go on radio and television a few times, get around the country, and so on—he can do most of what he has to do. Another way of putting this would be to say that above the minimum amount necessary to run a campaign the additional expenditures do not appear to confer significant advantages. Like other goods, money is subject to diminishing returns. People may get tired of being bombarded with literature and harangued by speakers. The candidates sometimes worry about overexposure lest they go the way of certain television celebrities who were seen once too often. Criticism of "trying to buy the election" may arise if too much time is taken on television. Indeed, there may be resentment if favorite programs are taken off the air to accommodate a candidate who seems to have had more than his say. We know that many voters are relatively impervious to bombardment by the opposition, and all the handouts in the world will not make them change. The actual result of extensive assault by the richer party may be to increase the polarization of the electorate as those who oppose that party find additional reasons to intensify their opposition.

However, given the necessary minimum amount of money on his side, the less affluent candidate can count on a good deal of free publicity. Presidential campaigns are deemed newsworthy by the press and are extensively reported. While Democrats may get somewhat less space than Republicans in papers, they still get some, and they do better in the magazines and on the air. Thus, they get through to their supporters. To some extent the candidates can make news. John Kennedy's grappling with the religious issue, Harry Truman's assaults on the opposition, Dwight Eisenhower's dramatic promise to go to Korea, all made headlines at little or no financial cost. The television debates in 1960 between Nixon and Kennedy attracted millions of viewers, numbers far in excess of the usual political broadcasts for which fees had to be paid.

The factor of skill must also be considered. Money can be spent for unrewarding purposes which actually rebound against the candidate. Democratic strategists during the 1930s were delighted at the expenditures made by the Liberty League on behalf of the Republican candidate, because they considered it to be an ideal target for their charges that the Republicans were the party of privilege. Money spent may unwittingly get the opposition to the polls. A poor performance on television may do the candidate no good no matter how much is spent. The man who says the wrong thing may deeply regret the wealth that made it possible for him to disseminate his statement widely. The methods by which money is raised, as Nixon learned to his sorrow, may do more to hurt a president when he is in office than they ever did (or could have done) to help when he was campaigning.

Other things being equal, of course, it would be nice to have more money to spend than the other fellow. But conditions are rarely, if ever, equal. The fundamental party allegiances of the population, the state of the economy, religious and ethnic affiliations, the personalities of the candidates—all appear to be more significant in determining the outcomes of elections than the differences in total party spending. Despite the understandable cries of harried party money raisers, the Democrats always seem to come up with enough to get by. There is always the hope of victory. The winner can expect to have his deficits covered at the next round of party "victory" fund-raising drives. It remains true that the most expensive election is the one you lose.

Money probably makes a greater difference at the prenomination stage than later on. Eisenhower and Taft spent about $2.5 million each on their nominating campaigns in 1952.[11] McGovern spent $11.8 million in 1972 on the way to his nomination.[12] The candidate who wishes to enter primaries and conduct a national drive to obtain delegates may be dissuaded through lack of the minimum amount necessary to get started. The lower visibility of primaries and the lesser attention paid to them by citizens may give an advantage to those with more to spend. Money, however, is only one factor. Estes Kefauver in 1952 put on a vigorous campaign despite his relative lack of wealth. Had he not been bitterly opposed by party leaders, or had he won all the primaries he entered, as Kennedy did in 1960, he might have won the nomination. As it was, Kefauver lost to Stevenson whose command of wealth was the least of his political assets. In 1968, Nelson Rockefeller spent over $7 million in his effort to impress Republican delegates with his strength in the public opinion polls, but the effort was fruitless.[13]

Other candidates may, however, have been adversely affected by lack of funds. Nelson Rockefeller in 1960 is a curious example. Apparently he decided not to contest the Republican nomination that year in part because he could not raise the cash, or, one assumes, the enthusiasm that cash contributions symbolize among like-minded party financiers.[14] During the 1960 Kennedy-Humphrey primary campaigns in West Virginia, charges of vast Kennedy spending were made. Certainly, Kennedy's ready cash did him no harm. In retrospect, however, it does appear that he was decidedly more popular with the voters than his rival, Hubert Humphrey. Would more money have enabled Humphrey to turn the tide? Humphrey's campaign was badly managed and severely under-financed and in part this led the press to accord him less serious treatment than he might otherwise have merited. Had Humphrey had as much money to spend on campaigning as Kennedy, for as long a period of time, the tide might conceivably have run in the other direction.[15] There were, nonetheless, other candidates—Johnson and Symington, for example—who had plenty of money but who chose not to contest the primaries.

It is exceedingly difficult to get reliable information on an event that involves a decision *not* to act. Such an event would be a decision by a political candidate not to run because he could not raise the money. There is, of course, no literature on this subject. But there have undoubtedly been some men whose inability to raise the cash has proved fatal to their chances of being considered for the nomination. Whether this failure represents inability to satisfy the monied classes or to convince any number of people that the candidate is serious and worthy is difficult to say in the abstract. A more important question concerns whether there has been systematic bias in favor of or against certain kinds of candidates that consistently alter the outcomes of presidential nominations. We can immediately dismiss the notion that the richest person automatically comes out on top. If that were the case, Rockefeller would have triumphed over Goldwater in 1964 and then again over Nixon in 1968, Taft over Eisenhower in 1952, and neither Humphrey nor Stevenson would have been nominated.

The ability to raise money is not only a matter of personal wealth but of being able to attract funds from others. Does this mean that only candidates attractive to the wealthy can run? It might be said that the problem is not so much whether it helps to be rich but whether men who favor the causes of the rich have the advantage over those who favor the poor. There is little evidence to support such a view. Given the nature of the American electorate, no candidate would openly admit to being the candidate only of the rich. Candidates holding a variety of views on economic issues—most of which are highly technical—manage to run for the nominations of both parties. If candidates are generally chosen from among people who differ but little on most substantive issues the reason is not because the rich are withholding their money from the more radical candidates but rather because the distribution of opinions in the electorate renders the cause of such people hopeless. Our conclusion is that it is nice to be rich; some people who lack funds may be disadvantaged. From the standpoint of the total political system, however, the nomination process does not appear to bar candidates who are otherwise acceptable to the electorate.

The Federal Election Campaign Act Amendments of 1974 were explicitly designed to reduce the influence of money in the electoral process. Whether they will actually accomplish this goal is difficult to calculate. The reform bill does establish a $1,000-per-person limit on contributions to any one candidate's primary, runoff, and general election campaigns, together with an overall limit of $25,000 on contributions by a single individual to all federal candidates in any one year. Organizations of all kinds are limited to $5,000 per candidate per contest. Since there is no limit on how large or small a donating group may be, or on how many donor organizations there are, it is possible that state and regional affiliates of unions or consumer groups or what have you could each contribute the maximum amount up to a total of $250,000.

The act also provides for public financing of presidential primaries, conventions, and campaigns. To be eligible for matching public funds, candidates in a presidential primary have to raise, on their own, at least $100,000, including $5,000 from each of twenty states or more. Only the first $250 of each individual contribution can be matched by the federal government up to a total of $5 million for each candidate, providing that no one primary candidate receives more than 25 percent and no party more than 45 percent of the monies available. Federal payments could not legally be made until January 1976, and only private gifts received after January 1975 are eligible for matching. It is clear that early money, widely dispersed in modest amounts, will be thrice blessed: once for helping a candidate get an early start, once for generating federal matching, and once for multiplying the disparity in private contributions by government aid. If three candidates raised $100,000, $200,000, and $300,000, the difference among them would be half as much ($100,000 and $200,000) before matching as afterward ($200,000 and $400,000).

The two major parties, if they wish, can get $2 million apiece for their national conventions from the Presidential Election Campaign Fund. This fund comes from the money automatically assigned to it when citizens check the proper box on their tax forms. Minor parties may receive lesser amounts based on the percentage of the total vote their candidates have received in a past or current election. Thus new parties have to compete at a disadvantage. To the extent that past presidential elections are used as a basis for calculating support, there is also a danger that a lapse of four years will distort a party's popularity, and the outpouring of third-party sentiment in one year will subsidize the perpetuation of the party four years later, when popular sentiments have shifted.

During the presidential election the major parties can get up to $20 million each from the public fund. They may, however, if they choose, opt for private financing. However, even if they do, the limit on expenditures still applies, and so the parties will undoubtedly take the public route. If they go public, however, they cannot also raise money privately. Again, minor parties are eligible on a proportionate basis, depending on the votes they received at the last general election, so long as they obtained a minimum of 5 percent of the vote.

Each candidate, finally, is required to establish a single central campaign committee through which all campaign contributions are funneled and reported. Specific banks must be designated as depositories of campaign funds. Many committees may be called to contribute funds, apparently, but only one chosen to spend them. These stipulations add to the already strong disclosure provisions of the 1971 Federal Election Campaign Act, the attempted circumvention of which was exposed during the Watergate revelations and subsequent trials and convictions.

Watergate was in part a scandal about campaign finance. It was revealed, for example, as the year of Watergate unfolded, that the Justice Department negotiated a settlement of an antitrust suit with the ITT Corporation soon after an ITT subsidiary, the Sheraton Corporation, agreed to supply $400,000 worth of services to the

Republican party if the party would locate its 1972 national convention in San Diego. Sheraton's offer was only part of a package put together by the San Diego city fathers, in competition with other cities around the country whose visitor's bureaus also wanted to attract one or both national party conventions.

Now the law provides public financing of $2 million to each national party for its national convention and forbids parties to spend more than that on the conventions. It is unclear, however, whether this ban includes the various "in kind" services that traditionally have been provided: automobiles from the major manufacturers, free hotel rooms for the national committee roughly on a ratio of one free room out of every ten paid for, special police protection and trash collection service, and so on. This is one of the most difficult of the questions to be faced by the new bipartisan Federal Elections Commission established for the purposes of monitoring compliance with campaign expenditures laws and distributing public money under provisions for public financing of elections.

There are four broad issues that the new regulations on money have posed. The least troublesome of these is the issue of public disclosure of campaign financing. All contributions in excess of $100 and expenditures by candidates and committees in excess of $1,000 for federal offices are required to be publicly reported under the Federal Election Campaign Act of 1971. The availability of this information led Common Cause, a political action group, to compile and publish lists of contributors for the congressional campaigns of 1972, thus documenting the unsurprising news that some senators and congressmen attracted donations from contributors having business before the committees on which they sat and that some Senate and House races attracted money from sources far away from the state or district concerned. As well they might; a few hundred thousand dollars invested in Delaware or South Dakota could produce a "right"-voting congressman or senator as readily as several million dollars invested in New York or California.

When these are matters of public record, voters can decide for themselves whether their representatives are still able to represent them adequately or not, and can vote accordingly. Against this clear public gain must be weighed the possible chilling effects of publicity on the financial angels of small, unpopular parties. Safeguards against this problem are not at present in the law, although it may be that the First Amendment protections of free speech will be successfully invoked against disclosure on these grounds.

A second feature of the new law is a provision for the public financing of presidential elections, which, as we have said, offers up to $20 million of public funds to each of the major parties, lesser amounts to minor parties, and matching sums to presidential candidates in primary elections. Among the policy issues raised by public financing are: How much should minor parties get? Shouldn't some method be found so that people rather than legislatures allocate public funds to the parties of their choice? In light of the nearly $100 million spent by the major party candidates in 1972, isn't $40 million too low to provide adequate political communication in a nation as large and diverse as ours?

United to this last question is, of course, the question of whether private expenditures should be prohibited where public expenditures are used. Any limitation on campaign expenditure acts as a limit upon political communication, a class of speech that one would think would be especially protected by the First Amendment to the Constitution. In practical terms, limits on campaign spending—now in force in all federal elections—constitute an incumbent's protective device, since challengers almost always have the greater burden of making their names known. When expenditures are limited, political competition is inhibited.

The final issue raised by recent legislation is the issue of limitations on contributions. Here, once again, a First Amendment problem is encountered, since voluntary political contributions by citizens of their own money can readily be construed as exercise of free speech. Against this must be weighed a general public interest in seeing to it that politicians are not unduly influenced by people who have large financial interests. May not those who contribute or raise money in large amounts thereby gain influence not available to others? Aware that the answer to this question is not a simple one and certainly does not dispose of the First Amendment problem, we would say, "Yes, but not overly much." What contributors or fund raisers (the financial middlemen) get to begin with is access to centers of decision-making. Control over money certainly makes it easier to get in and present one's case. Persons of wealth, however, are likely to have substantial economic interests which would provide them with good access whether or not they made contributions. If no significant interest feels disadvantaged by what these contributors want, they may well be given the benefit of the doubt. But in matters of great moment, where the varied interests in our society are in contention, it is doubtful whether control over money goes very far with a president. There are many reasons for this.

In the first place, there are many issues on which a candidate is likely to be already publicly committed. Suggestions that he change his position during the campaign are likely to be met with little favor. If the matter is important enough to be mentioned, it has to be considered in relation to its vote-getting potential. Forced to make a choice, nominees are far more likely to prefer votes to dollars. And even if a miscalculation is made in public, candidates generally prefer not to reverse their field and appear vacillating and inconsistent. Money may be given in the expectation of future favors. To spell this out in detail would appear unseemly, however, and is likely to be rejected outright.[16] The moral sense of the candidates would most likely forbid such a thing. If not, the good political sense of their advisers (certainly after, if not before, Watergate) would suggest that the consequences of discovery are much worse than any possible benefits. Thus, any strings attached to a gift are likely to be vague and cloudy, subject to all sorts of interpretations. When they are not, as in the now infamous milk deal during the Nixon administration, the costs of corruption are as likely to be as high for the contributors as for the public.

Once a president assumes office, he is in a much stronger bargaining position. Contributors are likely to need him much more than he will need them; he can do more to affect their fortunes than they can to affect his. A president may at that point refuse to acknowledge any alleged agreement of policy concessions in return for contributions. Wealthy contributors frequently give to both parties and, in any case, are often found on opposite sides of public issues. For candidates to give in to one of them may simply incur the wrath of others.

A decline in contributions from one source may be made up by funds from another. The president's need to gain or maintain support from the voters, the limits placed on his powers of decision by what congressmen, bureaucrats, and interest groups will accept, and his own preferences, all serve to place drastic limits on benefits contributors get from campaign contributions. In brief, money becomes much less important to the things a president needs to do while he is in office. Contributors may be heard to complain in the hurt tones of Henry C. Frick, who, after visiting Theodore Roosevelt at the White House, said, "We bought the son of a bitch and then he did not stay bought." [17] The foregoing analysis should help to explain why presidential politicians do not "stay bought" whatever their debt to their financial supporters.

It would be amazing if the exponential growth in regulation of private industry did not lead businessmen to seek advantages and governmental officials to confer them. The fact is that what government does—an airline route or a television license here, a tax ruling or an import quota there—can have an enormous impact on the fortunes of private people. Businessmen, we have learned from investigations of the fund-raising practices of the appropriately named Nixon CREEP (Committee to Reelect the President), feel they must act defensively. They may give to a campaign fund not so much to steal a march on their competitors as to make sure they are not left behind. Thus airlines may give to protect their routes. Because government power is so pervasive, businessmen, not knowing when or where they might need a friend, frequently give to the campaigns of both parties as a hedge against future adversity.

And, as we know all too well, favors may be bought and sold. One remedy is to remove the offenders who violate criminal statutes and to replace them with officials having higher moral standards. Another is to remember the biblical injunction against temptation. If we assume today's governmental officials are no worse than they were a decade or a century ago, their temptation to corruption would still be greater than before because their opportunities are so much better. One can (and should) deplore the milk deal; one might also ask what the federal government is doing fixing the price of milk. If there were fewer temptations, there would be fewer buyers and sellers.

Though it is true that the parties usually seem to raise enough money to get by, finding money is likely to be a traumatic experience. Each successive financial campaign tends to be run by different people who have to start from the beginning. Experience is not accumulated as it might be. When Adlai Stevenson was nominated in 1952, he downgraded large contributions and appointed Beardsley Ruml who tried to get most of what he needed from small contributions. Ruml did get more than usual from that source but not nearly enough.[18] Edwin Pauley, who raised funds for Truman, was an oilman who had a wide acquaintanceship among men of wealth and who was adroit in having his claims recognized by groups like road builders and construction firms who could expect to benefit from Democratic policies. Until the Kennedy campaign, the Democrats continued to live, at best, from hand to mouth, day to day, crisis to crisis. President Truman in 1948—few wished to contribute to a sure loser—found himself stranded without funds in the middle of Oklahoma on his campaign train, whereupon the governor and a few others on the train decided that this could not be allowed to continue and found the money. Humphrey was nearly out of money in the midst of his seemingly hopeless 1968 campaign when a plea for funds was inserted as an afterthought at the end of his nationwide television speech from Salt Lake City in which he pledged a bombing halt in Vietnam. Enough money came in to pay for the program twice over. Again, the essential wherewithal was forthcoming but the attendant tension is hardly the best atmosphere in which to conduct a political campaign.[19] In 1964, "when Republican chances of victory over Johnson were never rated much brighter than those of a snowflake in Austin," the Republicans raised more money than they had in any previous campaign. And, contrary to previous campaigns, the money came not from big business but primarily from "small donations sent in by hundreds of thousands of contributors, many of whom had never before contributed to a national campaign." The GOP collected 651,000 small, individual contributions in 1964. Candidates who generate intensely enthusiastic followings seem to be more capable of raising money from small contributions than standard representatives of the parties. For example, George Wallace has always raised a great deal of money this way, and he was the first Democrat to qualify for federal primary matching funds, some eighteen months before the 1976 election.[20]

The fund-raising dinner has in recent years become a major source of money. To the accompaniment of rubbery chicken or, in the more affluent affairs, good steak, the well-heeled come to listen to exhortations at up to $1,000 a plate. The advantages of this system to the parties are many. Attendance is visible. Those who do not come may be conspicuous by their absence. Those who wish to be regarded favorably by the parties' officeholders may decide that it is a good idea to come. Dinners are easy to organize, and a large profit is usually cleared. Such disadvantages as there may be to this system do not seem to accrue to the party coffers so much as to the party faithful. These loyal souls may, if fund-raising meals continue to proliferate, find it necessary to give up one of their expensive hobbies, politics or eating.

One of the more promising fund-raising gimmicks, the selling of advertisements in the program book of the Democratic National Convention at $15,000 a page, had to be abandoned in 1965 because of adverse publicity. Lacking this source, Humphrey turned in 1968 to the device of securing loans to cover campaign expenses as they arose. Prominent contributors would sign notes with banks and would then be paid back as funds from more traditional sources (dinners and so on) arrived. Most of the debt left by the Democrats in 1968 involved these outstanding loans.[21]

After the election of 1960, President Kennedy shifted the emphasis in fund-raising back from numerous small contributors to a few large ones. A Presidents' ($1,000 a year) Club was formed, whose members were rewarded with invitations to White House social functions and other notable occasions. Under LBJ this club became the primary source of Democratic fund-raising to the detriment of formerly broad-based efforts (Dollars for Democrats). The plan worked well in 1964 (when 4,000 members joined), but as Johnson's popularity declined, so did the membership (to 200 in 1966). From 1966 to 1968, Johnson was involved too deeply in other problems to concern himself with party affairs and the decline continued.[22]

In order to pay off the sizable debt left over from the 1968 presidential campaign, the Democrats took to the airwaves and put on a number of fund-raising telethons. These raised more than $2 million each, after costs. In recent years the Democrats have also practiced other methods of debt reduction, including the painful business of negotiating with creditors to see if they would settle for less than 100 cents on the dollar. Political parties and candidates have in consequence of these sorts of maneuvers gotten a bad name for themselves as credit risks. As a result, television stations and newspapers usually require payment in advance. Airlines and the telephone company—both regulated industries, after all, and hence vulnerable to the wrath of newly elected officials—have been edging gingerly toward similar requirements.

With the increase of government regulation of campaign giving, candidates have switched to the attraction of small donations by mass appeals through the mails. Mail solicitation for commercial purposes is a large and sophisticated business, and a whole new class of professional political managers who know about such things—which mailing lists yield the best results, how to write a mail solicitation, how to organize and account for returns—has grown up.

Control over Information

Control over information is another major political resource. Information does many things besides help voters to change their minds—that rare phenomenon. It helps people keep in touch with the progress of the campaign, gives the party faithful indications of the effectiveness of their side, and acquaints voters with the major arguments that the candidates are making. Information helps to guide and channel both the enthusiasm and content of participation, and therefore control over information and its dissemination is a significant political resource.

As we scan the major media of information it appears that, generally speaking, newspapers are a good deal more partisan in their straight news coverage than are the radio and television stations. A political party that feels discriminated against over the air can take its case to the Federal Communications Commission which may require the offending station to make a prompt restitution of the balance of coverage, on pain of removal of the station's license to broadcast.[23] There is no such legal limitation on the "freedom" of newspapers and magazines to be one-sided in the presentation of the news, and, indeed, it has again and again been discovered that the printed media avail themselves rather extensively of this freedom. Many newspapers enjoy monopoly positions in their communities, and much of the political information available comes from the press. For these reasons the character of press coverage of presidential elections is a matter of strategic importance.

It will come as no surprise to regular readers of the newspapers to learn that partisanship in news coverage generally tends to favor that side which is most often endorsed editorially by the press, namely, the Republicans. Repeated studies have shown that the Republicans are normally the favorite party of the newspaper executives who determine editorial policy in most newspapers. And they have also shown that whatever biases exist in news reporting, in the placing of stories in the papers, in the location and size of headlines, and so on systematically favor the Republicans.[24] The election of 1964, with a slight edge to President Johnson, provided the only exception; in 1968 the newspapers returned to form.

Yet, paradoxically, Democratic candidates for president do not seem to be harmed excessively by pro-Republican sentiments in the press, even among voters who rely heavily upon newspapers as sources of civic information. In recent decades Democrats like Franklin Roosevelt, Harry Truman, and John F. Kennedy have gained office despite the fact that a vast majority of the press was against them. If electoral votes had been apportioned within each state by the number of newspaper endorsements for each candidate, the 1968 count would have been Nixon 521, Wallace 17, Humphrey 0; if they had been apportioned on the basis of the circulation of these papers, the count would have been Nixon 471, Humphrey 60, Wallace 7; the actual result, of course, was Nixon 302, Humphrey 191, Wallace 45.[25]

Despite the seeming Republican edge, the days of the crusading editor who owned his own paper and used it as a vehicle to propagate his own political doctrines are largely gone. In our time, newspapers with substantial circulations are much more likely to be part of a corporate chain devoted primarily to making money for their stockholders.[26] The costs of publication are high. In order to show a profit, papers must have a substantial circulation and a good deal of advertising. This is difficult to achieve in the midst of competition among several papers and accounts for the trend toward consolidation. Reader attention is gained by emphasizing stories with high human interest appeal—sports, crime, local personalities, and the high jinks of movie stars. Political news, though it does have a place, is subordinate because most readers are not terribly interested in politics. An excessive emphasis upon public affairs, therefore, is unlikely so long as appeal to readers is a prime consideration. This certainly has drawbacks for civic education. But for present purposes, it means that the possibilities for political propaganda are much less that they otherwise might be, because public affairs do not get much space.[27] Advertising is gained by convincing businessmen that it will pay them in terms of increased sales. The periodic appeals of conservatives requesting businessmen to place or withhold advertising as a form of political coercion usually falls on deaf ears, because the motives of those who pay are commercial rather than political. Both the paper and its advertisers are likely to shy away from many forms of political controversy; it tends to make enemies rather than friends and is commonly believed to be "bad for business." The result is that much of the time newspapers are rather bland. Such political opinions as they do express are watered down so they will not give offense. Their political opinions, far from being their central concerns, tend to be sporadic and aimless, rather than representative of a coherent political ideology.[28]

These tendencies are strengthened by a prevailing belief that papers ought to be nonpartisan in their news stories and present both sides of the issues of the day. However much the norm of impartiality may be honored in the breach, it provides a standard which serves to some extent to hold down partisanship. More than that, the belief that it is a newspaper's function to report what happens rather than to editorialize in its news columns has many other attractions for editors. It enables them to escape to some extent from the hostilities engendered by political controversy; it lessens problems of editorial judgment, thus decreasing the amount of work they have to do; it enables them to select items that they think will enhance their readership; it provides editors with a rationale for defending themselves against the charge of giving too much prominence to causes and candidates that may be unpopular with advertisers or some influential readers. This norm leaves the papers open to manipulation by political strategists who can create sensational news stories. During the heyday of Senator Joseph McCarthy, for example, newspapermen slowly became aware of the extent to which they had aided him by publicizing his charges, because they were "news," rather than ignoring or carefully evaluating them.[29] During presidential campaigns, application of the same standard gives the candidate who is opposed by newspapers the opportunity to enter at least some of its news stories because whatever he says is "news." If he should be an incumbent, his exposure will be greater because the president of the United States, as the outstanding public official and symbol of the nation, gets attention for the smallest things that he and his family do.

The desire to cut costs has at least one favorable consequence for increased impartiality in news stories. There is today a growing reliance on material put out by the giant news services, the Associated Press, United Press International, and to some extent the *New York Times*, *Los Angeles Times*, *Washington Post*, and *Chicago Daily News* services. These news-gathering agencies serve an exceedingly wide clientele which includes a broad spectrum of opinion. They therefore endeavor to prepare stories that will prove acceptable to various shades of opinion.[30] Presenting what happened with a minimum of slanted commentary is a good way to do this, though the wire services are by no means perfect in this respect. The final product, however, is closer to the canons of impartiality than would be the case if each paper prepared stories in accordance with its editorial position.

While it remains true that candidates favored by newspapers receive better treatment and somewhat greater coverage than others, there is one compensating factor in presidential campaigns that has not received the attention it deserves. If the papers are generally conservative and Republican, political correspondents are comparatively more liberal and Democratic.[31] The stories they send, though subject to the mercies of the editor in the home office, serve to a certain extent to redress the balance on the paper. This is particularly the case in the rather subtle question of how candidates are portrayed. The feeling that some candidates are more responsive, more open, more friendly, more intelligent than others may get communicated through little human interest stories and result in an impression contrary to that preferred by the owners of the paper. Such appeared to be the case in 1960 with John F. Kennedy, who was popular with the reporters; and the extra attention he received resulted in complaints from Richard Nixon, who was not so popular with them.[32] By 1968, Nixon was a battle-scarred veteran who could watch with grim satisfaction as the press pursued the early Republican front-runner, the relatively inexperienced George Romney. Jules Witcover comments:

> Romney, Nixon reasoned correctly, had not yet learned the lessons about the press that Nixon's experience had taught him, and even if he had, he could not go into hiding. A moratorium on politics by a former Vice-President, Presidential candidate and conspicuous globe-trotter would make little difference, since his face and his views already were widely known in the country; Romney, however, needed exposure in large doses on the national scene if he hoped to graduate to the status of a national candidate. That exposure, Nixon was confident, would be Romney's downfall. . . . Meanwhile, Nixon himself could sit back, let Romney's destruction happen, and emerge all the stronger by virtue of the contrast between the way he and Romney conducted themselves in the pre-election year shakedown.[33]

In 1972, Nixon carried his strategy of avoidance even further, programming himself into local television spots in key places around the country and totally bypassing exposure to possible hostile questions from news correspondents.[34]

Are ordinary citizens actually influenced in their opinions and voting choices by the newspapers they take? We use the word "take" advisedly because the fact that a newspaper enters a home is no guarantee that its political news and editorials will be read. Most people pay little enough attention to politics; they often read nothing or just scan the headlines without taking away much of an impression. Analyses of tons of newspaper clippings showing political propaganda by newspapers mean nothing insofar as the effect is concerned if these stories are never read.

When stories and editorials are perused with some care, the reader's perception of what has been written may differ markedly from the intentions of the writer on the newspaper. An editorial may not be clear in intent, particularly if it is hedged by qualifications or watered down to minimize offense as is often the case. Frequently, the reader pays attention only to those parts of the piece which substantiate his own opinions. Opinion studies have demonstrated the remarkable capacity of people to filter out what they do not wish to hear and come away with quite a different impression than an objective analysis of an editorial or article would warrant. Indeed, the reader may interpret the story to make precisely the opposite of what it intends; a criticism of Harry Truman for being vituperative, for example, could be taken as a commendation of his fighting spirit,[35] just as a condemnation of Gerald Ford for being obstinate could emerge as praise for his high principles.

Stories and editorials may also be interpreted as they were meant to be and still be rejected as invalid. There is a great deal of suspicion of the press in the United States. Party identification is so powerful a force that it is likely to overwhelm almost anything a paper says. Obviously, millions of citizens have no difficulty remaining and voting Democratic while reading Republican newspapers. Group loyalties are another force that may lead to rejection of opinions in newspapers. Face-to-face groups in unions, on the job, in fraternal, religious, and ethnic organizations, may generate opinions of their own. If these differ from those in the newspaper, the members of the group are provided with defense against the persuasion of the press. Group pressures of this kind are likely to be far more influential than what is written in a paper. The group may also reinforce what the paper says, but this represents an intensification rather than a change of opinion.[36]

No doubt the monopoly position of most newspapers in local communities makes the dissemination of opposing views more difficult than it might be in the presence of competition from a newspaper of a different outlook. But there are ways of getting around this. Other publications may enter the home—magazines and pamphlets that are religious, ethnic, union, fraternal, and even political in their focus—and these may contain contrary notions of public policy and candidate preference. True, only a relatively few persons read the political magazines. But these people are likely to be opinion leaders, people who take an active interest in public affairs and from whom others seek advice. The availability, therefore, of little magazines of many shades of opinion permits the opinion leaders to receive and then disseminate on a personal basis information that may counteract whatever is in a newspaper.

Consider a puzzle concerning the political impact of the *New York Daily News*, a sensational tabloid with a circulation in the millions. It is apparent that if those who read the *News* all through the 1930s and '40s had voted against Franklin D. Roosevelt, as the paper repeatedly recommended in vitriolic terms, Roosevelt would certainly never have carried New York City by the huge margins he did. At the same time it seems strange that so many people who not only voted for but revered FDR in New York continued to read a newspaper whose editorials bitterly attacked their hero. The Democratic readers of the *News* apparently managed to get the best of both worlds. They read the paper they liked and voted for the man they favored without noticing the apparent contradiction—because, for them, there was no contradiction. They either did not pay attention to the editorials, or they blocked out the unfavorable ones completely, or they interpreted them to mean something favorable to FDR. Voting studies document instances where people who wanted to vote for Harry Truman in 1948 convinced themselves that the incumbent president was against price controls; some people who preferred Dwight Eisenhower in 1956 apparently had no difficulty in believing that he surely favored medical care for the aged.[37]

Or, let us consider the case of the opposite of the *New York Daily News*, the gray, sober, responsible *New York Times*. After the *Times* came out for John F. Kennedy in the closing weeks of the 1960 presidential campaign, various political pundits speculated on the probable impact of this endorsement by so august and respectable a source. Our theory about voting behavior would lead us to be wary of claiming much influence for the *Times*, not because its readership is too indifferent to heed this call to reason but because of the kind of people who read this paper. One has to be terribly interested in politics to read through the *Times* as far as the editorial page. People who read that far are among the small, interested minority who comprise the core of the strong party identifiers. Precisely because of their interest, they are likely to identify with a major party and to resist changing their allegiance. A call from the *Times*, therefore, however respectable, could hardly shake these devoted party people in their fundamental loyalty. The vacillating, the doubtful, and the uninformed who cannot make up their minds are far more likely to read comic books or *Modern Romance* than the *New York Times* with its surfeit of dull news about political events.

What, then, is the significance of newspapers in presidential campaigns? We have suggested that the press is by no means immensely influential. Its major importance probably lies in two directions: presenting some kind of information about the candidates and the campaign to its readers and intensifying the predispositions held by people who tend to agree with the paper's preferences. Under some circumstances, also, the press, if united, can force politicians to pay attention to a particular range of issues, not by telling people what to think so much as, in Bernard C. Cohen's excellent phrase, telling them what to think *about*. If one asked the candidates, they would undoubtedly prefer to have the press on their side instead of against them. But they can and do win in the face of opposition from the press.

It may be that the newspaper a person reads subtly conditions his attitudes in ways now unsuspected and that this has some effect on his opinions and voting choice.[38] One study, by Robert S. Ericson, suggests that when a newspaper in a monopoly position endorses a presidential candidate, that endorsement slightly influences the prevailing trend. Ericson found no influence for the press in 1968, a close election, but some in the polarized contest of 1964, when the usual Republican predominance lessened, and in 1972, when it intensified. The press matters more, it appears, as a conveyer of information during landslides when its effect on the outcome matters less.[39]

Undoubtedly whatever impact the press has varies enormously with circumstances. Against a well-known and immensely popular president like Franklin Roosevelt in 1936 or Lyndon Johnson in 1964, with substantial publicity resources of his own, the impact of the press may be negligible. Against a little-known candidate like Adlai Stevenson in 1952, the attitudes communicated by the press—say, aloofness, overintellectuality, indecisiveness—may be more significant. Yet we know from voting studies that in 1952 Stevenson was favorably regarded by Democrats who identified him with his party.[40] The sheer number of different issues that may become relevant during a presidential campaign may also neutralize or intensify the influence of the press depending on whether they are "pocketbook" issues that are grasped with relative ease by voters or "style" issues that owe their existence as issues to the attention paid them by the media of mass communications.

It might appear that radio and especially television have significant impact on electoral outcomes because more people get their news from these sources today than from any other. This may well be true for local, state, and congressional elections where voter interest and information is low. It is probably more true for primary elections at these levels where sheer name recognition may count a great deal. But, whatever may be true under other conditions, it evidently does not hold for presidential elections. Studying several gubernatorial, congressional, and presidential elections, Gary C. Jacobson found "only a small, statistically insignificant relationship between the candidate's relative proportion of broadcast media exposure and the proportion of the votes he receives" at the presidential (but not at the other) levels. In presidential contests, he explains, voters reach their saturation level of exposure long before any disparity in attention to or communications from the candidates makes a difference.[41]

Incumbency as a Resource: The Presidency

The presidency is one resource which, in any given election year, must of necessity be monopolized by one party or the other. When an incumbent president seeks reelection, he enjoys many special advantages by virtue of his position. He is, to begin with, much better known than any challenger can hope to be. Everything the president does is news and is widely reported in all the media of information. The issues to which the president devotes his attention are likely to become the national issues because of his unique visibility and capacity to center diffused public attention on matters he deems important. To this extent, he is in a position to focus public debate on issues he thinks are most advantageous. The president can act and thereby gain credit. If he cannot act, he can accuse Congress of inaction, as Truman did in 1948 and Ford did in 1975. Should he face a crisis in foreign affairs, and there are many, he can gain by doing well or by calling on the patriotism of the citizenry to support its chief executive when the nation is in danger. An example of this occurred during the 1964 campaign, when United States vessels in the Gulf of Tonkin were fired upon and President Johnson took to the airwaves to promise rigorous defensive measures. In late July, just before the incident, he attracted 59 percent of the voters, to 31 percent for Goldwater; in early August, just after the incident, the president's score went up to 65 percent, and Goldwater's declined to 29 percent.[42] The Tonkin Gulf episode also shows that the president cannot count on continued popularity if his policies do not appear successful to the electorate. President Nixon, to make a similar point in a different context, made repeated use of national television to mobilize support for his Vietnam policy. So long as his administration's actions were in accord with general public desires for withdrawal, even if gradual, the president did well in the polls. When he sent troops into Cambodia instead of withdrawing them from Vietnam, however, it was less clear that his fellow citizens approved of that course of action.[43]

As the symbol of the nation, the president can travel and make "nonpolitical" speeches to advance his candidacy subtly, while his opponent is open to charges of "blind partisanship" in what are becoming unceasingly troubled times. Should his opponent claim that he can do a better job, the president need hardly make the obvious response that he is the only candidate who has had experience in a job for which there exists no completely appropriate prior training. Presidents, moreover, as Nixon did in 1972, can campaign by doing their jobs while the challenger, as McGovern discovered, has to manufacture positions that may dissolve upon close scrutiny or criticism.

The life of the incumbent, however, is not necessarily one of undiluted joy. If the economic situation takes a turn for the worse, if a race riot erupts, if another nation comes under Communist influence, he is likely to be blamed as the man who was in office at the time. Whether he is really to blame or not, he is held responsible and has to take the consequences. Herbert Hoover felt deeply the sting of this phenomenon when the people punished the "ins" for a depression that Hoover would have given much to avoid. Gerald Ford may fall into the same fissure.

Moreover, the incumbent has a record. He has or has not done things, and he may be held accountable for his sins of omission or commission; not so the man out of office, who can criticize freely without always presenting realistic alternatives or necessarily taking his own advice once he is elected. The "missile gap" of 1960 turned out to be something of a chimera after Kennedy got into the White House, and he never found it possible to act much differently toward the Matsu-Quemoy situation than did Dwight Eisenhower, despite their overpublicized "differences" about this question during the campaign. Richard Nixon could complain about the problem of "law and order" in 1968 without promising anything more concrete than a new attorney general, which he would have appointed anyway. The incumbent is naturally cast as the defender of his administration and the challenger as the attacker who promises better things to come. We cannot expect to hear the man in office say that the other fellow could probably do as well or to hear the challenger declare that he really could not do any better than the incumbent, although both statements may be close to the truth.

While his opponent can to some extent permit himself to be irresponsible or carried away by exuberance, the president cannot detach himself from office while campaigning, and he must recognize that other nations are listening when he makes statements. The president's very superiority of information may turn out to be a handicap as he cannot make certain statements or reveal his sources for other statements without committing a breach of security. His opponent can attack his record, but the incumbent may have difficulty finding a comparable record to assail on the other side—unless, of course, a McGovern comes along who strives and succeeds at making his proposals the issue.

Incumbency as a Liability: The Vice-Presidency

Yet the incumbent president does have some advantages; it is the candidate who seeks to succeed an incumbent of his own party who suffers the most. His is the unhappy lot, as Stevenson discovered in 1952, Nixon in 1960, and Humphrey in 1968, of getting the worst of all possible worlds. He suffers from the disadvantages both of having to defend an existing record and of being a new man. He cannot attack the administration in office without alienating the president and selling his own party short, and he cannot claim he has experience in office. It may be difficult for him to defend a record he did not make and may not wholly care for. His is the most difficult strategic problem of all the candidates.[44]

Thomas Riley Marshall, the genial Hoosier who was Woodrow Wilson's vice-president, once observed that the office he had in the U.S. Capitol was so little protected from tourists that they used to come by and stare at him like a monkey in the zoo. "Only," he complained, "they never offer me any peanuts."

This is the way vice-presidents have viewed their constitutional office, not just its physical setting, for a long time. "Not worth a pitcher of warm spit" was the bowdlerized version of John Nance Garner's rueful conclusion in the mid-thirties. "A mere mechanical tool to wind up the clock" was the way the first vice-president, John Adams, described himself. "My country has in its wisdom contrived for me the most insignificant office that was the invention of man."

The main constitutional function of the vice-president is to wait. Clearly this is not much of a job for a major political leader, used to active leadership. Yet suppose a sudden tragedy (be it physical, mental, or moral) should befall the president. Can we afford in the inevitable days of uncertainty that follow such an event to replace him with anything less than a major political leader who can step into the breach immediately, do the president's job, and do it well?

This is the first and fundamental dilemma of the vice-presidency and as the quotation from John Adams amply testifies, it has been with us since the founding of the Republic. From this dilemma flow the problems characteristic of the modern vice-presidency.

We can date the modern vice-presidency from April 12, 1945, the day Franklin Roosevelt died. The next day his successor remarked to some newspapermen: "Boys, if you ever pray, pray for me now. I don't know whether you fellows ever had a load of hay fall on you, but when they told me yesterday what had happened, I felt like the moon, the stars and all the planets had fallen on me."

Harry S Truman had been a respected but not a leading senator before he assumed the vice-presidency. In his three months in that office Vice-President Truman saw President Roosevelt only a few short times. As vice-president he had not been told of the Manhattan Project to build the atomic bomb. Sticking closely to the duties prescribed under the Constitution, Mr. Truman spent the vast bulk of his time on Capitol Hill, presiding over the Senate.

His knowledge of the affairs of the executive branch and of foreign and military operations was the knowledge of an experienced legislator and not the inside information routinely available to top policy-makers in the Roosevelt administration. Mr. Truman wrote later, "It is a mighty leap from the vice presidency to the presidency when one is forced to make it without warning."

Since Harry Truman made the leap in the waning days of the Second World War, the world has grown more complicated, and so has the presidency. Efforts have accordingly been made to update the vice-presidency to meet modern conditions. The vice-president now sits with the National Security Council as a matter of right; under President Eisenhower, the vice-president attended all meetings of the cabinet at the president's invitation and presided in the president's absence. In addition to his Capitol Hill quarters, Vice-President Johnson had a suite of offices in the Executive Office Building adjacent to the White House. For a while President Nixon moved Spiro Agnew to an office down the hall from his own. Nelson Rockefeller has not only been made head of the Domestic Council by President Ford, but has also been allowed to bring his own men in as top staff assistants in this presidential agency.

Since 1945, presidents have made greater efforts to involve vice-presidents in various administrative activities: goodwill tours abroad, occasional attempts to promote legislation on Capitol Hill, honorific jobs "coordinating" programs to which the president wants to give a little extra publicity, and, especially, political missionary work around the country—speeches and appearances in behalf of presidential programs.

These are the tasks of the modern vice-president. In return for continuous briefing on the entire range of problems confronting the government, vastly improved access to the ear of the president, and a closer view of the burdens of the presidency, the modern vice-president must carry some of these burdens himself.

Which burdens he carries, how many, and how far are up to the president. Naturally a vice-president may withhold his cooperation; but if he does, he impairs his relationship with the president. This is bound to affect his capacity to fulfill the constitutional obligation of the vice-presidency, which is to be genuinely prepared in case of dire need.

The vice-president is in no sense the second in command in a president's administration. In truth, he is entirely removed from any chain of command at all in the government. This guaranteed the independence of the vice-president in the days of Aaron Burr, John C. Calhoun, Charles Dawes, and other free spirits who have occupied the office.

Today, the situation is quite different: it is much easier for high members of a president's administration to maintain independence from the presidency. Top administrative officials can constitute a loyal opposition on government policy within the executive branch because their obligations run in at least three directions: upward to the president, downward to the agencies whose programs they supervise within the administration, and outward to the clientele their agencies serve.

Political executives serve the president best who serve their clients with devotion and promote the interests of their agencies with vigor. They know, moreover, that if in the process they conflict too much with presidential plans or priorities the president can always fire them. If the president fails them in some serious way, they can resign as Attorney General Richardson did when President Nixon removed Special Prosecutor Cox during the memorable "Saturday night massacre" of October 1973.

The vice-president can hardly fulfill his constitutional responsibilities by resigning, nor, in midterm, can he be dismissed. He has no anchor in the bureaucracy, no interest group constituency. Thus, uniquely in the executive branch, the modern vice-president must discipline himself to loyalty to the president.

This sometimes has painful consequences for vice-presidents, especially when they attempt to emerge from the shadow of the president and run for the presidency on their own. It is scarcely necessary to note Vice-President Humphrey's difficulty in persuading opponents of the Vietnam war that he and President Johnson were not Siamese twins.

Voters with longer memories may recall Vice-President Richard Nixon's similar problem in 1960, when Senator Kennedy wanted to get the country "moving again." Mr. Nixon somehow had to offer a new program of his own while defending the eight Eisenhower years, wrapping himself in the mantle of his popular predecessor, but taking no notice of the occasional potshots the general peevishly took at him. Neither Nixon nor Humphrey was fully able to run independently on his own record.

There seems, in short, to be no way for a vice-president to avoid the dilemmas built into the office: Unless he is scrupulously loyal to the president, he cannot get the access to the president that he needs to discharge his constitutional function; when he is loyal to the president, he is saddled, at least in the short run, with whatever characteristics of the president or his program the president's enemies or his own care to fasten on him. He sits there in the limelight, visible, vulnerable, and, for the most part, powerless.

Nevertheless, as long as vice-presidents have some chance eventually to run for the presidency, as they presently do, and are not arbitrarily excluded from further consideration as independent political leaders in their own right, there will be plenty of takers for the vice-presidential nominations. This contributes to the strength of political parties.

Vice-presidential nominees can balance tickets, help to unite a warring party, and campaign effectively with party workers and before the public—as, for example, Senator Lyndon Johnson did with conspicuous success in the election of 1960. Thus, vice-presidential nominees can help elect a president. It is after the campaign is over that the vice-president's problems begin.

Unless, of course, by a stroke of good fortune, he and his running mate lose.

Convertibility of Resources

Clearly, the social framework within which presidential election strategies must be pursued distributes advantages and disadvantages rather importantly between the parties. We have attempted to explain why the unequal distribution of key resources such as money and control over information do not necessarily lead to election victories for the parties and candidates who possess and use most of these resources. Might there not, however, be a cumulative effect that would greatly assist those who possessed both more money and more control over information? This effect may exist, but it could obviously not be of overwhelming importance since the Democrats, who are usually disadvantaged in these respects, have won most elections since the 1930s. We can suggest three reasons for Democratic strength despite these disadvantages. First, the Democrats are able to convert other resources into money and control over information, thereby narrowing the gap during campaigns. Second, the Democrats have superior access to other important resources which may overwhelm the Republican superiority in money and control over the media of information. Third, the Democrats are better able in general to convert some resources into others than are their opponents.

Once the Democratic party assumed the presidency in 1933 and held it for twenty years, it was able to use the resource of official position to collect campaign funds because contributors wanted access to the winner. The party could also get greater news coverage because the president's activities are newsworthy no matter what his party. The alliance of the Democrats with the large industrial unions has, at times, meant that the party has received contributions in the coin of personal electioneering for which the Republicans had to lay out cash or do without. The superiority (perhaps the mere existence) of Democratic organizations in cities of large population with strategic impact on the Electoral College has sometimes led to the availability of election workers who did not have to be paid in cash—at least not during the campaign and not at all if the party lost the election. The appeals of the Democrats to ethnic, racial, and religious groups has meant that publications of these specialized groups might serve to offset the preponderant Republican orientation of the daily press.

The fact that the Democrats have approximately a two-to-one lead over Republicans in party identification is perhaps the most effective resource in the Democratic arsenal—so effective, indeed, that it is apparently more than enough to compensate for whatever advantages the Republicans gain through wealth and the mass media. For unless the Republicans manage to do something special, or the Democrats oblige, as they did in 1968, by falling into spectacular disarray, or in 1972, by selecting a candidate who appealed to purists but not to the people, the voters will elect a Democrat by following their usual partisan dispositions. To be sure, other factors—turnout, for example—are not always equal; otherwise the Republicans would never win. But in the sheer numbers of nominal supporters the Democrats are ahead at the start. Republicans need a break to win; Democrats just have to play by the rules.

Implicit in these remarks is the proposition that the Democrats in our era are better able to convert their resources into success at the polls than are the Republicans; that is, the party identification of a significant majority of the electorate can more easily be turned into electoral victory than money or control over information can be turned to winning the allegiance of citizens to a different party. Party identifications change but slowly and change significantly only under the impact of events in the society that profoundly affect the mass of citizens. No one really knows short of that how to go about changing the party identifications of masses of people in the same partisan direction.

The Republicans can use their advantage in turnout to overcome the Democratic advantage in party identification. They can try to make party identification seem less relevant at election time by putting up an attractive candidate who is "above" partisanship. They can capitalize on errors by Democrats or on dissatisfaction with a Democratic administration. No one can claim to predict the outcomes of elections yet to come; certainly we cannot. Nothing that has been said here means that a Republican might not win handily, as Eisenhower did in two elections and Nixon did in 1968 and 1972 after the Vietnam issue decimated the Democratic party leadership and the Democratic party undertook to reform itself in a way that gave at least a temporary advantage to a candidate whom the majority of voters perceived as an extremist. Speaking in terms of probabilities over several elections, however, it seems to us that the Democrats are likely to win more often than they lose. When Republicans win, the cause will normally be found in something the Democrats did to make it possible.

Notes

1. Our discussion of money in elections owes a great deal to the work of Herbert Alexander who, over the years, has built up an unequaled store of knowledge on this subject. Recent legislation affecting money in politics includes the Federal Election Campaign Act Amendments of 1974, 2 USC 431, and the Federal Election Campaign Act of 1971. For a wide-ranging set of materials on election reform up to and including the 1971 act, see U.S. Senate Select Committee on Presidential Campaign Activities, *Election Reform: Basic References* (Washington, D.C., 1973). A compact summary of the state of the law as of 1975 is contained in U.S. Senate Subcommittee on Privileges and Elections of the Committee on Rules and

Administration, *Federal Election Campaign Laws* (Washington, D.C., 1975). For a useful discussion of the new law's political implications, see the American Bar Association, *Symposium on Campaign Financing Regulation* (Chicago, 1975).

2. For 1960 figures, see Herbert E. Alexander, *Financing the 1960 Election* (Princeton, 1962), p. 10. Figures for 1964 are contained in Herbert E. Alexander and Harold B. Meyers, "The Switch in Campaign Giving," *Fortune*, November 1965, pp. 103–8. Figures for 1968 are contained in Herbert Alexander, "Financing Parties and Campaigns in 1968: A Preliminary Report" (mimeo, Citizens Research Foundation, Princeton, 1969). Figures for 1972 are contained in Herbert Alexander, *Financing the 1972 Election*, forthcoming.

3. Alexander Heard, *The Costs of Democracy* (Chapel Hill, 1960), pp. 7–8; Herbert E. Alexander, "Financing the Parties and Campaigns," in *The Presidential Election and Transition, 1960–61*, ed. Paul T. David (Washington, D.C., 1961), pp. 116–18; Alexander and Meyers, "The Switch in Campaign Giving"; Alexander, "Financing Parties and Campaigns in 1968," p. 2; Alexander, *Financing the 1972 Election*.

4. Heard, *The Costs of Democracy*, pp. 18–22, 39; Alexander, "Financing the Parties and Campaigns," p. 118; Alexander and Meyers, "The Switch in Campaign Giving"; Alexander, *Financing the 1972 Election*.

5. Alexander and Meyers, "The Switch in Campaign Giving."

6. Alexander, *Financing the 1972 Election*.

7. Heard, *The Costs of Democracy*, p. 6.

8. Ibid., p. 41; Herbert E. Alexander, *Financing the 1964 Election* (Princeton, 1966), pp. 68–69.

9. Heard, *The Costs of Democracy*, pp. 49–53.

10. For expenditure figures, see ibid., pp. 17–24, and, for 1956 on, see Alexander, *Financing the 1972 Election*. The following table is adapted from figures in both these books.

	Democratic Percentage of Two-Party Vote	Democratic Percentage of Two-Party Expenditures
1932	59	49
1936	62	41
1940	55	35
1944	52	42
1948	52	39
1952	44	45
1956	42	41
1960	50	51
1964	61	37
1968	49	35
1972	37	33

On the state level, however, the story may be different. See Murray Levin and George Blackwood, *The Compleat Politician* (Indianapolis, 1962), pp. 227–43.

11. Alexander, "Financing the Parties and Campaigns," p. 119.

12. Alexander, *Financing the 1972 Election*.

13. Alexander, "Financing Parties and Campaigns in 1968," p. 9.

14. See Theodore H. White, *The Making of the President, 1960* (New York, 1961), pp. 71–74.

15. See ibid., pp. 92–110, and Harry W. Ernst, *The Primary That Made a President: West Virginia, 1960* (New York, 1962), especially pp. 16–17, 29–31. Several factors appear to have contributed to Humphrey's difficulty in raising money. First and probably foremost, he had very little of his own to draw upon. Second, Adlai Stevenson was being indecisive and refused to withdraw from contention. Thus, Stevenson's backers were encouraged to wait and see rather than switch monetary support to Humphrey. Had Stevenson not been in contention, Humphrey might have gotten more money. And third, Humphrey apparently was unwilling to do things that would severely alienate the other candidates or otherwise jeopardize his future associations in the party. He may, therefore, have been restrained from actions that would have aided him. A revealing passage in White, *The Making of the President, 1960* (pp. 109–10) indicates what may have been involved: "In New York, from which so much Stevenson money had originally come to Humphrey's coffers, Governor Abraham Ribicoff, acting on Kennedy's instructions, warned all Stevensonians that if they continued to finance the hopeless campaign of Hubert Humphrey, Adlai Stevenson would not even be considered for Secretary of State. Where necessary, Kennedy lieutenants were even rougher; in Connecticut, Boss John Bailey informed former Connecticut Senator William Benton . . . that if he continued to finance Humphrey (Benton had already given Humphrey $5,000 earlier in the spring), he would never hold another elective or appointive job in Connecticut. . . ." Benton disputes this story. "It was wholly out of character for John Bailey to say anything like the words Teddy White ascribed to him. . . . John Bailey did get in touch with me, but what he said was this: 'Since you gave $5000 to Hubert's campaign I want you to even the account by giving $5000 to Jack Kennedy's campaign.' I told John that if Jack was nominated for the presidency, I would give him $10,000, which I later did." Quoted in Sidney Hyman, *The Lives of William Benton* (Chicago, 1969), p. 529.

16. In October 1968, for example, a multimillionaire named Stewart Mott offered to raise a million dollars for Hubert Humphrey, then in desperate need of cash. Mott "made it clear that the Presidential candidate would have to modify his views on Vietnam." Humphrey refused Mott's offer. Herbert Alexander and H. B. Meyers, "A Financial Landslide for the GOP," *Fortune*, March 1970, p. 187.

17. Quoted in Jasper B. Shannon, *Money and Politics* (New York, 1959), p. 35.

18. Heard, *The Costs of Democracy*, pp. 249–58.

19. See ibid. and Shannon, *Money and Politics*, p. 59. On pp. 13–65, Shannon presents a colorful history of American experience in raising money for presidential campaigns.

20. Alexander and Meyers, "The Switch in Campaign Giving," pp. 103–8. In 1968, the pattern of small giving continued, augmented by the return to the Republican fold of many large contributors who had defected to President Johnson in 1964. See Alexander, "Financing Parties and Campaigns in 1968."

21. Alexander, "Financing Parties and Campaigns in 1968," p. 64.

22. Alexander and Meyers, "The Switch in Campaign Giving," pp. 105, 186.

Maurice Stans started an analogous "R. N. Associates" for candidate Nixon in 1968. Jules Witcover, *The Resurrection of Richard Nixon* (New York, 1970), p. 239.

23. Television stations have few programs of news commentary and these are not usually overtly partisan. (To be sure, the wealthier party may buy more TV time for its candidate, but we have already discussed the limitations of this resource.) Radio news commentary is more ubiquitous, but only those who initially agree with highly opinionated commentators are likely to tune in regularly. Consider, however, the impact of television coverage of the 1968 convention in Chicago. One incident will suffice to give a sense of the options open to television news directors under special circumstances: "Alioto rose on screen to nominate [Humphrey]; back and forth the cameras swung from Alioto to pudgy, cigar-smoking politicians, to Daley, with his undershot, angry jaw, painting visually without words the nomination of the Warrior of Joy as a puppet of the old machines. Carl Stokes, the black mayor of Cleveland, was next—to second Humphrey's nomination—and then, at 9:55, NBC's film of the bloodshed had finally been edited, and Stokes was wiped from the nation's vision to show the violence in living color.

"The Humphrey staff is furious—Stokes is their signature on the Humphrey civil-rights commitment; and Stokes' dark face is being wiped from the nation's view to show blood—Hubert Humphrey being nominated in a sea of blood." Theodore H. White, *The Making of the President, 1968* (New York, 1969), pp. 300–302.

On the evening of August 28, 1968, according to Richard Pride and Barbara Richards, "NBC showed the same violent event, which lasted less than five minutes, from three different camera angles with three separate reporters and led viewers to believe it was one continuous battle lasting several hours." "Denigration of Authority? Television News Coverage of the Student Movement," *Journal of Politics* 36 (August 1974), p. 640.

24. See Nathan B. Blumberg, *One-Party Press? Coverage of the 1952 Presidential Campaign in 35 Daily Newspapers* (Lincoln, Neb., 1954); Edwin Emery and Henry L. Smith, *The Press in America* (Englewood Cliffs, N.J., 1954), pp. 714 ff. Arthur Edward Rowse, *Slanted News: A Case Study of the Nixon and Stevenson Fund Stories* (Boston, 1957).

25. "634 For Nixon, 146 For Humphrey (and 12 For Wallace)," *Editor and Publisher*, November 2, 1968, pp. 9–10.

26. A. J. Liebling, with characteristic pungency, puts the proposition this way: "With the years, the quantity of news in newspapers is bound to diminish from its present low. The proprietor, as Chairman of the Board, will increasingly often say that he would *like* to spend 75 cents now and then on news coverage, but that he must be fair to his shareholders." *The Press* (New York, 1961), p. 5.

27. Bernard C. Cohen, in *The Press and Foreign Policy* (Princeton, 1963), presents figures from a variety of sources on foreign affairs news (Chapter 4). His conclusion: "The volume of coverage is low."

28. Following is an example, atypical but illuminating, of this aimlessness at work. Former House Speaker Joseph Martin in his memoirs describes the appearance of an editorial mildly critical of presidential candidate Thomas E. Dewey in Martin's

own newspaper (Martin was editor and publisher) on the day of Dewey's arrival in Martin's hometown during the 1948 campaign. "Behind all this fuss was a very simple explanation. Having a small staff, the *Evening Chronicle* bought 'boilerplate' editorials prepared by a syndicate. The day of Dewey's visit, the editorial in question happened to be on top of the pile, and a man in the composing room slapped it into the paper. Ironically, he was one of the most ardent Dewey supporters in North Attleboro. As for myself, I never read the editorial until it was well on its way to fame." Joseph W. Martin, Jr., *My First Fifty Years in Politics*, as told to Robert J. Donovan (New York, 1960), pp. 196–97.

29. See Richard Rovere, *Senator Joe McCarthy* (New York, 1959), pp. 137, 162–69.

30. See Frank Luther Mott, *The News in America* (Cambridge, Mass., 1952), p. 110; and Emery and Smith, *The Press in America*, pp. 541 ff.

31. See William L. Rivers, "The Correspondents after 25 Years," *Columbia Journalism Review* 1 (Spring 1962). On p. 5 he says, "In 1960, 57 per cent of the daily newspapers reporting to the *Editor and Publisher* poll supported Nixon, and 16 per cent supported Kennedy. In contrast, there are more than three times as many Democrats as there are Republicans among the Washington newspaper correspondents; slightly more than 32 per cent are Democrats, and fewer than 10 per cent are Republicans. . . . More than 55 per cent of the correspondents for newspapers consider themselves liberals; 26.9 per cent consider themselves conservatives."

32. See White, *The Making of the President, 1960*, pp. 333–38. Corroborative testimony is given by Benjamin C. Bradlee, *Conversations with Kennedy* (New York, 1975). On Barry Goldwater's press relations, see Charles Mohr, "Requiem for a Lightweight," *Esquire*, August 1968, pp. 67–71, 121–22.

33. Witcover, *The Resurrection of Richard Nixon*, p. 173. See also pp. 188–92.

34. Timothy Crouse, *The Boys on the Bus* (New York, 1972, 1973), pp. 189–90; Theodore H. White, *The Making of the President, 1972* (New York, 1973), pp. 251–68; Witcover, *The Resurrection of Richard Nixon*; and Joe McGinniss, *The Selling of the President, 1968* (New York, 1969).

35. Elmo Roper has observed that "on the civil rights issue [in 1948], Mr. Dewey draws the support of voters favoring exactly opposite things, and more than that, each side thinks Dewey agrees with them." Hugh A. Bone, *American Politics and the Party System* (New York, 1955), p. 447.

36. This paragraph summarizes the major findings of researchers on what has come to be called the "two-step flow" of information. See Elihu Katz and Paul F. Lazarsfeld, *Personal Influence* (Glencoe, Ill., 1955).

37. Key, *Public Opinion and American Democracy*, p. 453.

38. An example would be in instances where candidates were not known to voters before the campaign or where they ran without benefit of party labels, as in local nonpartisan elections. See Charles R. Adrian, "Some General Characteristics of Nonpartisan Elections," *American Political Science Review* 46 (September 1952), pp. 766–76; Charles E. Gilbert and Christopher Clague, "Electoral Competition and Electoral Systems in Large Cities," *Journal of Politics* 24 (May 1962), pp. 323–49, especially p. 344; and Raymond E. Wolfinger and Fred I. Greenstein, "Regional

Political Differences in California," *American Political Science Review* 63 (March 1969), pp. 74–86.

39. Robert S. Ericson, "The Impact of Newspaper Endorsements on Presidential Elections," paper delivered at the annual meeting of the American Political Science Association, 1974.

40. Campbell, Converse, Miller, and Stokes, *The American Voter*, pp. 58, 530.

41. Gary C. Jacobson, "The Impact of Broadcast Campaigning on Electoral Outcomes," paper delivered at the annual meeting of the American Political Science Association, 1974.

42. American Institute of Public Opinion Survey, released October 18, 1964. For other examples, see Nelson W. Polsby, *Congress and the Presidency* (Englewood Cliffs, N.J., 1971), p. 45.

43. Witcover, *The Resurrection of Richard Nixon*, pp. 462–63.

44. The material in this section is adapted from Nelson W. Polsby, "Any Vice President Is in Dilemma," Topical Comment, *Los Angeles Times*, August 28, 1968.

CHAPTER THREE

Nomination: Before the Convention

Obtaining the presidential nomination of a major political party in this country has never been a simple process. Today, however, this process has grown even more difficult. There are new rules governing the conduct of candidates, activists, and party regulars in the preprimary period, during the actual delegate selection phase, and at the national party conventions themselves.[1]

Before the Primaries

Once upon a time, not so long ago, there was a gap between presidential election campaigns, a little breathing space during which, we assume, politically active citizens occupied themselves with such unexciting business as, for example, making a living like ordinary people (for those out of office) or governing (for those in office). What has caused this space to shrink so drastically, in spite of the entreaties of reformers and the bleats of journalists?

Essentially, as we see it, the spreading out of preconvention party skirmishing, extending first to the primary phase and now to an ever lengthening preprimary period, is, in part, a direct result of rules changes governing delegate selection to the national convention— and especially, of course, the national convention of a party that has no incumbent president eligible for reelection.

These rules changes have had the net effect of increasing the number of different people each candidate for the nomination must reach and, if possible, convince of his worthiness. The more people you have to reach, the more time and the more money it takes to do the job. We reserve for later a consideration of whether this can be called a democratization of the candidate selection process. There is something to be said on both sides of that proposition. For the moment, however, we must put ourselves in the shoes of the candidate for a presidential nomination who confronts the following rules of the game:

1. (For Democrats) Convention delegates must be selected in the year of the convention according to rules mandating that state parties "assure that such delegates have been selected through a process in which all Democratic voters have had full and timely opportunity to participate . . . [further] the convention shall require that: A) The unit rule not be used in any stages of the delegate selection process; and B) All feasible efforts have been made to assure that delegates are selected through party primary, convention or committee procedure open to public participation within the calendar year of the National Convention." [2] The Republican party has faintly echoed these changes by calling on states to publicize the process of delegate selection.

2. Candidates of either party may be eligible for the funding of their primary up to $4.5 million each if they can raise at least $5,000 cash in each of twenty states (or more) before the primary (only the first $250 of each contribution being eligible for matching).

3. In the Democratic party, any candidate in a statewide primary who receives more than 15 percent of the vote obtains a proportionate share of the delegates (unless the national committee approves a winner-take-all procedure for an election process taking place at the congressional district level).

If rule 1 of the new ball game is that the more people you have to sell, the longer it takes, rule 2 is as follows: The more restrictions that are placed upon the expenditure of money, the harder it is for newcomers to public notice to get into the race. Anybody whose name is known ahead of time—movie stars, sports figures. incumbents of high office—gets a boost. The upshot of these changes in rules of the game is to make it more (rather than less) important for serious candidates to contest primary elections. For one thing, proportionate rules for counting votes will encourage Democrats to contest more primaries for the simple reason that there are delegates to be had. For another, primaries generate attention, and this means more people will be enticed out of the woodwork to make financial contributions that the government will then match. The rules also, as we shall see, make bargaining at the convention more difficult.

In part, no doubt, candidates will be reading the lessons of 1972 into future election years. For among the axioms of conventional wisdom to bite the dust in 1972 was the notion that an early announcement of candidacy was a sign of a weak candidate and that it therefore behooved front-runners to avoid an early disclosure of their plans, with all the inconvenience and running around that an active campaign entails.

In some respects, the 1972 preconvention race in the Democratic party provided an interesting transition between old and new practices. Democratic party rules were written in such a way as to placate those elements of the party who were most disaffected in the debacle of 1968, namely, the left wing. There is reason to believe that this was done in part because party leaders who both acquiesced to and enforced these changes were reasonably confident that placating the left in this fashion would merely legitimize throughout the party the eventual selection of a broadly based, centrist candidate.[3] Early in the 1972 election season, at least two such candidates were extremely visible to party leaders: Senator Edward Kennedy and, after the Chappaquiddick incident put Kennedy out of action, Senator Edmund Muskie of Maine. By early 1971, Muskie was leading President Nixon in Gallup trial heats. Consequently, giving in on party rules must have seemed to party leaders a low-cost proposition. As the leading Democrat in all polls, Muskie concentrated his early efforts upon securing endorsements from party notables. However, by the time of the primary elections, when Muskie got around to announcing his candidacy formally, Senator George McGovern had already won the allegiance of and organized the most energetic segment of the party. McGovern's was the only organization that employed grass roots activists in large numbers. Like Goldwater among Republicans in 1964, McGovern won not because he was the most popular candidate among his fellow partisans, but because he was best organized to move into state primaries and state party conventions and take them over from party regulars.

Party rules could not have created Goldwater-type Republican activists who were far more conservative than ordinary Republican voters. Party rules may have strengthened but they did not create Democratic party activists who differed widely from ordinary Democratic voters on a wide range of political issues. The growing gap between activists and rank-and-file voters in both parties raises fundamental problems of political philosophy. Should intensity of preference (and the possession of resources making it possible to express preferences intensely on policy issues) count as heavily as it now does in the nominating process? Should power in political parties go to those who participate the most, or to those in the populace they are supposed to serve?

In practice, this does not pose a choice between the many party voters and the few party activists. What is really at stake is a choice between "regular" party leaders and workers, whose commitments to public policy are not so intense that they have lost interest in what ordinary people think, and "activist" party leaders and workers, for whom public policy, not pandering to the public, is the central issue. Both of these groups participate more than ordinary voters. One group seeks to give "the people" what they want; the other, considering themselves "the people," seek to give themselves what they want. This reality, we believe, is concealed by party reform rhetoric in which rules changes shifting power from one elite group to another are justified on the grounds that "the people" rather than an elite group are the true beneficiaries of the change.

When party activists and party voters held similar preferences these questions did not arise—what was good for the activist was good for the voter and vice versa. But those days disappeared for the Republicans in the 1950s and for the Democrats in the 1960s. Today, Republican activists are far more conservative and Democratic liberal activists far more liberal than the voters identifying with these parties. Should the parties seek to represent their own activists or their strong party identifiers or their voters or the entire population? Should they represent the regulars who work in their party organizations or enthusiasts who appear in force during the presidential election year? If parties are supposed to represent enthusiasts, then changes in the rules are working in the right direction, but if they are supposed to represent their identifiers or their voters or their regulars then they are not. If representation means having delegates to national conventions who meet certain biological criteria—sex, race, age—then the parties represent certain groups well and others badly. If representation means that delegates are in accord with the candidate preferences, policy positions, and social philosophies of voters in their own party, then they are hardly representative at all. The rules favor representation of activists who emerge in the presidential election year and whose preferences may well be distant from those of party identifiers or voters in general. But these rules did not emerge out of thin air; they are responsive to strong currents, especially within the Democratic party, identifying representation with biological quotas and favoring representation by people willing and able to engage in high rates of political activity for short periods of time. Inevitably, these developments reinforce one another so that the objectives and strategies of the nominating process have been transformed. It may be useful, therefore, in appraising the extent of the changes that have come about, to consider them not only in their own right but in relation to past practices.

Goals

The delegates to national party conventions are selected state by state, in conventions or primaries, or by a combination of the two methods.[4] They represent the outcomes of processes that are slightly different in their legal requirements and political overtones in each of the states, the District of Columbia, and the territories—all of which send delegations to both party conventions. But when delegates arrive at the convention, they enter into a social system in which their roles are reasonably regularized. Not surprisingly, they try to behave in a way that will maximize their political power to nominate a candidate who can win the election or to assure that their own views will be expressed at the convention. The rational dice player will place his bets in accordance with his chances of winning under the rules of the game he is playing. Similarly, the rational delegate will be expected to be reasonably well informed about how his behavior affects his chances of achieving his goals, and he will behave in accordance with his information, his position in the game, and the goals he intends to achieve.

At most party conventions, the great search has been for "The

Man Who Can Win," for without hope of victory, over the years there would be little reason for a heterogeneous party to stay together. Even if the parties were far more cohesive than they are today, they still could not disregard the need to get into office now and then by nominating a popular candidate. But increasingly, as more and more delegates are selected under rules favoring enthusiasm over party regularity, delegates look for a candidate who represents them, not necessarily the voters.

The desire to nominate a winner is widespread, but it is not equally distributed among delegates. It is the professional politician's reason for being there, but the purist is more interested in his relationship to the candidate than the candidate's relationship to the people. Preoccupation with winning is weaker among delegates with deep and intense policy commitments and stronger among those who are not so fiercely committed to specific policies.

Capitalizing on the desire to nominate a winner, candidates seek to demonstrate that they can win and others cannot. They cite polls and make complicated electoral analyses in order to convince delegates on this point. Frequently, there appear to be several strong candidates, and disagreements about which one is the most probable winner often take place because the delegates have private preferences and lack enough information about what the voters are likely to do.[5] To the extent that delegates are purists, however, candidates have an incentive to sing an Ivory Soap commercial—99 and 44/100 percent pure. Candidates will not only want to show they share delegates' policy preferences at the convention but also that they will take risks—even court disaster—to promote them in the campaign. Whereas the politician wishes to demonstrate flexibility in adapting to popular preferences, the purist wishes to reveal rigidity in adhering to the policy positions of the delegates.

Politicians seek to maintain or increase their own political power. In order to do so, most of them feel that they must, in general, increase the potential vote for candidates whom they sponsor. The more leaders who agree on a candidate and the more interest groups and state party organizations that are working for his election, the greater are the chances that he will win office and provide those politicians who supported him with access to political power. Party unity, therefore, is perceived by politicians as an important prerequisite to the achievement of victory. Unless party leaders achieve a consensus among themselves, the chances are diminished that they will be able to elect a president. As a result, party politicians tend to nominate candidates who at the least are not obnoxious to, and ideally are attractive to, as many interest groups and state party leaders as possible.[6] If winning becomes less important, or purism more important, or both, the incentive to find a candidate with broad appeal will decline. Compromise will be more difficult not only at the electoral level but within the convention because purist principles frown upon it. Whatever candidates do to make themselves more acceptable to people other than their die-hard supporters, will tend to erode their original base of support.

But these are only tendencies; circumstances alter cases not only for politicians but for purists as well. Throughout the ever lengthening preprimary, primary, and state convention days, purists mobilize around candidates whom they come to care about. It is not so easy for them to disregard their candidate's preferences at convention time because of the emotional ties that have grown up between them even if, in principle, issues should count more and personalities less. The tendency for winners to establish themselves early also means that successful candidates, more than their supporters, have a personal organization that, with nomination assured, looks forward to the election campaign to follow. To impose their views on candidates, therefore, purist delegates would have to organize themselves exceedingly well in a few days at the convention and persuade a majority of all delegates, including politicians, that their party's chances in the general election should be subordinated to a phrase in a plank of a party platform or a provision in party rules. Unless the proportion of purists is very large and the organization of their candidate is very weak, the candidate can do a great deal to moderate the terms of debate.

These situational factors explain why behavior at the 1972 "McGovern" Democratic convention was not quite what his purist supporters would have preferred. McGovern was better organized than the women's or youth caucuses, for instance, which helps explain why statements on abortion and marijuana did not make it into the Democratic platform despite the fact that a majority of his delegates preferred legalizing them both.[7]

Things can (and in 1976 may well) change. The abolition of winner-take-all primaries at the state level in favor of proportional or district delegate selection may make it more difficult for any one candidate to come to the convention with a majority. In this case, candidates may be weaker and delegates stronger. The prohibitions against unit rules and instructing delegates, which used to force all of a state's votes to be cast in the same direction, will also make bargaining more difficult, because fewer delegates will come pre-packaged in cohesive voting blocs organized by state leaders.

The members of each party may love their party on a sentimental basis. But do they love one another? The convention tests party unity by determining whether the disparate elements that make up each party can agree on one candidate to represent them—a candidate who cannot possibly be equally attractive to all of them. Party unity may aid in securing victory, and this provides an incentive for keeping all the factions under the same party umbrella. But the differences among delegates may be so great that no one is quite sure whether they can agree. The much maligned party platform is exceedingly important in this regard, not so much for what it makes explicit as for the fact that it is written at all. The platform tests and communicates the ability of the many party factions to agree on something, even if on some crucial points major differences have to be papered over.[8] Nixon in 1960 wanted a reasonably strong platform on civil rights that would reflect his views and not alienate black voters. As a result, he had a staff member draw up a lengthy statement of his own views. During the course of the meetings of the platform subcommittee dealing with civil rights, Nixon's spokesmen actively participated in the discussion and bargaining. When it began to look as if the subcommittee report would be most unsuitable, the Nixon staff contacted the leaders of state delegations from which the members came. Nevertheless, Nixon's views became the minority report of the subcommittee by an eight to seven vote. Finally, Nixon himself was called in. He spoke to members of the full platform committee, and his staff followed up by seeking pledges of support. The Nixon draft won by a vote of 55 to 45.[9]

One of the important estimates that rival party leaders must make is how far they can go in attaining their preferences without completely alienating some faction, resulting in its withdrawal from the convention or refusal to support the party nominee in the election. This information may not be available until party factions begin to bargain at the convention. The McGovern organization in 1972, for example, did not realize until too late the depth of disaffection by the AFL-CIO union leadership. The angry speech by

I. W. Abel of the Steel Workers Union was the only five minutes the AFL-CIO had on the platform of the convention. While Hubert Humphrey in 1968 might have been willing to write a plank acceptable to opponents of the Vietnam war, President Johnson was not. Consequently, Humphrey never got the enthusiastic support of key Democratic activists who disagreed vehemently with Johnson's conduct of the war. Where they did not damn Humphrey outright, they simply failed to show any enthusiasm. By the time they realized he still might be preferable to Nixon, it was too late; Humphrey never recovered from the demoralization of the early days of his campaign.

Delegates like a winner; they also want to have a claim on him so that he will consider their views favorably. Thus, they seek a candidate who is known to be friendly to them, whose policy views tend to coincide with theirs, or who will be indebted to them because they have provided support toward his nomination. Jim Farley's famous list establishing priorities for distributing patronage—FRBC (For Roosevelt Before Chicago)—illustrates this point. It helps to explain the rush to get on the bandwagon by delegates who wish access to the winning candidate.

But this rush may slow to a walk if there is no hope or no point in getting on—no hope because delegates are too far apart, no point because (for politicians) the candidate is thought to be a sure loser or (for purists) because they would rather be right.

The urge to find or start a bandwagon is likely to be strongest for workers in the organizations of candidates. For them politics is not only about policy but about careers. They have invested huge amounts of time, at low or no wages, to move ahead in political life. Though they may have started as adherents of a candidate or a cause, they naturally want to do something with the skills they have learned and the contacts they have made. Their best chance, of course, is to stick with their own candidate; but if the nomination is beyond their reach, they may be tempted to stay in politics by seeking access to the winning candidate. Rank-and-file delegates, who lack this opportunity and hence this temptation, are more likely to prefer purity and say they are being sold out. What the politician would regard as a necessary accommodation, the purist, precisely because of the gap between promise and performance, would consider an act of betrayal.

At a contested convention there will be few chiefs and many

Indians. Purist delegates may stick with their candidates to the end; it will be difficult, and in some cases impossible, to lead them to another. Had McGovern not made it in 1972, for instance, it is doubtful that his organization would have been able to transfer many of its votes to another candidate. Regular delegates come from state parties with internal lives of their own. They spend over 1,400 days every four years as members of their state parties and less than a week at the national convention. So far as they are concerned, it would be unwise to commit acts at the convention—such as supporting a candidate unpopular in that state, or compromising at the wrong point in a fight over the platform—that would lead to years of bitter internal rivalry. Yet it is not always possible to avoid mistakes. Delegates may misjudge who will run well in their state and provide a "coattail effect."

Sometimes nominees run better in states that opposed them at the convention than in those that gave them support.[10] In any event, it is clear that in order to interpret or predict a state's behavior a presidential aspirant must acquire information on internal party affairs which may prove indispensable to planning his strategy and may enable him to take advantage of or to avoid dangerous party splits.

All this supposes that delegates are identified with their state party and expect to maintain that identification for years to come. This, indeed, is the hallmark of the professional politician. But the amateur purist may not feel that way at all. Encouraged by the new party rules, which open delegate selection to people who have literally just come in off the streets, they may have little past party experience. Neither having come from their state organization nor expecting to go back to it, they have little reason to worry about how their behavior will affect their party, if, in fact, they think of it as theirs. As a few McGovern delegates put it, "Democratic Party? Why I've never voted for a Democrat in a general election. . . . I was in the streets in Atlantic City in 1964 and Chicago in 1968. . . ."[11]

We have seen that some delegates have strong policy preferences. Black delegates may care deeply about racial questions. Union officials and industrial executives may be unwilling to support candidates presumed to be hostile to the interests they represent. Delegates from the District of Columbia may consider crime to be of paramount importance while the men and women from New York may be adamant about welfare. There are consistent liberal and conservative blocs in both major parties. To some extent, therefore, intense policy preferences may restrict the actions of delegates who share them; delegates may seek the candidate who has the best chance of winning among those who meet their specifications on crucial policies.

The major goal of the presidential aspirant in the convention is to win the nomination; but in addition the nominating convention must be regarded as the first part of the election campaign. This is all the more reason why prospective candidates, even while belaboring one another in an attempt to get the nomination, must give due consideration to the necessity for party unity in case they win. There are several ways in which this party unity is achieved. One device available to the winner of a contested nomination is to select the disappointed presidential aspirant with the second most votes in the convention as a vice-presidential nominee, as Kennedy selected Lyndon Johnson in 1960.

"My most critical problem," Richard Nixon wrote of the 1960 convention, "was to see that our Convention ended with all Republicans united behind the ticket. If this were to be accomplished, I knew I had to take some decisive action with regard to Nelson Rockefeller. . . . My goal was to beat Kennedy—not Rockefeller. . . . I felt it was essential that he be an enthusiastic rather than a reluctant supporter of my candidacy after the Convention. His differences with [Eisenhower] Administration policies had to be ironed out." So Nixon took the initiative in meeting Rockefeller and from 10:00 o'clock one evening until 4:30 the next morning they hammered out a joint statement.[12] Afterwards, Nixon was inevitably (and as it happens quite wrongly) accused of "selling out" to Rockefeller, but this did not deter him in his search for party unity.

In 1968, Nixon's problem was to bring the South into his electoral coalition, and so he made a special effort in that direction in the convention, promising southern delegates that he would select no vice-presidential nominee who would "tear the party apart."[13] Johnson's moves to ensure unity at the 1964 Democratic convention included naming Senator Hubert Humphrey to the vice-presidency in order to appease the liberals and compromising on the Mississippi Freedom Democratic party challenge to the Mississippi delegation by seating the latter but allowing the former the status of observers.[14]

McGovern's choice of Eagleton in 1972 was designed to balance his ticket with a young moderate who was acceptable to the AFL-CIO.

An extreme purist, of course, would insist that a vice-presidential running mate should not so much balance as overbalance a ticket. So far, only Barry Goldwater has taken this path, with his nomination of William Miller ("He'll drive Lyndon crazy," Goldwater said) in 1964. In the future, however, we may expect more one-sided tickets. The more purist the parties become, the less they will be able, or desire, to balance their tickets.

Incumbent presidents and other obvious choices, such as Richard Nixon in 1968, are in a good position to treat the convention as the opening gun of their campaign. They can participate wholeheartedly in the party rituals, the speech-making, informal social gatherings, and the self-congratulation that give the party faithful at the convention a sense of identity and mission and that project over television an image of unity, purpose, and togetherness. Such nominees also can manipulate the party platform to offset their real or imagined weaknesses with the electorate and to capitalize on their strengths. In contested conventions, the platform must be negotiated among representatives of the leading contenders and major segments of the party, and so it is less easy to write a platform that the eventual winner can call his own and comfortably campaign on.

Thus, we can describe briefly the major goals of most delegates to national conventions. They want to gain power, to nominate a candidate who can win the election, to obtain some claim on the nominee, and to protect their central core of policy preferences.

Uncertainty

It is far easier to describe goals than to attain them. The attainment of each participant's goal requires a great deal of information about the future. What will the electorate do at the polls months after the convention? Who will other delegates to the convention support and for how long? What will be the effect of initial declarations and switches of support on other delegates? What bargains can particular candidates make? Are they willing to bargain at all? What will be the consequences of the nomination for one's state party? For the careers of the candidates' organizers? For the national parties?

Answers to these and other questions about convention events are either entirely obvious, because a majority has been formed beforehand, or extremely uncertain. There are good reasons for this. The answers depend, first, on national and world conditions, which we have not learned how to predict—war, depression, inflation, urban unrest. To pick an extreme example, the candidate who appears likely to win in peacetime may not be able to command the support of the electorate during open warfare unless he happens to be the incumbent president. Second, the answers depend on a complex series of events involving the actions, reactions, and intentions of others. To obtain a claim on the winner, a delegate (or delegation) often must contribute to his support at the convention by guessing who will win in time to "get on the bandwagon." But more than one bandwagon may appear to be in the making, and delegates and their political leaders may have difficulty deciding when is the best time to make the jump and gain great bargaining advantages for themselves. Then, too, a delegation's estimate of who will win may be determined, in part at least, by the estimate it makes about what other delegations are going to do. And their behavior, in turn, may be influenced by what still others do or say they are going to do. This situation may result in a self-fulfilling prophecy where a delegation's estimate of who is most likely to win leads to actions that influence others in the same direction and confirms its original expectation. A third difficulty in acquiring the necessary information results because delegates are required not merely to predict an isolated set of occurrences (although this would be difficult enough) but to gauge the outcome of complex chains of events. If Nominee A receives support from delegation B and wins decisively in primary C, then he will be in a position to bargain with delegation D and to use this leverage to gain support from party leader E, which in turn will lead to the possibility of heading off rival nominee F, and so on.

There are some potentially reliable sources of information—primaries, polls, balloting on procedural motions or on the platform, successive nominating ballots, shifts by key delegations—which are avidly observed. But these publicly available indicators of what might happen in the future do not necessarily have meaning in themselves; they are given meaning by interested observers. Unless the significance attributed to the indicators is widely shared and clear beyond any doubt, so that one overwhelming favorite emerges, the delegate is still left with the troublesome problem of interpretation.

Many of the standard indicators may be perceived to be ambiguous. Did Senator John F. Kennedy emerge from the 1960 Wisconsin primary with a margin of only 100,000 votes, or did he win by the substantial margin of 100,000? [15] Did Robert Kennedy win a "smashing victory" over Eugene McCarthy in the 1968 California primary by receiving 46 percent of the vote to McCarthy's 42 percent, or did he fall short? [16] Was McGovern's 1972 30 percent plurality in Wisconsin a major victory and his defeat in Pennsylvania to be discounted? Perceptions (and hence interpretations) of identical indicators may vary widely depending on the delegate's predispositions, or on the amount of reinforcement or counterinterpretation to which he is subjected. Unless a delegate's interpretation of events coincides with those made by others, his predictions and the actions based on them may be invalidated. At best, the delegates swim in a sea of uncertainty.

One may well ask whether the new rules for selecting delegates will increase or decrease uncertainty. Insofar as the occurrence of contested conventions is concerned, the new forces appear to be moving in opposite directions. The increased use of primaries, together with partial governmental financing, makes the emergence of early front-runners somewhat more likely; but the allocation of delegates by proportion of votes received makes it less likely that any single candidate will gain a majority by convention time. On the assumption, then, that we are talking about a contested convention, in which the outcome is not known beforehand, all the forces at work promise to increase uncertainty. Unity within state delegations is less likely because a variety of candidates, under proportional or districting rules, have a chance to acquire delegates. Majority rule within the delegation is forbidden as falling under the prohibition against unit rule voting. And the fragmentation of delegations into varieties of special caucuses makes not only unity but communication more difficult.

If we look at the problem from the standpoint of candidates, we see that they have all the old problems and a few new ones. The rise of purism means that willingness to bargain cannot be taken for granted. The primary system is biased in favor of candidates with early and intense followings—candidates more likely, therefore, to come from the far left or right rather than the center. The new rule forbidding non-Democratic voters from participating in Democratic primaries will mean that "swing votes" from the center will be more

difficult to mobilize. The decline of leadership within state delegations means that many more people must be brought into the act.
Thus the next contested conventions may well be "brokered"
conventions, but with too few brokers present to do the job or too
many, if everyone gets into the act. And once the convention
splinters, it may take more than a kingmaker to put it back together
again.

What delegates believe about what is happening determines the
premises of many decisions. One report on this subject was made by
Colonel Jack Arvey who led the forces in Illinois that wanted to
draft Adlai Stevenson in the 1952 Democratic convention:

> Cook County Chairman Joe Gill and I were having dinner . . .
> when one of our ward committeemen came running over to tell us an
> important roll call vote was under way on the seating of Virginia. . . .
> Gill and I hurried back into the hall. Illinois had already been recorded
> 45–15 against seating Virginia. It suddenly dawned on us what was
> happening. The strategy of the Kefauver backers and the Northern
> liberal bloc was to try and make impossible demands on the Southern
> delegates so that they would walk out of the Convention. If the total
> Convention vote was thus cut down by the walkout of delegates who
> would never vote for Kefauver, then the Tennessee Senator would have
> a better chance of winning the nomination. Our Illinois delegation
> quickly huddled and then changed our vote to 52–8 in favor of seating
> Virginia.
>
> The eight opposed included Senator Douglas and other backers of
> Kefauver.[17]

Suppose that "eight" was "forty-eight" splintered six ways? And
suppose there was no one with whom to bargain, that is, too few
leaders who could speak for anyone else? This is the sort of situation
that future candidates may find themselves confronting.

Power

In the past, a relatively few party leaders controlled the decisions
of a large proportion of the delegates to conventions. Delegates to
national conventions were chosen as representatives of the several
state party organizations, apportioned according to a formula laid
down by action of previous national conventions. While it is true
that official decisions are made by a majority vote of delegates,

American party organizations were often centralized at state and local levels. This meant that such hierarchical controls as actually existed on the state and local levels asserted themselves in the national convention. Until recently the probabilities were fairly good that both major parties at any given time would have succeeded in electing a substantial number of governors and mayors of important cities; the chances were also fairly good, therefore, that a substantial number of delegates would be controlled hierarchically. Some states, of course, may be badly split with no one holding the lever to much more than his own vote.[18]

Normally, state party organizations are unified by incumbent governors. Without the centralizing forces of state patronage and coherent party leadership embodied by a man in the governor's chair, state parties tend to fragment into local satrapies or territorial jurisdictions which can be played off one against another by astute aspirants for the presidential nomination. The lack of strong leadership at the state level also means that within the delegation a set of presidential preferences and strategies for pursuing them is less likely to be worked out in advance and agreed upon by all elements. Decentralized state parties thus become happy hunting grounds for early starters in the presidential sweepstakes. They can move into a vacuum, make alliances and receive commitments, and build delegate strength from the ground up.

The importance of governors at national conventions (and along with them hierarchical control of state delegations) has diminished over the last quarter-century. There has been a little noticed but important secular decline in the number of governorships that are up for election in years during which presidents are also running for office, as the table on page 102 indicates. From the thirty-three governorships that were open to election in 1944, the number declined to twenty-one in 1972 and stands at twenty-four in 1976. Many states are changing the two-year gubernatorial term to a four-year term and are providing for the gubernatorial election in the middle of the president's term of office. This is intended to isolate gubernatorial elections from national electoral currents. But it may also mean that the number of state delegations to national party conventions controlled by governors will decrease as the motivation of governors to protect their own fortunes by finding popular presidential candidates also decreases. This trend thus far has had its most pronounced effect upon the Republican party, where the number of Republican governors up for election in presidential years declined from twenty in 1944 to eleven in 1968.

Number of Gubernatorial Elections
in Presidential Election Years
(Excluding Hawaii and Alaska)

Year	Number of Elections
1944	33
1948	31
1952	31
1956	31
1960	27
1964	26
1968	25
1972	21
1976	24

SOURCE: *World Almanac*, 1944, 1948, 1952, 1956, 1960, 1964, 1968, 1972.

Number of Republican Governors
up for Election in Presidential Election Years
(Excluding Alaska and Hawaii)

Year	Number of Republican Governors up for Election
1944	20
1948	19
1952	15
1956	16
1960	11
1964	7
1968	8
1972	11

SOURCE: *World Almanac*, 1944, 1948, 1952, 1956, 1960, 1964, 1968, 1972.

This fact helps account for the willingness of Republican delegates to nominate Barry Goldwater even though he could reasonably have been expected to hurt the party's chances in many states. There were Republican state leaders in 1964 who winced at the thought of a disastrous defeat in November, but there were fewer such leaders than there might have been because there were fewer (that year, sixteen) Republican governors at the Republican convention. The advantages accruing to Goldwater by declaring an early candidacy under these circumstances are obvious. Governors might have had sufficient hierarchical control over their delegations to keep them from precipitously joining the Goldwater bandwagon. The absence of central leadership on a state-by-state basis meant that delegates were freer to follow their personal preferences and also free to weigh ideological considerations more heavily than they could have if they had been responsible to a leader who would suffer badly if Republicans were defeated for state offices.

The power of elected leaders over their state party organizations varies. Governor Thomas E. Dewey of New York is an example of a governor who was able to wield virtually absolute control over his Republican delegation when he was in office.[19] Other governors may be able to throw their votes to certain candidates but not to others because the delegates would not permit it. The delegation may agree to stick with its leader for a specified number of ballots and no further. Then internal bargaining may take place with the governor acting as first among equals, but no more than that. The desire to maximize the delegation's bargaining power by maintaining a united position may cause a governor to make concessions to some of his delegates.

Barring catastrophic events—depression, war, scandal—the president's power is most certainly strong enough to assure him of renomination within the limits imposed by the anti-third-term (the Twenty-second) amendment to the Constitution. This is not merely because his is the greatest, most visible office in the land with all sorts of patronage and other controls over the potential delegates. There is, in addition, the fact that his party can hardly hope to win by repudiating him. To refuse him the nomination would, most politicians feel, be tantamount to confessing political bankruptcy or ineptitude.

This rule was not broken in 1968. President Johnson had scheduled the convention of the Democratic party to coincide with his birthday in anticipation of his renomination. The fact that his birthday fell in late August left his successor, Hubert Humphrey, with little time to heal the wounds and raise the money needed for victory in November. The challenges of McCarthy and Kennedy in that year demonstrated, however, that the costs of party insurgency are high: not only do insurgents rarely win their party's nomination; their party usually loses the election in such years.

The presidential power over national conventions has historically extended to (1) the right to renomination, or to designate the party nominee, effectively exercised in eighteen of the twenty conventions since the Civil War in which the president interested himself in the outcome; (2) the power to dictate the party platform; (3) the power to designate the officers of the convention; (4) the power to select many delegates. This last privilege was especially potent historically in the case of Republican delegations during the days of the one-party Democratic South, when Republican presidents, until the passage of the Hatch Act, drew upon a corporal's guard of federal patronage appointees to man this sizable convention bloc.

The constitutional amendment limiting presidents to two terms may eventually change the power of a two-term incumbent radically, but we doubt it. The party still must run on the presidential record, and the outgoing president still seems likely to control the management of the convention. Before President Roosevelt broke the two-term tradition, outgoing presidents controlled conventions even when no one expected them to run again. Presidents Truman and Johnson were also very influential in 1952 and 1968 when they were not candidates for reelection.[20]

In the absence of hierarchical control by an incumbent president, decision-making at conventions is ordinarily coordinated by a process of bargaining among party leaders. We think of bargaining as a method by which activities are coordinated in situations when controls between individuals approach equality, where no leader by himself can fully dominate another. Each leader represents a state party or faction within a state which is independently organized and not subject to control by outsiders. In the presence of disagreement and the absence of coercion, leaders must persuade one another, compromise, and form coalitions if they are to gain sufficient support to carry the day. Although the leaders may differ in their preferences among possible candidates, they believe that participating in the bargaining process will aid them in achieving their goals and inform them of the goals and tactics of others, which in turn may help them in attaining their own goals.

Prerequisites to bargaining may be summarized as (1) no hierarchical controls, (2) interdependence of bargainers, (3) disagreement among bargainers, and (4) expectation of gain. When the president is of the opposite party, or of the same party but chooses not to intervene, the convention becomes a bargaining system because no political leader besides the president is in a position to control the national convention by himself. The interdependence of party leaders may be established by reference to the custom of American democracy which allows the voters to replace the elected officials of one party with those of another at general elections. In order to mobilize enough nationwide support to elect a president, party leaders from a large number of constituencies must be satisfied with the nominee. Without agreement on a nominee, none of them is likely to enjoy access to the eventual president; hence, party leaders are interdependent and expect to gain from the outcome of the bargain. Because of the different amounts of access to different aspirants that delegates carry with them into the convention, delegates are likely initially to disagree on their preferences.[21] Most politicians believe that bargaining is necessary and not dishonorable, although Senator Goldwater in 1964 and Senator McCarthy in 1968 took the position that the gains to be expected by bargaining were greatly outweighed by the loss of ideological purity and commitment.[22]

Suppose differences in style—purists versus politicians—or issues —race, income distribution, defense—make bargaining unproductive? The parties might split apart or, if conventions are unable to decide, the choice might be shifted to a national primary. The future of the American party system, for good or ill, then, may be determined by the ability or willingness of delegates to agree on the minimum essential: a presidential candidate.

Preconvention Strategies

The selection of a presidential nominee is the business that dominates the convention. From this it follows that decisions preceding the presidential nomination are important or unimportant largely depending upon their implications for the presidential nomination. Decisions not taken unanimously that precede the presidential nomination in the convention are almost always tests of strength between party factions divided over the presidential nomination. These decisions are usually more important for the information they communicate on the strength of the candidates than for their actual content.[23]

Perhaps the first strategic decision facing an avowed candidate is whether to attempt to become a front-runner by raising enough money in twenty states to qualify for the federal subsidy of his primary campaigns, entering primaries, barnstorming the country, and publicly seeking support at state conventions. The advantage of this strategy is that a candidate may build up such a commanding lead (or appear to do so) that no one will be able (or will try) to stop him at the national convention. The possibility that a candidate might become unstoppable early, reinforced by the larger number of primaries, the prospect of a federal subsidy for primary contestants, and the proportionate allocation of delegates obviously makes early entry more desirable for all candidates than it has been in the past. The disadvantage is that an open campaign may reveal the inability of some candidates to acquire support or may lead other candidates to band together in order to stop the front-runner. Adoption of this position depends for its success, then, upon the front-runner's ability to predict accurately both how he will fare compared with others in open competition and what others will be able to do when they discover his lead. He may, for example, try to anticipate whether his activity will stimulate a coalition of opponents who are otherwise unlikely to get together. If such a coalition seems likely, the candidate may issue communications playing down the extent of his support. But this tactic may discourage new supporters who would have been attracted by a display of strength. Since even losers stand to gain delegates if they get 15 percent of the vote, and since funds depend on visibility, running openly is much more attractive than it used to be.

The dark horse is a possible candidate who avoids primaries and much open campaigning. Like Stuart Symington in 1960, or Richard Nixon in 1964, he is content to be everyone's friend and no one's enemy.[24] As Abraham Lincoln wrote to a supporter in 1860 describing his dark horse strategy: "My name is new in the field, and I suppose I am not the first choice of a very great many. Our policy, then, is to give no offense to others—leave them in a mood to come to us if they shall be compelled to give up their first love." [25] The strategy of the dark horse is to combine with others to oppose every front-runner. His hope is that when no front-runner is left he will appear as the man who can unify the party by being acceptable to all and obnoxious to none. The dangers the dark horse faces are that he will enter the convention with too little support to make a strong bid or that some other dark horse will prove preferable. How much support is enough to make a serious bid but not enough to be shot at as a front-runner? How far behind the front-runner can a candidate permit himself to get without becoming entirely lost from sight? Either an intuitive ability to guess or an exceedingly accurate apparatus for collecting information on the present strength of candidates, as well as on the likely effect of different levels of strength on other delegates, must be part of the serious dark horse's equipment. The best chance for a dark horse in the future is likely to be a deadlocked convention. Well-known party leaders who have run before and have achieved great visibility, like Hubert Humphrey or Edmund Muskie in 1976, can afford the luxury of hoping lightning will strike, without doing too much to stimulate it. If the candidates who contested the primaries and arrived at the convention with pledged delegates are unacceptable to a majority, the party will either have to go back to someone it passed over or break up.

Primaries

In the years from 1968 to 1972 the Democratic Commission on Party Structure and Delegate Selection issued rules changing past party practice. They wanted to make delegate selection more open and representative. So they issued eighteen new regulations opening up meetings to all comers, giving those who come the right to vote, scheduling their choices closer to the election, and seeking to include various demographic groups in proportion to their size in the population. This had the immediate effect of increasing the number of primaries. Seeing that their delegates could be challenged in eighteen new ways, state party leaders in numerous states decided to let all the candidates contend in primaries. Thus, from 1968 to 1975 fourteen states (in addition to the other states that had previously selected their delegates in primaries) adopted primaries as their method for choosing delegates to the Democratic National Convention. More important, as a recent study explains:

> The increase in the number of "effective" primaries was even greater, however, because (required) reforms upgraded previously less significant arenas into serious campaign sites. In fact, the biggest rise in the number of delegates along the primary route came not from new entries but from changes in old ones. In 1968, nearly half of all primaries had been "advisory," i.e., either voters would express a

Presidential preference but delegates would be chosen *independently* in party conventions, or, more commonly, a Presidential preference could not be logically connected with the separate vote for delegates. By 1972, the linkage between candidate preference and delegate selection had been tightened so much that the free agents of past primaries—"favorite sons," "bosses," and "uncommitted" delegates—had almost disappeared.[26]

Primaries are important largely because most of the delegates are selected in them and also because the results represent an ostensibly objective indication of whether a candidate can win the election. The contestants stand to gain or lose far more than the growing number of delegate votes that may be at stake. A man situated as Richard Nixon was in 1960 would be ill advised to enter a primary unless the information at his disposal led him to believe that he was quite certain to win. This stricture applies with special force to any candidate who is well ahead in delegate support. All he can gain is a few additional votes, while he can lose his existing support by a bad showing in the primary since this would be interpreted as meaning that he could not win in the election. The candidate who is far behind or who has to overcome severe handicaps, however, has little or nothing to lose by entering a risky primary. If he wins, he has demonstrated his popularity; if he loses, he is hardly worse off than if he had not entered the primary at all. Such was the case when John F. Kennedy quieted the apprehensions of Democratic politicians about the religious issue by winning in Protestant West Virginia.[27] In 1964 Goldwater needed a primary victory in California to show uncommitted delegates that he had voter appeal, even though at the start of the primary campaigns he had been a prominent candidate. He accepted the risk of losing the nomination if he lost the primary because he needed proof of popularity to get the votes necessary for nomination.[28] Nixon, who had lost the presidency in 1960 and the governorship of California in 1962, had a similar problem in 1968. He had to enter the primaries in order to dispel his "loser" image.[29]

In a primary in which there are many contenders, a defeated candidate may attempt to gain advantage from what may be regarded as an ambiguous result by claiming that the man who actually won was allied to him ideologically. The results may then be viewed as a victory for the ideology rather than defeat for the candidate. After Robert La Follette had won an overwhelming victory in the 1912 Republican primary in North Dakota, Theodore

Roosevelt issued a statement "claiming an immense progressive victory." He even went beyond this to count the La Follette delegation as part of the Roosevelt camp once it had cast "a complimentary vote for La Follette." [30] In the same way, Rockefeller supporters in 1964 hailed the New Hampshire Republican primary, which Henry Cabot Lodge won, as a defeat for Goldwater and a victory for the moderate wing of the Republican party. Something similar went on in 1968; supporters of both Eugene McCarthy and Robert Kennedy claimed that all those who had voted for either man in the primaries had voted against Hubert Humphrey.[31]

One strategy for primaries, the write-in, offers the maximum possibility of gain with the minimum possibility of loss. If a candidate gets virtually no votes, he can easily explain this by saying that he did not campaign and that it is difficult for people to write in names. If he receives over 10 percent of the vote, he can hail this as a tremendous victory under the circumstances. In Nebraska in 1964, Nixon received 35 percent of the vote as a write-in in the primary and it was "claimed that 'Nebraskans have nominated the next Republican candidate for President . . .' a claim that was forgotten after the Nixon debacle in Oregon just three days later." [32]

If a write-in candidate should win, he can build his victory up to the sky, stressing the extraordinary popularity required to get people to go to all the trouble of writing in a name.[33] But the man who is behind cannot rest content with being able to explain away a poor showing; he must win to establish himself as a contender. The strategy of the write-in, consequently, is most accessible to the man who is ahead and hopes to solidify his position while minimizing his risks.

Entering and winning primaries may be of little value unless the results are widely interpreted in such a way as to improve a candidate's chances. The contestant who loses but does better than expected may reap greater advantage from a primary than the one who wins but falls below expectations. It is, therefore, manifestly to the advantage of a candidate to hold his claims down to minimum proportions. Kennedy tried in 1960 to follow this advice in Wisconsin—he claimed Humphrey had been Wisconsin's third senator —but the press, radio, and TV took note of his extensive organization and of favorable polls and in advance pinned the winner-by-a-landslide label on the senator from Massachusetts.[34] Early predictions in the 1968 New Hampshire primary were that Eugene

McCarthy would receive somewhere around 10 percent of the vote. When he eventually polled 42 percent—against Lyndon Johnson's 48 percent write-in vote—it was widely interpreted as a victory, in part because it was so unexpected.[35] The same was true of McGovern in 1972. The public media have taken most of the control over "expectations" away from the candidates.

The significance of primaries has, not surprisingly, risen with the importance of public opinion polls. As knowledge of popular opinion has increased, the media of information have disseminated this data. Why should politicians guess if they can get direct access to public or (if they can afford it) private opinion through polling? The result has been a syndrome in which leaders in opinion polls go on to contest primaries, the winners of the contested primaries do well in future polls and proceed to take the nomination—not always, to be sure, but very often. William H. Lucy, who has done the required research, concludes:

> There have been several strong relationships between polls, primaries, and presidential nominations since 1936. At those 20 national conventions, the nominee has been the preconvention poll leader 19 times. The preprimary poll leader became the nominee 85 percent of the time. The preprimary poll leader continued as the postprimary poll leader 90 percent of the time. Only once has the preprimary poll leader lost primaries and then permanently lost the poll lead. Ninety percent of the winners of the seriously contested primaries who also led the final preconvention polls won the nomination. And 75 percent of the cumulative winners of seriously contested primaries were nominated.[36]

The political consequences are as clear to Lucy as they are to us.

> If primary winners are nearly always nominated, then it behooves would-be leaders to bargain with candidates early in the primary process in order to be on board when their support is still valued. Or, if the preprimary poll leader is nearly always nominated, then this fact would be a cue for party leaders to start to choose sides even before the primaries began. In addition, if candidates leading the polls believed that success in the primaries depended but little on support by political leaders, then the assets with which they would be willing to negotiate with political leaders might be reduced in number and value. As compared with political leaders, those with plentiful campaign funds or media skills might increase their bargaining potential. If primaries were not important enough, however, the Democratic Party has made sure they will not be overlooked.[37]

More than the media, however, the political parties have acted in a way that makes it difficult to avoid primaries. It is no one thing but the whole confluence of events that has conspired to reemphasize primaries.

National party conventions are nowadays convocations of the party faithful only when an incumbent president is due for renomination. Otherwise, the convention is the last stage in a process in which primaries are playing an increasing role. In 1968, only seventeen states selected delegates by primary; in 1972 twenty-three states did so. Obviously, the number of delegates selected in this fashion is on the rise, from 36.7 percent in 1968 to roughly two-thirds in 1972 for the Democrats, and, undoubtedly, even more in 1976.

So, now, who runs in primaries? In an increasing number of states, *all* recognized candidates are placed on the ballot by a state official whether they wish to enter the fray or not. A convergence of opinion, whether justified or not, that no candidate is legitimate without exposure in primaries makes it difficult to stay out. The more primaries there are, the harder they are to miss. And there is an added inducement for candidates to enter. Delegates on a statewide basis are to be allocated proportionally, which means that even losing candidates can frequently pick up a few delegates.

Since primaries have become so important—almost but not quite indispensable—for presidential nominations, it behooves us to learn more about how they operate. Which candidates, and the interests they represent, are advantaged or disadvantaged by primaries? Will radicals, conservatives, or moderates do better or worse with more extensive use of primaries? Are citizens' preferences more or less likely to be reflected in the results? If not citizens, then, whose preferences will be met? How do the rules for counting votes affect the results? We begin with this last important question because it turns out that the way votes are counted in large measure determines whose preferences count the most. The latest example—the Democratic primaries of 1972—have the most to teach us.

No one pretends that primaries are perfect representations of the electorate that either identifies with a particular political party or is likely to vote for the leading vote-getter. For one thing, voters are not allowed to rank their preferences, so a candidate's popularity with voters who give their first-choice votes to others is unknown. It is quite possible for a candidate to be the first choice of a plurality of voters but to be only the fourth or fifth choice of all voters taken together. In 1972, for example, the candidates of the Democratic party right and left—Wallace and McGovern, respectively—won pluralities in more states than any other candidates, yet they obviously could not have been elected because they also attracted widespread opposition, opposition that was ineffectively expressed in the primary process. Voter turnout in primaries is usually much lower than in the general election and is likely to contain a larger proportion of dyed-in-the-wool party supporters than would be true in a general election. Austin Ranney has shown that between 1948 and 1968 average turnout in primaries was merely 27 percent of all people of voting age compared with approximately double that in the presidential election.[38] It is not so much low turnout, however, as the combination of low turnout with plurality elections that biases the results. In 1972 Senator McGovern had a plurality in seven states. In those states his proportion of the total vote cast in the general election ranged from 4 to 24 percent. Clearly, his primary voters could not have been a representative sample of those who actually voted in November.[39]

Nevertheless, it may appear that McGovern was entitled to most of the primary delegates because he won more often than any other candidate. This would depend, however, on how the votes were counted. There are three basic ways of counting votes. One is winner take all: whichever candidate gets a plurality of votes in the entire state gets all the delegates. Another is proportional: all candidates who pass a certain threshold, say, 15 percent, divide the delegates among them in accordance with their percentage of the vote. A third is congressionally districted: after delegates are allotted (by population or past party vote or both) to districts, the candidate who wins a plurality gains all of the votes in that area. What would happen if all the votes in the 1972 Democratic primaries were recomputed by following any of the three rules consistently—rather than according to the actual mélange of rules that determined the 1972 delegate allocation: winner take all, proportional, or congressional district? Which candidates and, more importantly, which interests would have prevailed?

Consider the situation in Pennsylvania. Had it been run under a winner-take-all rule, Humphrey would have gained all 182 votes. Under the actual districted rule, however, Humphrey received only 93 votes, substantially more, in fact, than the 66 he would have gotten had proportional rules been in effect. Two close students of the situation point out: "In fact, the *difference* [in delegates] between winning Pennsylvania Winner-Take-All and . . . proportionately is greater than the total number of delegates available in twelve out of the first fifteen primaries." [40] The point is not that Humphrey "wuz robbed" since McGovern might well have been nominated anyway, but that the rules matter a great deal. And they contribute to the interpretation of the results: McGovern's 39 votes were considered excellent in a state where he was not expected to run well, and Humphrey's total of 93 was downgraded for the opposite reason, whereas the entire 182 might have been considered a real victory.

Comparing 1972 delegate strength in fifteen primaries held before California's, one can see the enormous differences in results given by varying the rules. The reason the actual results differ from the three pure plans is that the candidates were helped and harmed in different ways. McGovern evidently gained in that he would have done worse if any of the three pure plans had been used. Had the district rule been uniformly employed, Wallace would have been the leading candidate before the California primary.

How the Rules of the Game Affected Delegate
Distributions, 1972 Democratic Primaries

	Winner take all	Proportional	Districted	Actual Results
Humphrey	446	314	324	284
Wallace	379	350	367	291
McGovern	249	319	343	$401\frac{1}{2}$
Muskie	18	82	52	$56\frac{1}{2}$
Others	0	27	6	59

SOURCE: James Lengle and Byron Shafer, "Primary Rules, Political Power, and Social Change," *American Political Science Review* (March 1976).

Rumination about the three rules reveals the kinds of constituencies (and hence interests) they are likely to favor. Winner take all favors populous and competitive states, which have a large number of delegates. These are, by and large, the states of the Northeast and California, known for their large concentration of urban, ethnic minorities and union labor. The proportional rule favors noncompetitive areas because these are the places where a high degree of support for a single candidate pays off. Among Democrats, such areas are found in the South, West, and Midwest. The congressional district rule would fractionate the large states where many candidates could get some support but not the smaller, less competitive ones that have only a few homogeneous districts. That is why Governor Wallace did so well there. It should be evident, as Lengle and Shafer conclude, that "the widespread adoption of Districted primaries after 1968, or the prohibition of Winner-Take-All primaries after 1972, were not, then, just inconsequential decisions to hand out delegates via a certain mechanism. They were far-reaching, if almost accidental, choices about the type of candidates who would bear the party's standard, the type of voters who would have the power to choose those standard-bearers, and the type of issues with which both groups would try to shape history. They were, in short, a decision on how to (re)construct the Democratic party." [41]

The new rules of the Democratic party require selection of delegates by either proportional or congressional district rules. Who will benefit? District rules provide more sites for electioneering than any other. Hence they will favor candidates with intense followings. Moderates, who may appeal to rank-and-file voters in the general election but are too bland to develop a devoted following within the party, will lose out. In the absence of an unusually appealing moderate, therefore, the Democratic convention is likely to be faced with a choice between candidates of relatively committed radical and conservative factions. Thus the capacity of the internal machinery of the party to reconcile differences from within is likely to be tested as seldom before in recent history.

State and District Conventions

In 1976 something like 70 percent of the delegates at the Democratic convention will be chosen in primaries. State and district conventions will still choose the other 30 percent. In the past this process has historically provided relatively few contests over the selection of delegates. But taking over the state and district conventions that chose the Republican delegations to the 1964 convention was the heart of Barry Goldwater's strategy and an important aid for George McGovern in 1972. The belated realization of anti-Johnson forces in 1968 that this was where so much of the action was prompted them to demand, and get, substantial changes in the rules governing the selection of delegates for the next convention. These included abolition of unit rule voting in state and district conventions and a rule that delegates to the national convention had to be chosen in the year of the convention itself rather than at some earlier time as had been the case in some states.[42]

Attempts to influence delegates chosen outside of primaries in the past were usually made after they were selected. The first strategic requirement for the candidate seeking to influence these delegations was an intelligence service, a network of informants who would tell him which delegations were firmly committed, which were wavering, and which might be persuaded to provide second- or third-choice support. Advance reports on the opportunities offered by internal divisions in the state parties, the type of appeal likely to be effective in each state, and the kinds of bargains to which leaders are most susceptible were also helpful. The costs of this information came high in terms of time, money, and effort, but it was worthwhile to the serious candidate who needed to know where to move to increase his support and block his opponents.

These days no one wants to wait for delegates to be chosen before trying to influence them. Delegates are far more likely to be committed to a particular candidate or point of view and, in any event, must be selected in the year of the election. The same forces that persuade candidates to begin their drive for the nomination ever earlier—five men had announced their candidacies for the Democratic nomination by February 1975, one solid year before the first primary election—impel them to begin the hunt for delegates ahead of time. Since fund-raising must go on in at least twenty states to attract federal matching money, it can be combined with delegate selection. Primaries are important, too, because the publicity candidates get and the signs that they are doing well encourage both contributions and volunteers.

The major change between past and present, however, stems from weaknesses in the party system. When and where there were strong party organizations in the past, aspiring candidates had to deal with them. Decisions on whether to enter a primary or influence delegate selection were mediated through party leaders. If they thought a contest in their state would be divisive, candidates would have to worry about incurring their enmity. The decline of party organization has lowered these obstacles. Relatively small numbers of activists without a continuing connection to the party may mobilize around a cause or a candidate and overwhelm the party regulars. If the test is numbers who will come to a particular meeting rather than present party position or past service, the activist surge is bound to carry the day as McGovern, as well as Goldwater, demonstrated so well.

Aspirants for nomination vary greatly in the degree to which they know other politicians throughout the country. Men like Richard Nixon, Hubert Humphrey, and Barry Goldwater, who have traveled extensively and given assistance to members of their party, may simply need to keep their files up-to-date in order to have a nationwide list of contacts. When the time comes, they know from whom they can request assistance in gathering information, persuading delegates, and generally furthering their cause. Candidates who lack this advantage, however, have to take special steps in order to build up their political apparatus. In paving the way for Franklin D. Roosevelt's nomination in 1932, James A. Farley began early by sending invitations to Roosevelt's inauguration as governor of New York to party leaders throughout the country. Most invitations were refused but a valuable correspondence grew out of this approach. Farley next sent a small manual containing a few facts about the New York Democratic party organization to people throughout the country. The response encouraged a follow-up pamphlet which presented, without comment, the New York gubernatorial vote in every county since 1916. It was intended to be impressive testimony of FDR's vote-getting ability. When many people wrote back expressing an interest in FDR's candidacy, offering suggestions, or just saying "thanks," Farley replied with a personal message and endeavored to keep up the contact through further letters, phone calls, and even a phonograph record. Later, in 1931, Farley took a trip through the West, ostensibly to visit the Elks Convention in Seattle, but actually to contact over 1,000 party leaders in all but three states west of the Mississippi. Upon his return, every one of Farley's contacts received a personal letter.[43]

No one today would emulate Farley. Candidates have to be well known to get a start. Instead of heading toward the Elks, a candidate's managers march toward the media. Senators Eugene McCarthy in 1968 and George McGovern in 1972 increased their visibility by doing better than expected in early primaries. They were thus able to build on past successes to create future ones until their luck ran out or they were nominated. Now everybody knows (or believes) that the early aspirant gets the nomination. Candidates will need more than they used to have and they will need it earlier than they used to have it to compete in the future.

Notes

1. Much of the discussion in this and the next chapter is drawn from our own observations of the nomination process over the mass media, for one of us in person at the Democratic National Conventions of 1960, 1968, and 1972 and the Republican National Convention of 1964, and from a set of basic texts on American parties and elections, including Moisei Ostrogorski, *Democracy and the Party System in the United States* (New York, 1910); C. E. Merriam and H. Gosnell, *The American Party System* (New York, 1929); Peter H. Odegard and E. A. Helms, *American Politics* (New York, 1938); Pendelton Herring, *The Politics of Democracy* (New York, 1940); E. E. Schattschneider, *Party Government* (New York, 1942); D. D. McKean, *Party and Pressure Politics* (Boston, 1949); V. O. Key, Jr., *Politics, Parties and Pressure Groups*, 4th ed. (New York, 1958); H. R. Penniman, *Sait's Parties and Elections* (New York, 1952); Hugh A. Bone, *American Politics and the Party System* (New York, 1955); Austin Ranney and Willmoore Kendall, *Democracy and the American Party System* (New York, 1956); William Goodman, *The Two-Party System in the United States* (Princeton, 1960); and Gerald Pomper, *Nominating the President: The Politics of Convention Choice*, 2nd ed. (New York, 1966).

We also found quite useful a more specialized literature on nominations, including Paul T. David, Malcolm C. Moos, and Ralph M. Goldman, *Presidential Nominating Politics in 1952*, vols. 1–5 (Baltimore, 1954); Paul T. David, Ralph M. Goldman, and Richard C. Bain, *The Politics of National Party Conventions* (Washington, D.C., 1960); and Richard C. Bain, *Convention Decisions and Voting Records* (Washington, D.C., 1960).

2. Commission on Party Structure and Delegate Selection, *Mandate for Reform* (Washington, D.C., 1970), pp. 14–15.

3. See William Cavala, "Changing the Rules Changes the Game: Party Reform and the 1972 California Delegation to the Democratic National Convention," *American Political Science Review* 68 (March 1974), p. 31, n. 20.

4. See *Nomination and Election of the President and Vice-President of the United States Including the Manner of Selecting Delegates to National Political Conventions*, 86th Congress, 2nd Sess. House Document No. 332 (February 15, 1960) for an exhaustive description of the selection process, state by state. This is updated in *Nomination and Election of the President and Vice-President of the United States Including the Manner of Selecting Delegates to National Political Conventions*, compiled under the direction of Felton M. Johnson by Richard D. Hupman and Eiler C. Ravnholt with Robert L. Tienken, Senate Item 998 (January 1964), pp. 43–46; and further, in *Federal Election Campaign Laws* (January 1975), compiled by the Senate Library for the Subcommittee on Privileges and Elections of the Committee on Rules and Administration, U.S. Senate (Washington, D.C., 1975).

5. See Paul Tillett, ed., *Inside Politics: The National Conventions, 1960* (Dobbs Ferry, N.Y., 1962), and Aaron B. Wildavsky, "The Intelligent Citizen's Guide to the Abuses of Statistics," in *Politics and Social Life*, eds. Nelson W. Polsby, Robert A. Dentler, and Paul A. Smith (Boston, 1963), pp. 825–44.

6. Key in *Politics, Parties and Pressure Groups*, p. 443, states succinctly the qualities of the ideally "available" presidential candidate. He includes such factors as residence in a large, politically uncertain state. He also says: ". . . A man must be a Protestant [this was published in 1958] of good American stock and name to be 'available.' He should not be too closely affiliated with any particular interest or group nor should he have committed himself on a great and contentious issue before the time is ripe. Yet he must stand for something or a complex of things—a general point of view—in public life." Other factors listed are appearance, personal vigor, the possession of an attractive wife and children, and the luck to be in the right place, age group, and so on, at the right time.

7. For an account see Sullivan, Pressman, Page, and Lyons, *The Politics of Representation*, especially pp. 41–70 for group caucuses, and pp. 71–115 for the platform.

8. See Herring, *The Politics of Democracy*, pp. 203–24; Edward F. Cooke, "Drafting the 1952 Platforms," *Western Political Quarterly* 8 (September 1955), pp. 465–80, and Part III of *Inside Politics*, ed. Tillett.

9. Karl A. Lamb, "Civil Rights and the Republican Platform: Nixon Achieves Control," in *Inside Politics*, ed. Tillett, pp. 55–84. Nixon was also concerned to see that his party made a good impression on television. Richard M. Nixon, *Six Crises* (New York, 1962), pp. 313–20.

10. This is a point made by David, Goldman, and Bain, *The Politics of National Party Conventions*, pp. 398–404.

11. Quoted in Sullivan, Pressman, Page, and Lyons, *The Politics of Representation*, p. 76.

12. Nixon, *Six Crises*, pp. 313–14.

13. See Witcover, *The Resurrection of Richard Nixon*, p. 343.

14. See Theodore H. White, *The Making of the President, 1964* (New York, 1965), Chapter 9.

15. See Ernst, *The Primary That Made a President*, p. 5, and White, *The Making of the President, 1960*, pp. 94–95, for indications that participants were not at all clear at the time how to interpret these results. Evidently John Kennedy was himself surprised at how badly he had done. See Bradlee, *Conversations with Kennedy*, pp. 16–17.

16. See Richard Scammon and Ben J. Wattenberg, *The Real Majority* (New York, 1970), pp. 135–40; David Halberstam, *The Unfinished Odyssey of Robert Kennedy* (New York, 1969), p. 214; Arthur Herzog, *McCarthy for President* (New York, 1969), p. 173; White, *The Making of the President, 1968*, p. 89; and Bruce Page, Godfrey Hodgson, and Lewis Chester, *An American Melodrama* (New York, 1969), p. 357, for alternative interpretations. Note also the reaction of one McCarthy worker to McCarthy's loss (by 49 percent to 42 percent of the 1968 New Hampshire primary to Lyndon Johnson, running as a write-in candidate: "Nor did anyone know what would be considered a good vote. We had to rely on the press after the vote was in to tell us whether it was respectable or not. If the press called 25% a good showing for McCarthy, then it would be so. If the press called 40% a decisive loss for McCarthy, it would be that. . . .

"When the votes were tallied, I was somewhat surprised that a full 48% of the voters liked LBJ enough to write in his name. But since all the newscasters said that our 42% was a great victory for McCarthy, we were ecstatic." Ben Stavis, *We Were the Campaign* (Boston, 1969), p. 25.

17. Jack Arvey, as told to John Madigan, "The Reluctant Candidate," *The Reporter*, November 24, 1953.

18. In 1960, for example, Minnesota Democrats split among delegates friendly to Senator Humphrey and Governor Freeman—and to both of them. Freeman nominated John F. Kennedy for president. Senator Eugene McCarthy nominated Adlai Stevenson. And most of the delegation ended up voting for Humphrey.

19. David, Moos, and Goldman, *Presidential Nominating Politics in 1952*, vol. 2, pp. 155–66.

20. For Truman, see Harry S Truman, *Years of Trial and Hope* (Garden City, N.Y., 1956), pp. 499–503, and Alben Barkley, *That Reminds Me* (Garden City, N.Y., 1954), pp. 225–32. For Johnson, see White, *The Making of the President, 1968*, passim.

21. For a general discussion of bargaining, see Robert A. Dahl and Charles E. Lindblom, *Politics, Economics and Welfare* (New York, 1953), passim, and several works by Charles E. Lindblom that have been written since then, especially his *Bargaining: The Hidden Hand in Government* (Santa Monica, 1955) and *The Intelligence of Democracy* (New York, 1965).

22. For Goldwater, see Nelson W. Polsby, "Strategic Considerations" in *The National Election of 1964*, ed. Milton C. Cummings, Jr. (Washington, D.C., 1966), pp. 82–110, and Wildavsky, "The Goldwater Phenomenon, pp. 386–413. For McCarthy, see Eugene McCarthy, *The Year of the People* (Garden City, N.Y., 1969), pp. 228–29.

23. One famous example has already been cited: the seating of Virginia in the 1952 Democratic convention. See Allan P. Sindler, "The Unsolid South," in *The Uses of Power*, ed. Alan Westin (New York, 1962), pp. 230–83. See also Abraham Holtzman, *The Loyalty Pledge Controversy in the Democratic Party*, Eagleton Series, no. 21 (New York, 1960). Another example is the seating of Texas delegates at the 1952 Republican convention. See Malcolm C. Moos, *The Republicans: A History of Their Party* (New York, 1956), pp. 468–79; William S. White, *The Taft Story* (New York, 1954), pp. 176–83; and David, Moos, and Goldman, *Presidential Nominating Politics in 1952*, pp. 69–85.

24. See the articles on Symington in Eric Sevareid, ed., *Candidates, 1960* (New York, 1959), and Ralph G. Martin and Edward Plaut, *Front Runner, Dark Horse* (Garden City, N.Y., 1960). See also Nixon, *Six Crises*.

25. Carl Sandburg, *Abraham Lincoln: The Prairie Years* (New York, 1926), vol. 2, p. 330. To an Indiana leader, Lincoln wrote that Republicans should "look beyond our noses and say nothing on points where we should disagree."

26. James Lengle and Byron Shafer, "Primary Rules, Political Power, and Social Change," *American Political Science Review* (March 1976).

27. See Ernst, *The Primary That Made a President*; White, *The Making of the President, 1960*.

28. James Reston, "The Organized Disorder in California," *New York Times*, June 3, 1964, p. 30.

29. See Witcover, *The Resurrection of Richard Nixon*, Chapter 10.

30. Elting E. Morison, *The Letters of Theodore Roosevelt* (Cambridge, Mass., 1954), p. 525. See also George E. Mowry, *Theodore Roosevelt and the Progressive Movement* (Madison, 1946).

31. See, for example, Jack Newfield, *Robert Kennedy: A Memoir* (New York, 1969), p. 293. For a different view, see Scammon and Wattenberg, *The Real Majority*, Chapters 7–8.

32. Robert D. Novak, *The Agony of the G.O.P., 1964* (New York, 1965), p. 368. In the 1964 Nebraska Republican primary the results were:

Goldwater	67,369	49 percent
Nixon (write-in)	42,811	35 percent
Lodge (write-in)	22,113	16 percent

33. General Eisenhower's write-in vote of over 100,000 in Minnesota in 1952 is, of course, an example of what we have in mind. See David, Moos, and Goldman, *Presidential Nominating Politics in 1952*, vol. 1, p. 32.

34. Ernst, *The Primary That Made a President*; White, *The Making of the President, 1960*.

35. See White, *The Making of the President, 1968*, p. 89; Page, Hodgson, and Chester, *An American Melodrama*, pp. 79–99; Herzog, *McCarthy for President*, p. 97; Newfield, *Robert Kennedy*, p. 218.

36. William H. Lucy, "Polls, Primaries, and Presidential Nominations," *Journal of Politics* 35 (November 1973), p. 843.

37. Ibid., p. 833.

38. Austin Ranney, "Turnout and Representation in Presidential Primary Elections," *American Political Science Review* 66 (March 1972), pp. 21–37.

39. For an interesting argument along these lines see Malcolm E. Jewell, "A Caveat on the Expanding Use of Presidential Primaries," *Policy Studies Journal* 2 (Summer 1974), pp. 279–84.

40. Lengle and Shafer, "Primary Rules, Political Power, and Social Change."

41. Ibid.

42. The Report of the McGovern Commission of the Democratic National Committee said: "A minority of the Rules Committee of the 1968 Democratic National Convention brought to the floor a proposal to further 'democratize' the selection of delegates to future conventions. They proposed that the 1972 Convention shall require, in order to give all Democratic voters . . . full and timely opportunity to participate in nominating candidates, that (1) the unit rule be eliminated in all stages of the delegate selection process and (2) all feasible efforts [be] made to assure that delegates are selected through party primary, convention, or committee procedures open to public participation within the calendar year of the national convention. This minority report of the Rules Committee, subsequently passed by the delegates assembled in Chicago, carried an unquestionably stern

mandate for procedural reform." *Mandate for Reform*, A report of the Commission on Selection to the Democratic National Committee. Democratic National Committee, April 1970, p. 15. In early 1971 Senator McGovern announced his candidacy for the presidency and resigned from the commission. His successor as chairman was Representative Donald Fraser of Minnesota.

43. James A. Farley, *Jim Farley's Story* (New York, 1948), pp. 11–13, and his *Behind the Ballots* (New York, 1938), p. 70; see also John F. Carter, *The New Dealers* (New York, 1934), p. 34.

CHAPTER FOUR

Nomination: At the Convention

❧~⚜~❧

Housekeeping

While the selection of a site for the convention has often been interpreted as one of the preballot indicators of various candidates' strength, in the past it usually was the rather routine outcome of the weighing of one major and several very minor factors. The major factor was the size of the convention city's proffered contribution to the national party committee; this money came partly from the city government (sometimes in the form of cash, usually in much larger contributions in kind, such as special travel arrangements, security and housekeeping services, etc.) but mostly from various business groups—hotels, restaurants—which stood to profit from a week-long visit of 6,500 delegates and alternates, their families and friends, and thousands of media representatives, dignitaries, and other convention personnel. The cloud over the offer of several hundred thousand dollars by the Sheraton hotel chain as part of San Diego's bid to host the 1972 Republican convention, as well as the reaction to Watergate, has changed all that. In the future the federal government will pay the major parties $2 million apiece to run their conventions, a payment that precludes private financing and may or may not (depending upon decisions of the Federal Election Commission) preclude contributions in kind. There is a variety of other factors, however, which may tip the balance between cities. One of these is the quality of facilities, the convention hall, hotel and entertainment accommodations, and the caliber of the local police force. For example, Philadelphia's James Tate headed as large and as loyal a Democratic organization in 1968 as Chicago's Richard Daley, and his city was closer geographically to Lyndon Johnson in Washington; but Philadelphia simply could not provide 20,000 first-class hotel rooms.[1] All things being equal, an incumbent president is likely to prefer a city near enough to Washington to allow him to keep close tabs on convention business and to travel easily back and forth to the convention while at the same time playing his role away from it as "president of all the people." And, naturally, the wishes of a sitting president will not be farthest from the minds of the site committee of the national committee, which does the choosing. In addition, they will have in mind some other marginal factors. The Republicans in 1968, by selecting Miami Beach for the first Republican convention ever held south of the Mason-Dixon Line, may well have facilitated a "southern strategy" if they intended to pursue one. Both parties prefer to bring their publicity and their business to cities and states where the mayor and the governor are friendly members of the party, since this may give added access to (and control of) public facilities. The attitude of California's Governor Jerry Brown toward the site selection committee of his party evidently tipped the decision of the Democrats toward New York City in 1976 and away from Los Angeles. The desire to maintain the autonomy of the convention against demonstrators in 1972, keeping in mind the Democratic debacle in Chicago in 1968, led to a choice of Miami Beach, where a causeway facilitated crowd control.

The time of a convention varies between mid-July and late August. There are two general statements to be made about it. One is that the out party will normally hold its convention before the ins, on the theory that their man will need more of a publicity boost earlier; in 1960 and 1972 this put Democrats before Republicans, and in 1964 and 1968, it was the other way around. Also, if there is an incumbent president, he will schedule the convention to fit his timetable. At its most momentous, this may coincide with an international peace offensive; in 1968, the date of the Democratic convention seems to have been set with nothing more in mind than the president's birthday.

Once assembled, the national convention is a mass meeting in which the participants necessarily play widely varying and unequal roles. The candidates and their chief supporters are busily, perhaps frantically, perfecting their organizations and trying to influence as many delegates as they can. In the old days, "bossed" or "pledged" delegations were either actively supporting their candidate or negotiating for the disposal of their votes. The leaders of these delegations were the men who conducted negotiations among the delegations when an impasse developed. There were also factional leaders and independent delegates within state delegations who played an important part in determining what their delegation or a part of their delegation would do. They bargained *within* their delegation rather than *among* the various state delegations. Now, the roles of both of these relatively autonomous types of politicians are bound to be sharply diminished, since more and more delegates will come to the convention pledged to one or another presidential candidate. This will mean that candidate organizations, not state party leaders, will have to do the bargaining. But it will be hard for them to bargain if they cannot transfer the votes of their supporters. Only then will they be attended to on an individual basis by the various contending factions. In setting the stage for the balloting, therefore, we will deal first with candidates and their organizations and then with the delegates—leaders of large delegations, independent delegates, state factional leaders, and finally the rank-and-file delegates.

Candidates and Their Organizations

There is a wide divergence among candidate organizations. They range from the comprehensive, integrated, and superbly effective to the fragmented, uncoordinated, and virtually nonexistent. We can only suggest the range of organizational coherence through some general comment and a few examples.

In 1960, Senator John F. Kennedy wanted a communications network that would provide him with a continuing and accurate stream of vital information.[2] He wanted detailed personal information about as many delegates as possible in order to know how they were likely to vote and how they might best be persuaded to stay in line or to change their minds. More than a year before the convention the Kennedy-for-President organization started a card file containing information on people throughout the nation who might be delegates and who might influence delegates. Included on each card was the prospective delegate's name, occupation, religion, party position, relation (if any) to the Kennedy family or its leading supporters, ambitions, policy preferences if strongly held, and likely vote. This was brought up-to-date before convention time and entries were made in a central register as new information developed. Thus when it appeared that a delegate needed to be reinforced or might not vote for Kennedy, his card was pulled and the information was used in order to determine the best way to convince him.

At the national convention, before the balloting for the presidential nomination starts, one or more days are consumed in a variety of party rituals: speech-making, seating delegates, presenting the platform, and so on. During that time delegates and their leaders mill about, exchanging greetings and gossip. It is this set of circumstances that challenges even the most efficient candidate organization.

In order to keep an up-to-date and, when necessary, an hour-by-hour watch on developments within the state delegations, the Kennedy organization assigned an individual to each state. This person might be a delegate or an observer such as a senator or a member of the candidate's staff. When it was deemed inadvisable to choose a delegate for fear that any choice would alienate one faction or another, a person outside the state was chosen. These liaison men kept tabs on individual delegates and maintained a running record of the likely distribution of votes. When necessary, the liaison men sent messages to the candidate's headquarters and reinforcements were sent to bolster the situation. At the Kennedy headquarters the seriousness of the report would be judged and a decision made on how to deal with it. Senator Kennedy himself might call the wavering delegate, one of his brothers might be dispatched, a state party leader might intervene, or some other such remedy might be applied.

In the hurly-burly, crush, and confusion of convention activity, it cannot be assumed that any messages sent are necessarily received or that decisions made are communicated to those who must carry them out. The Kennedy organization took great care to prepare a communications center which would receive messages and locate the people at which they were aimed and which could send out instructions and receive feedback on the results. Each key staff person was required periodically to phone his whereabouts to a central switchboard. This made it possible for the Kennedy forces at the convention to deploy and reassign their people on a minute-by-minute basis, as developments seemed to require.

A system set up only to deal with emergencies would have limited usefulness to a candidate who wanted regular reports so that he could appraise them in a consistent way. Every morning every liaison man assigned to the Kennedy headquarters attended a staff meeting at which he deposited with the secretary a report on his activities for the previous day. These reports were sent to what was called the "secret room" and the information was transferred to state briefing files. From these files, a daily secret report on delegate strength was written and given to the candidate and his top advisers.

At the morning staff meetings, Robert Kennedy would ask each liaison man for his estimate of the number of Kennedy votes. Keenly aware of the dangers of communicating an attitude suggesting that he wanted high estimates, Robert Kennedy challenged the liaison men if he felt that their estimates were too high, but not if they appeared too low. On occasion he would reprimand a liaison man for including a delegate as a certain Kennedy supporter when other information indicated that this was not true. The success of this procedure was indicated by the fact that when the alphabetical balloting had reached Wyoming on the first (and last) ballot, the Kennedy organization's estimate of their delegate strength was proved correct within a one-vote margin.[3]

The danger of confusion and mishap is multiplied during the balloting because the convention floor is filled and it is difficult to move about freely. To deal with this, the Kennedy organization arranged for telephones on the convention floor. Six were set up beneath the seats of chairmen of friendly delegations who were seated around the gigantic convention hall. These phones were connected to the Kennedy headquarters outside the hall. Inside the headquarters, staff members sat near the telephone and simultaneously scanned several television sets to look for possible defections. Had the telephones failed to work (they were pretested), walkie-talkie radios were available to take their place.[4]

By comparison with the Kennedy efforts, most of the organizations that have successfully nominated presidential candidates in American history have been uncoordinated, diffuse affairs. For example, in 1952 none of the various factions in the Democratic party that favored the nomination of Adlai Stevenson had the wholehearted cooperation of their candidate; information-gathering was casual and tactical maneuvers were in some cases hit upon accidentally or as afterthoughts. The factions working for the Stevenson nomination did not cooperate with one another to a significant degree and in fact squabbled among themselves on occasion. Yet Stevenson was nominated; his success came about because he was the second choice of an overwhelming number of delegates who could not agree on any of their first choices and the first choice of a significant number of leaders in spite of his disinclination to pursue the nomination in an organized fashion.[5]

We have devoted so much space to the Kennedy organization because, unlike the Stevenson example, it is clearly a harbinger of the future. McGovern's was very much like it only more so—more telephones, more communications apparatus, more file cards. These extremely organized efforts created some tension within the McGovern camp because delegates who prided themselves on independent thinking did not always appreciate a series of communications on each issue coming before the 1972 convention, telling them how to vote or—equally insulting—allowing them a free choice if a given matter was not considered important.

An interview one of us had with a black delegate from a sparsely populated state suggests how things worked. The delegate was for Rep. Shirley Chisholm for president and had been selected because she had shown up at a meeting to back her candidate. Even before she left home she received calls from the McGovern forces asking her to vote against the Humphrey challenge to the seating of the California delegation. (The California primary had been contested under the existing winner-take-all rule, though the national committee had in general required a proportional vote principle; this slim reed was used by Humphrey forces to mount a challenge to the credentials of the McGovernite California delegation.) But the delegate approved the challenge because it meant more votes for Chisholm. She was not moved by the argument that McGovern would thereby lose his majority; he was not her choice. As soon as she arrived, she was visited at her hotel by McGovern people. When she took her seat on the floor, she felt she had been moved away from Native American delegates on whom she might be a bad influence. Listening to the convention proceedings, she observed the leader of an adjoining delegation pick up the phone, get his instructions, and pass them on to the delegates. A couple of large black McGovern men came over and asked whatever could be on her mind. She replied that if she wanted anyone looking into her head she would find a psychiatrist. Besides, if they continued to try to sway her, she would make a fuss. They left. Finally, as the crucial vote neared, the ultimate weapon was unveiled. She was asked to meet Coretta King, the widow of the martyred black leader. She was glad to make Mrs. King's acquaintance; but she didn't change her mind and voted against McGovern on the California challenge.

At the end of the interview, this spirited delegate claimed to be puzzled about the way the convention worked. We attempted to assure her that she needed no instruction from us. But she persisted, "You are a professor and you have been to conventions before; tell me, if this is supposed to be the 'new politics,' what was the 'old politics' like?"

The McGovern organization worked wonderfully on the platform. A free vote was permitted on giving Indians first choice in the distribution of federal land. Proposals for a guaranteed national income of $6,500 and for minority rights for homosexuals were opposed and defeated. Last-minute additions to reassure supporters of Israel and a commitment to remain in Western Europe were supported and passed. Commands went down the line, obedience came up the line, since it was all for the cause.

Delegates and Caucuses

There are four identifiable categories of convention activists: (1) a small number of managers of candidate organizations; (2) a shrinking proportion of state leaders who control votes other than their own and who participate in high-level negotiations on the disposition of these votes; (3) a growing number of delegates of independent standing who may control only their own votes or those of a faction within their home state but who, because of their special skills at negotiation and maneuver, or because of their high personal prestige, or simply because of the open and unbossed character of their state delegation, play significant roles at the convention; and

(4) members of demographic caucuses. The rise of these caucuses deserves special comment.

The demographic identities of the delegates to the Democratic National Convention of 1972 were, as at other conventions, determined in part by the kinds of people who supported candidates who had won delegates in primaries and state conventions. This time, in addition, new rules modified the demographic makeup of the delegations. The Democratic Commission on Party Structure and Delegate Selection, headed by George McGovern, required state parties to take "affirmative steps to encourage representation . . . of young people [and] . . . minority groups in reasonable relationship to their presence in the population of the States." [6] The best study we have of the immediate effects of this requirement is William Cavala's aptly titled article "Changing the Rules Changes the Game," which deals with California. After observing what happened there, we shall note the effects on the composition, policy preferences, and behavior of delegates as a whole.

California had a winner-take-all primary in 1972, the last in the country. According to past practice, the candidate who won this primary election would choose his delegates on the basis of recommendations made by his leading supporters around the state. The major criterion for delegate selection was the degree to which a person's past record or present resources suggested he could help the party in the coming campaign—high party officials, officeholders, and financial contributors. Most of these are white, male, and over thirty.

This traditional system had its drawbacks. It gave candidates a splendid opportunity to unmake friends by failing to appoint people to the delegation. And space was always limited. This meant a certain amount of bargaining: people who wanted to be selected could refuse to help with the campaign or delay their contributions until they had first been rewarded with a delegate's position. Thus California political leaders did not oppose changes in the rules that imposed de facto quota requirements and removed the choice of delegates to the congressional district level. At the time, this seemed to be an opportunity to connect convention rewards with party performace.

In each congressional district, delegate selection meetings were held well in advance of the primary in behalf of each candidate. Some of these meetings were dominated by traditional interest group forces. But these were mostly the meetings of the traditional centrist candidates—Humphrey, Jackson, and the early front-runner, Muskie. Not so the meetings of the eventual winner of the primary, George McGovern. At the McGovern district meetings there were large turnouts of white liberal activists who had not previously been involved in local and state politics. "In contrast to campaign professionals," Cavala writes, "who saw delegates as basically campaign personnel, the assembled activists viewed them as moral ambassadors. . . ."[7] Thus prior experience in campaigns was often viewed as a disqualification, presumably on the ground that the nominee had been tainted, and offenders were hooted down. Activists found the instructions on quotas congenial because they believed in both demographic (race, age, sex) and issue representation. They soon broke up into black, Spanish-American, and women's caucuses, whose members bargained with one another for representation. The concern of these caucuses was with group and not party or candidate interests. Hence women who had been active for McGovern were slighted in these mini-caucuses in favor of those whose attention was focused on women's rights. Racial minorities received a double bonus. The McGovern campaign committee urged extra representation in districts where minorities predominated in order to enhance electoral prospects. This was done. But they did not anticipate that areas with few minority people would also feel it necessary to have minorities on their slate.

What about white males over thirty years of age? They, presumably, did not have a shared interest requiring separate representation. Only 8 percent of the McGovern delegates selected at district meetings met this description. Jewish males, who had in the past supplied a great deal of the money for Democratic politics in the State of California, and many of whom backed McGovern, were evidently not considered a minority because they were nowhere to be found. To find Jews one had to look at the female side of the delegation. The final result was a delegation consisting of 41 percent minority group members, whose presence in the general California population hovered around 18 percent.

As an aid in obtaining party unity during the campaign for the general election, the primary winner traditionally chooses a few delegates from the losing slates. A few members of the winning slate are asked to resign, and supporters of other presidential nominees are salted in. However, the new breed of delegates refused to give up a single place. Consequently, organized labor, which had supported Humphrey, had hardly any representation in the California delegation, and officeholders were noticeable by their absence. Hence the manpower and money these groups provided in the campaign came to McGovern late and in lesser amounts.[8]

At the Democratic convention itself the various demographic caucuses started with a whoop and ended with a whisper. The opening days witnessed a flurry of activity. Their members expected great things of them and so did the McGovern campaign. The excluded middle—white male delegates over thirty—had no place to go until the states started their own caucuses. One day, for instance, in a search for delegates to interview, we approached a man on the street in Miami Beach who readily agreed to talk. Surprised that he took so little persuading, we asked why he seemed less busy than other delegates. "Well," he said, amid bites on a huge pastrami sandwich, "the blacks have their caucuses, the kids go to the youth caucus, the women to the women's caucuses but [plaintively] there is no place for me." Not long afterward he became active in his state caucus because, increasingly, that was where the action was.

The demographic caucuses were hampered by the clash between group interests and candidate-campaign interests as well as by organizational defects. The McGovern people generally contacted delegates through the state caucuses because everyone could be found there. If delegates had to make a choice between a state or a group caucus, the state won out because voting was on a state basis. Besides, the state caucuses met where the delegations were housed while delegates had to travel considerable distances for the group caucuses. Biology, moreover, is not necessarily ideology. Black delegates disagreed over who should mediate black interests and what their most important priorities were. McGovern, who wanted to ensure his nomination, was less happy about a separate black position than Humphrey, who figured that the more black delegates who went for Chisholm, the easier it would be to dislodge the front-runner from his black support.

Women were divided over support for their special issues, such as abortion, versus helping McGovern, who recognized that the issue would be a liability in the general election campaign. The women's caucuses, moreover, had differences of opinion with the Latin American caucus over abortion. The youth caucus, whose members had come to support McGovern, were cross-pressured. The Mc-

Govern organization did not want to be challenged from the left. Its leaders could not exactly say children should be seen, not heard, but they implied it. And, this time, they had their way.

The demographic caucuses, in addition, had difficulty in establishing and maintaining their boundaries against non-delegates. After all, if race or sex or age is the criterion, why shouldn't non-delegate "spokespersons" for these interests also be included? The caucus of black delegates ended up opening their meetings to all black people.

In time, the McGovern organization and the state delegations increasingly came to be recognized by delegates as the places where instructions originated and were delivered.[9] In the future, however, if conventions are more closely contested and if demographic groups become more experienced, they may become an important part of the strategic environment. For if states lack leaders (that is, people who can commit one delegate's vote other than their own—and deliver), candidates may seek to simplify their task by bargaining with larger numbers through group caucuses. Whether the prospect of power will increase or decrease the willingness of these groups to seek unity no one can say. Since demographic caucuses may well be important in the future, however, it is worth knowing how representative were delegates chosen under the new quotas as compared with delegates in previous years and what their preferences were compared with those of voters who identified with the Democratic party.

The new rules succeeded in increasing the proportion of black people, women, and youth at the Democratic convention. Black people were overrepresented compared with their proportion in the total population (16 percent to 11 percent) but this accurately mirrored their contribution (17 percent) to Democratic party identifiers. They were also at the Republican convention in rough proportion (5 percent) to their 4 percent of party identifiers.

Women constituted 40 percent of Democratic delegates, a threefold increase over the 1968 Democratic convention. Youth (i.e., those under age thirty) comprised 23 percent (as compared to 3 percent in 1968) of delegates for the Democrats, while they constituted 28 percent of the population over eighteen and 25 percent of Democratic party identifiers. Around 16 percent of youth identified with the Republican party, but this group made up just 8 percent of Republican delegates. Although people over sixty-five made up 15 percent of the general population, only 4 percent of that age group were at the Democratic convention and 9 percent at the Republican.

But this breakdown covers only demographic groups; what happens if we stratify delegates by income and education? At the end of 1971, 48 percent of Democratic identifiers had a family income of less than $9,000; another 30 percent had incomes of from $9,000 to $15,000. Thirty-six percent of Democratic delegates had incomes of over $10,000; and another 50 percent had family incomes of over $20,000. The gaps between rank-and-file and delegate income were even greater on the Republican side. Forty-three percent of Republican identifiers had incomes of under $10,000 as compared with 23 percent of delegates with incomes of under $20,000; 15 percent of Republican identifiers had incomes of over $15,000, and 23 percent of Republican delegates had incomes of over $50,000.[10]

Educational differences were even more striking. About three in five delegates from both parties had college degrees compared to one in four among rank-and-file Democrats and one in three of rank-and-file Republican identifiers. Among the Democratic delegates, 65 percent of McGovern's people had college degrees compared to 33 percent for Wallace, 40 percent for Humphrey, and 56 percent for Muskie. Professional people predominated among the delegates with lawyers in the forefront, except among McGovern supporters where teachers were predominant.

Who was absent? Only the representatives of capital and labor. Self-employed businessmen constituted only 8 percent of Democratic delegates (compared to 29 percent in 1968) and made up 18 percent of Republicans, not much for the alleged party of business. Workers were hardly to be seen. As Jeane Kirkpatrick concludes, "The delegates to both conventions were an overwhelmingly middle to upper class group. . . ."[11]

What difference does all this make? Did the policy positions of delegates in 1972 agree more than heretofore with those of citizens? Herbert McClosky's classic study comparing delegates to the 1956 conventions with ordinary voters uncovered an important source of difficulty for the Republican party that has persisted through the years: that Republican voters and Democratic voters tend to think more or less alike on most policy issues and that they in turn have had attitudes close to those of Democratic leaders but relatively removed from the attitudes of Republican leaders.[12] This suggests that Republican activists, by satisfying themselves with a candidate and platform, would court unpopularity and defeat. Indeed the 1964 experience is frequently cited as evidence of this.

Today, quite similar risks seem to have passed to the Democratic camp. In 1972, on the broadest range of issues, Democratic delegates, especially McGovern delegates, were far from most citizens including supporters of the Democratic party. In fact (see the table on page 135), they differed from the preferences of Democratic voters on most issues even more than Republican delegates. On welfare policy, most voters gave priority to work while most Democratic delegates were more interested in eradicating poverty. On busing, only 3 percent of the McGovern delegates were strongly opposed, in contrast to 71 percent of voting Democrats. On law and order, over three-fourths of the delegates cared more about the rights of the accused compared to one-third of the voters. On Vietnam, 7 percent of the voters but 57 percent of the McGovern delegates were opposed to giving any aid whatsoever after American withdrawal. Only on inflation were Democratic voters and delegates agreed on the importance of governmental action.

Politics involves feelings not only about issues but also about groups. Toward one group—politicians—delegates in both parties were more favorable than voters. On unions, business, and liberals, Democratic voters and delegates were together. But on political demonstrators, civil rights leaders, black militants, the military, and people on welfare, Republican delegates were closer to Democratic voters who were very far indeed from Democratic delegates. On all issues and group attitudes, McGovern delegates differed more with Democratic voters than the supporters of any other candidate including George Wallace.

Differences between Republican and Democratic voters still persist. Democrats are more liberal on crime, welfare, and busing and more sympathetic to union leaders, the aspirations of black citizens, and demonstrators. But, as Kirkpatrick emphasizes, ". . . the same issues and symbols which separated the Democratic from Republican voters still further separated Democratic voters from their own party elite." [13] Are these differences caused by the new quota rules of the Democratic party or by divergences between voters and activists on other grounds? All McGovern supporters were alike, male and female, white and black, young and old. Thus the quotas clearly cannot be blamed for the disparity in views

Differences Between Democratic Rank-and-File Identifiers and
Selected Groups of Convention
Delegates
(The larger the number, the greater the difference)

| Attitudes toward: | Delegates for: | | | | | |
	McGov-ern	Hum-phrey	Wallace	Muskie	Repub-lican	Demo-cratic
Welfare	110	35	46	60	19	76
Busing*	147	54	26	67	9	108
Crime	107	45	54	54	21	79
Civil rights leaders	94	59	74	69	4	67
Welfare recipients	76	69	32	50	1	64
Political demonstrators	123	61	5	68	5	90
Police	33	7	11	7	18	16
Military	97	5	30	30	29	52
Blacks	34	45	6	37	26	34
Conservatives	89	42	66	48	41	64
Liberals	78	24	99	37	73	46
Union leaders	10	43	52	21	52	15
Politicians	55	76	16	66	75	57
Inflation*	21	5	30	9	20	14
Abortion*	89	43	2	67	50	68
Laying off women first*	54	32	4	38	18	42
Women's liberation†	61	32	55	21	57	25
Business interests†	57	2	2	15	45	35
Black militants†	93	26	15	32	9	61
Vietnam	109	29	14	62	34	79
Ideological Self-Classification†	83	40	80	54	59	59
MEAN DIFFERENCES	77.0	36.9	34.2	43.5	31.6	54.9

* These data on rank-and-file indentifiers—used to compute differences—were taken from the C.P.S. Pre-Election (Post-Convention) Study.
† These data on rank-and-file identifiers—used to compute differences—were taken from the C.P.S. 1972 Post-Election Study.
The remaining data on rank-and-file identifiers were taken from the Pre-Convention Study.
N.B.: The difference scores above were computed from preponderance scores carried to the first decimal place.
SOURCE: Jeane J. Kirkpatrick, "Representation in the American National Conventions: The Case of 1972," *British Journal of Political Science* 5 (July 1975), p. 304.

between 1972 Democratic delegates and voters. Yet it is still possible that the entire process that brought delegates to the Democratic convention, and not the quotas, made them less representative than they had been. Perhaps what has happened is that activists in both parties, increasingly manifesting high social and economic status, have grown at once farther apart from one another and from the voters. The participant sectors of the parties are far more polarized than they were in the 1940s and 1950s in two directions—one party from the other at the elite level and elites in both parties from their followers.[14]

It remains to be seen whether the 1972 Democratic convention produced a sample of Democratic activists that is in some way atypical. There is certainly good reason to believe so a priori, since at the convention a substantial majority of delegates voted for George McGovern, who lost 40 percent of the vote of Democratic identifiers in the general election. In addition, there are the striking differences in policy attitudes between McGovernites and the rest of the Democratic party as displayed in the preceding table. But the question remains: Are these the only Democratic activists? Or can we find a population of Democratic party leaders whose attitudes fall closer to the mainstream of the voting population?

Evidently we can. A recent survey comparing the policy preferences of Democratic and Republican county chairmen with rank-and-file party identifiers discloses findings "rather similar to McClosky's"—Republican chairmen are much more conservative than voters, whereas Democratic chairmen and voters have more congruent preferences.[15]

There is something about having a winning presidential candidate, however, which appears to help mute ideological extremism over the short run. A scholar who has made a study of political attitudes among Republican delegates suggests that while many of the former Goldwater activists remained active in Republican organizations after 1964 they made individual ideological accommodations to the comparatively moderate forces that captured the G.O.P. after 1964. In the short run, the Nixon candidacies may have tempered the conservative zeal of many former Goldwater supporters and resulted in their "professionalization." The comments of a state committee-woman who was recruited as a Goldwater volunteer in 1964 characterizes this pragmatic evolution: "I was a Republican amateur in 1964 but I wouldn't support Goldwater today. Our leader must reflect majority opinion, namely the views in the middle because a man is elected to represent this country's beliefs, not to force his own on the country. Nixon is doing a great job at this even though conservatives have given him a hard time. . . . After the primary we worked for the ticket because party unity is the result of both free discussion and being a good loser if necessary." [16]

Why might Democratic delegates be different? According to Austin Ranney, a political scientist member of the McGovern commission that wrote the rules for 1972, "Most of the guidelines were consciously designed to maximize participation by persons who are enthusiasts for a particular presidential aspirant or policy *in the year of the convention.*" [17] Evidently enthusiasts for McGovern were different. If a more centrist Democratic candidate had emerged from the 1972 convention, the discrepancies we are exploring would not have existed or been noticed. On the other hand, it must be recognized that it is undoubtedly in the nature of centrism and moderation to be relatively poor at stimulating precisely the enthusiasm among party activists that is increasingly needed to win under the guidelines as they are presently written.

Straws in the Wind

When an incumbent president desires renomination, his influence is normally great, his party can hardly hope to win by repudiating him, and his nomination is virtually assured.[18] Sometimes, the titular leader of the party or some other candidate is so far ahead, as Nixon was in 1960 and 1968, that there is nothing left for the delegates to do but ratify the decision that has already been negotiated by leaders of the state parties.

But here we are mainly concerned with those contested nominating conventions where there is uncertainty at the time of the convention about who will be the nominee. In an uncertain convention, delegates crave information on what is going to happen and when. For some of them, of course, the convention is a spectator sport, since they will be acting under instructions from the voters in their state primary or from their state party leaders. But many now have an independent voice, so they will want to know who is ahead and who is behind and what the chances are of majority agreement on one of the leading candidates. Rumors are rife because no one has been able to establish an unshakable claim of victory, because it is to the advantage of more than one aspirant to be thought to be winning, and because people like to speculate. In the grip of uncertainty, the delegates grasp for any objective information that may be gleaned from the events of the convention itself.[19]

Before the balloting on the candidates begins at the convention, there often are votes on the seating of contested delegations, on a plank in the platform, or on some rule governing convention life such as a loyalty pledge; or there is conflict over the person who is to be permanent chairman. If some of the candidates become identified with one or the other side on these preliminary votes, the results may be considered a test of who is likely to win the nomination. Thus, candidates who identify themselves with one side or another may prejudice their chances of nomination. They must calculate the effects of the loss of such a vote. In 1932, Franklin Roosevelt nearly lost his bid for the nomination by coming out against the two-thirds rule then required for nomination. Fortunately for his chances, FDR's supporters at the convention discovered that the opposition to the change in rules was greater than the opposition to him and he beat a hasty retreat from his previous position.[20]

A challenge to the seating of delegates may also tell the story. Eisenhower's victory in 1952 was signaled by challenges to Taft delegates, and McGovern showed he would win in 1972 by beating Humphrey's forces on California. The decision of the credentials committee to allow delegates from California, who would support McGovern, to vote on the challenge was an early and significant sign.

Many of the same strategic considerations hold in relation to any conflict that may develop over the permanent chairman. This struggle may be important because the chairman has significant procedural powers at the convention. He can speed up adjournment to give a particular candidate time to make bargains, or he can harm another's chances by refusing to recognize a state delegation about to go over to that candidate at a crucial moment. The importance of being chairman was demonstrated at the 1920 Republican convention when Senator Henry Cabot Lodge wanted to permit party leaders to find a way out of an impasse that had developed. Shortly after the fourth ballot, Senator Reed Smoot of Utah moved to adjourn the proceedings. A resounding "no" echoed throughout the auditorium as Lodge put the motion to a vote and immediately declared the convention adjourned.[21] Twenty years later, at another

Republican convention, Senator John Bricker of Ohio asked Chairman Joseph Martin for a recess before the sixth ballot; this would have given the Taft and Dewey forces time to make a deal. Partial to the Willkie cause, however, Martin refused the request and the balloting continued, ending with victory for Willkie.[22]

Unless victory appears assured, it may be unwise for a candidate to challenge a popular chairman. An alternate strategy is to accept an unfavorable chairman but to put forth a stream of publicity stressing the chairman's partiality, so that he feels under continuous scrutiny and may bend over backward to avoid charges of favoritism. Nowadays, however, the usual practice is for representatives of the leading candidates to agree upon major personnel of the convention—keynoter, permanent chairman, platform committee chairman—by negotiation well ahead of the convention itself.

Virtually any action can take on added significance if it reveals information hitherto unavailable to all. In the 1932 Democratic convention a vote on seating a contested delegation was taken under conditions that freed many of the delegates from the unit rule. This revealed which delegations were closely divided, information that imposition of the unit rule had helped to hide.[23]

Such apparently trivial matters as the date or the place in which the convention meets may take on special meaning if those decisions are believed to affect the fortunes of candidates. The fact that the 1844 Democratic convention was delayed while Van Buren's letter opposing the annexation of Texas was having its effect was known at that time to be prejudicial to his chances. Locating the 1928 Democratic convention in Houston, Texas, was widely interpreted as a move to mollify people in the South and led to the conclusion that this was necessary because party leaders intended to nominate Al Smith.

While candidates are being nominated, and during the balloting, demonstrations—partly spontaneous, largely prearranged—take place on the floor. These raucous displays are meant to let everyone know that a candidate has many loyal supporters. A demonstration at a crucial moment, it is hoped, might succeed in igniting the spark of enthusiasm among the multitude of uncertain delegates. But, as supporters of Adlai Stevenson learned in 1960, this has the possibility of working only when delegates are really uncertain and uncommitted.

Despite the fact that everyone seems aware of what is going on, the same old tricks are played at every convention. Part of the reason is that once a practice has begun, unanimous consent is necessary to eliminate it; otherwise, the candidate who received no ovation would be deemed to have no support or not enough sense to stimulate it artificially. Another part of the rationale behind demonstrations should be clear from our argument: reliable information may be so scarce that, despite all warnings, delegates may be swayed (as was the Republican convention of 1940 that nominated Wendell Willkie) by the most immediate, tangible evidence before them—the roar of the crowd. Despite the jeers of sophisticates, it would not be impossible for the same phenomenon to occur again if delegates are exhausted by balloting that does not lead to a decision.

The Balloting

Politicians who wish power in government try to contribute to the majority essential for the nomination of the candidate they believe will be the winner. This explains the so-called bandwagon behavior which has been seen in operation at many conventions. When politicians believe that one presidential aspirant is certain of nomination, they will attempt to go on record as voting for that aspirant as quickly as possible. Delegates committed to a favorite son candidate will trade their votes for access (or what they hope will be access) to the candidate they think most likely to win nomination. Note the differences in these two statements. In the first, delegates *know* which candidate will win and hope to earn his gratitude by voting for him. In the corollary, delegates are less certain of the outcome, hence their commitment to an aspirant is more costly for him. The prospective candidate, in these circumstances, often makes promises of access to delegates in return for their support.

Purists will try to keep pure. If they can't get all they want, they may be "half-safe" by finding a candidate ideologically and stylistically compatible. A compromise candidate, however, would be far less congenial to them. If they get on any bandwagon, it is more likely to be one taking them out of the convention. Splitting the party would be better, so far as purists are concerned, than injuring their integrity.

An aspirant who leads in votes for the nomination must actually win the nomination by a certain point in time, or else his chances of eventually winning decline precipitously, even though he remains temporarily in the lead. This is true when delegate support is given candidates because of the expectation of victory. When this victory falls short of quick materialization, delegates may question their initial judgment. Thus, the longer a candidate remains in the lead without starting a bandwagon, the greater the possibility that his supporters will reassess his chances of victory and vote for someone else. In order to maximize access, delegates prefer to support the eventual winner before he achieves a majority. They are therefore guided by what they expect other delegates to do and are constantly on the alert to change their expectations to conform to the latest information. This information may be nothing more substantial than a rumor, which quickly takes on the status of self-fulfilling prophecy, as delegates stampede in response to expectations, quickly realized, about how other delegates will respond. The strategies that a candidate adopts depend, therefore, not only on showing that he can win but also on his position in the convention. So long as he keeps gaining support, no matter how slightly, he is still in contention because it is assumed that he may have more strength in reserve. But the front-runner who begins to manifest any decline, or even in some cases a leveling off in votes, on successive ballots can expect to see uncommitted delegates conclude that he has shot his bolt and begin to shift their support to more promising prospects.

Considered as a source of information, the balloting indicates whether a candidate is gaining or falling behind. One strategy sometimes used in this connection is to "hide" a few votes on early ballots by giving them to others and reclaiming them little by little to show a steady increase.[24] Or a candidate may decide to bide his time and delay making his bid. In that case a weak initial total of votes is not likely to be commented upon because the front-runner occupies the center of attention. Later, a dark horse may occasion surprise by his rapid climb and hope that most delegates will decide to hitch their wagons to a rising star.

The importance of indicators of uncertainty in contested conventions has been empirically validated. Eugene B. McGregor, Jr., proves that "the candidate making the largest gain from the first to the second ballot went on to win the nomination . . . in . . . eight out of the ten most recent multi-ballot conventions . . . held since 1892. . . ." The exceptions, such as the 103-ballot Democratic convention in 1924, are the result of "extreme ideological divisions" such as urban Catholic "wets" versus rural, Protestant "drys" in that case.[25]

Aspirants sometimes combine their voting strength in the convention in order to prevent a front-running candidate from gaining a majority. They will then negotiate the nomination among themselves. If the front-runner's victory promises other aspirants insufficient access, they may defeat him by preventing a bandwagon in his favor. An apparently successful case of combining against the front-runner occurred in 1920 when Harry Daugherty, Harding's manager, realizing that General Leonard Wood had to be defeated to give Harding a chance, offered to lend Illinois Governor Frank Lowden every vote he could spare until the governor passed Wood in the balloting. Then the alliance would be terminated. "Certainly you couldn't make a fairer proposition." Lowden responded, and the agreement was consummated.[26] The good old days of "lending" votes may, however, be no more because under the primary rules governing the obligations of delegates, candidates will be unable to exercise this kind of control over them.

The rational aspirant who leads but lacks a majority will bargain and promise access to leaders representing the requisite number of votes, if he believes that no bandwagon will appear unstimulated. He may offer the vice-presidential nomination to one or more leaders of important states; he may hint at cabinet posts, patronage, or preferred treatment; he may explore concessions on policy. But this account is too simple. Before he can bargain, the candidate must know with whom to bargain. And among those delegations or caucuses that might be swayed he must find the ones amenable to what he can offer. The necessity of maintaining an apparatus for obtaining this information was evident in the past but it will become indispensable in the future because there will be so many more "bits" of data to keep in mind.

The front-runner may reasonably expect to win without cost (that is, without making promises) unless leaders of opposing factions reach agreement on a ticket and appear likely to combine against him. Early front-runners often win nominations precisely because they face a divided opposition.

The case of the Democrats in 1960 is a perfect example of this. In the preconvention maneuvering, Adlai Stevenson might have cut into John Kennedy's liberal and labor support had he made himself available as a candidate. Many party regulars from the urban political machines and, in particular, ex-President Truman had no special liking for Kennedy, and Senator Johnson could draw on a rather substantial reservoir of strength from southern delegations who were determined not to walk out even though they knew they would not approve of the civil rights plank of the platform.

These groups could not get together and settle on a candidate who was more satisfactory to all of them than the front-runner, Senator Kennedy. Labor clearly would accept no one to the right of Kennedy; the southerners could abide nobody to the left of him. Adlai Stevenson was perhaps the leading candidate whose ideological location, prominence in the party, and public record could pass muster with all these groups, but he had alienated Truman and in any case refused to go to work in his own behalf. And so Kennedy's opposition stayed divided.

If a candidate thinks he can win on his own, he may be reluctant to risk sacrificing his ambition by "making a deal" to combine against a front-runner. Yet if he hesitates too long, he may lose all. This is apparently what happened to Thomas E. Dewey in the 1940 Republican convention. As Senator Arthur Vandenberg recorded in his diary, "I offered to flip a coin with Dewey to see which side of the ticket each would take. Dewey never saw me again until the final voting. But it was too late. He missed the boat when he clung to his own first place ambitions. Between us we could have controlled the convention if it had been done in the first instance." [27]

The candidate who wishes to get support must show that he already has some to begin with. This is particularly the case when one contender is considering throwing his support to another in order to assure the latter's nomination. There would be no point in sacrificing one's chances in favor of another candidate who would then not have enough votes to win. This kind of situation occurred around the time of the fiftieth ballot at the 1924 Democratic convention. Al Smith informed Senator Oscar Underwood of Alabama that if two more southern states would give Underwood their support, Smith would also give the senator his support. The Underwood forces accepted the offer but they were unable to find other southern states that would support their candidate, and so the scheme fell through.[28] Although the rule requiring two-thirds support for nomination no longer exists, this convention may repay further study of what happens when style and issue positions are incompatible.

The bargaining process itself may be an excellent source of information on what delegates are likely to do under a variety of circumstances. A series of probing actions may be carried out to discover what delegates want, what they will take, what they will give in return. Out of the negotiations may emerge the beginnings of a commonly held picture of the shape of events to come.

Bargains may be tacit rather than explicit, made through intermediaries rather than by principals. Exactly what was promised may not be entirely clear or may be distorted later on, if this is deemed advantageous. The delegate who wishes to collect what he believes to be his due may have trouble securing effective guarantees. Thomas Dewey never quite manifested the same understanding that Charles Halleck did about an offer of the vice-presidency in return for support in the Republican convention of 1948.[29] One delegate to the 1960 Democratic convention told reporters that he was the nineteenth person to be offered the vice-presidency by the Kennedy forces. Under the circumstances, he allowed as how he would take cash.[30] Proffering positions in return for support has declined of late, possibly because contested conventions have also declined. Despite the distaste with which these deals are regarded, they may rise again; what else will candidates have to bargain with?

It is possible that much less comes out of the convention in terms of reward for support than is commonly supposed. An incoming president, for example, may well decide to handle patronage through the dominant party faction in a state rather than suffer the disabilities of supporting a weak dissident faction that helped him at a convention. Nevertheless, if delegates believe that rewards are likely to follow support, as many apparently do, their actions will conform to this belief.

One by one the leading candidates try their luck. Timing is of the essence. Each candidate seeks the strategic moment to push his candidacy. A miscalculation, a decision, perhaps, to move ahead before sufficient support is available for the final push, may prove fatal to a candidate's chances. In a closely contested convention the prize may go to the candidate who possesses sufficient information about the intentions of others to make the successful move.

Whispering campaigns are begun, saying, "Candidate X is certain to, win; get on the bandwagon while you still have a chance." Rumors appear that a crucial delegation will swing to a particular candidate. The balloting may remain substantially unchanged and reveal no secrets. It is difficult to know what to believe. No mass meeting of thousands of delegates can hope to find out who is acceptable to most of them. It is up to the leaders to assert control.

In the absence of quick agreement at the convention, the demonstrations and adjournments give party leaders, if there are any, time to meet and see if a candidate can be found who can receive a majority of votes. This is the "smoke-filled room" of convention lore. Its participants try to work out an agreement that will meet their desires. But they are severely limited in their choice by their estimate of what the people will accept at the polls and what the other delegates will stand for. Delegates have independent influence and different interests and there may be only a limited range of agreement among them.

The essential trick is to convince others that one's preferred view of what will happen, or must happen, is the correct one. This is apparently what took place in the 1920 Republican convention when Harry Daugherty succeeded in convincing party leaders that a deadlock was inevitable and that only Harding could break it. Much the same kind of thing occurred in 1844 when Gideon Pillow and George Bancroft spread the word that Cass, Calhoun, or Van Buren could not possibly win but that Polk would carry the day.[31]

In order to break a deadlock, it is necessary to convince some delegates that the candidate they prefer cannot win and that they would be well advised to switch to a man who can. The leaders at the 1920 Republican convention decided to communicate this point convincingly by calling for several additional ballots during which nothing changed.[32] This also helped to assure losing party factions that their candidates had had a fair chance. At the 1924 Democratic convention, however, which went to 103 ballots, the lengthy voting apparently did not communicate the hopelessness of their cause to the leading candidates. Not only did incompatibility and intransigence block bargaining, but short-lived booms kept arising, an indication that the delegates shared no common view of future events.[33] The shock to loyal party members was so great that many years later John Nance Garner chose to submerge his own chances and throw the 1932 convention to Franklin Roosevelt rather than risk another agonizing stalemate.[34]

The Vice-Presidential Nominee

When the convention finally selects its presidential candidate, it turns to the anticlimactic task of finding a running mate. Vice-presidential nominees are chosen to help the party achieve the presidency. Party nominees for president and vice-president always appear on the ballot together and are elected together. Since 1804, a vote for one has always been a vote for the other.

The vice-president occupies a post in the legislative branch of the government that is mostly honorific, and his powers and activities in the executive branch are determined by the president.[35] The electoral interdependence of the two offices gives politicians an opportunity to gather votes for the presidency. Therefore, the prescription for an "ideal" vice-presidential nominee is the same as for a presidential nominee, with two additions: he must possess those desirable qualities the presidential nominee lacks, and he must be acceptable to the presidential nominee.

The vice-presidency is the most frequent position from which presidents of the United States are drawn. Over a third of our thirty-seven presidents were at one time vice-presidents. (Four were first elected to the presidency in their own right; eight first took office upon the death of a president; and of course Mr. Ford succeeded because of President Nixon's resignation.) American history has given us thirteen good reasons—one for each man who succeeded to the presidency—for inquiring into the qualifications of vice-presidents and for examining the criteria by which they are chosen.

The presidential candidate who has firm control over his nomination is in a position to use the vice-presidential slot to help win the election. This is what Abraham Lincoln did in 1864 when he chose a "War Democrat," Andrew Johnson, whom he hoped would add strength to the ticket.

In the same way, John F. Kennedy chose Lyndon Johnson to help gather southern votes, especially in Texas; and Richard Nixon chose Henry Cabot Lodge in 1960 to help offset the Democratic party advantage in the Northeast. In 1964 President Johnson chose a man who was helpful in unifying the party and maintaining its good electoral prospects. Johnson's own credentials as a liberal Democrat down through the years were not strong; when Kennedy picked him as vice-president he was opposed on these grounds by many labor leaders and by leaders from several of the most important urban Democratic strongholds. In choosing Senator Hubert Humphrey, a longtime liberal leader, President Johnson adhered to the familiar strategy of ticket balancing. President Ford with his midwestern and congressional background may have had the same thing in mind when he chose a more liberal eastern establishment figure, Nelson Rockefeller, to be his nominee for vice-president; a midterm nominee would ordinarily be expected to stand during the next election.

Recent vice-presidential candidates have sometimes been distinguished men who had a great deal to recommend them. But the help they could offer their parties was undoubtedly an important consideration. Spiro Agnew was chosen in 1968 because, with the Democrats badly divided and Nixon assured of the nomination, it was important to find a running mate who was not hated by anyone. Nixon had seen the results of a poll indicating that all of the leading candidates for the vice-presidency would hurt his chances of election more than they would help him. Agnew was little known outside his home state of Maryland, had been a Rockefeller supporter, had defeated a Democratic segregationist in his gubernatorial race, was a member of one of the "newer" ethnic groups (Greek-Americans), and impressed Nixon with his personal qualities. At the time of his selection, he was, as he himself said, not exactly a household word. No one suspected that he would later become one—as the first vice-president to resign in disgrace in return for avoiding a criminal indictment.[36]

Sometimes a presidential candidate will try to help heal a breach in the party by offering the vice-presidential nomination to a leader of a defeated party faction. Or the presidential candidate may try to improve his relationships with Congress by finding a running mate who has friends there. Franklin Roosevelt chose Harry Truman for both these reasons. There is less chance today, when party factions are so far apart, that they will be disposed to make such accommodations. Humphrey balanced his ticket in 1968 by choosing Senator Edmund Muskie, a quietly eloquent, moderate man, a member of an ethnic group (Polish-Americans) concentrated in the cities of the eastern seaboard, to balance off his own Midwest populist background and fast-talking style.

A Republican presidential candidate from the East will try to pick a vice-president from the Midwest or Far West. It has been thought desirable for both to reside in large, two-party "swing" states. With the mode of delegate selection among Democrats biased in favor of one-party states (owing to the abolition of the unit rule and the winner-take-all primary), however, this tendency may no longer prevail. A liberal Democrat running for president will try to find a more conservative running mate—unless the idea is to emphasize the differences between the parties, in which case the vice-presidential nominee should be more extreme in his or her views than the main contender. And so on. If it is impossible to find one person who combines within his heritage, personality, and experience all the virtues allegedly cherished by American voters, the parties console themselves by attempting to confect out of two running mates a composite father-son image of forward-looking-conservative, rural-urban, energetic-wise leadership that evokes home-town, ethnic, and party loyalties among a maximum number of voters. That, at least, is the theory behind the balanced ticket.

There have been times when a president has insisted on having his personal choice selected as vice-president. Andrew Jackson was adamant about running with Martin Van Buren, and Franklin Roosevelt went so far as to write out a refusal to accept the Democratic nomination in 1940 when party leaders balked at the thought of Henry Wallace.

The presidential nominee clearly is expected to have a lot to say about who will run with him on the party ticket. More and more in recent years the expectation has been that the presidential candidate makes the choice himself after due consultation with party leaders. Indeed, failure to act decisively may well be regarded now as a sign of weakness. Yet there have been times when presidential candidates have not wished to become involved in internal party battles and have let the convention decide. William Jennings Bryan would not even allow his own Nebraska delegation to signal his preferences by voting on the vice-presidential nomination at the 1896 Democratic convention, and Adlai Stevenson preferred to let Estes Kefauver and John F. Kennedy fight it out for the prize in 1956. George McGovern undoubtedly wishes he had let the delegates decide in 1972, thus avoiding responsibility for selecting Thomas Eagleton. Throwing the decision up for grabs may become more common if it gets to be all anyone can do to make it through to the presidential nomination.

When especially able men have appeared in the vice-presidential office from time to time, this may have been more because of the blessings of Providence than because of wise actions on anyone's part. If good results require noble intentions, then the criteria for choosing vice-presidents may leave much to be desired. Why should the great parties, we might ask, not set out deliberately to choose the candidate best able to act as president in case of need? Should ticket-balancing and similar considerations be condemned as political chicanery?

In a speech to the Harvard Law School Forum in 1956, former Vice-President Henry A. Wallace declared: "The greatest danger is that the man just nominated for President will try desperately to heal the wounds and placate the dissidents in his party. . . . My battle cry would be—no more deals—no more balancing of the ticket." In 1964, the Republican party evidently also endorsed this view. The selection of the 1964 Republican nominee, Representative William Miller, was intended to violate criteria used in the past for balancing the ticket. Although he came from a region different from Barry Goldwater and is a Catholic, Miller was chosen primarily because of his ideological affinity with the presidential candidate. The special style of Goldwater and his supporters required that consistency of views, opposition to the other party on as many issues as possible, and refusal to bargain prevail over the traditional political demands for compromise, flexibility, and popularity.[37]

From the standpoint of the electoral success of candidates, balancing the ticket seems only prudent. But there are reasons as well for ordinary citizens to prefer that candidates make an effort in this direction. One of the chief assets of the American party system in the past has been its ability (with the exception of the Civil War period) to reduce conflict by enforcing compromise within the major factions of each party. A refusal to heal the wounds and placate dissidents is nothing less than a declaration of internal war. It can only lead to increased conflict within the party. Willingness to bargain and make concessions to opponents is part of the price for maintaining unity in a party sufficiently large and varied to be able to appeal successfully to a population divided on economic, sectional, racial, religious, ethnic, and perhaps also ideological grounds. To refuse entirely to balance the ticket would be to risk changing our large, heterogeneous parties into a multiplicity of small sects of "true believers" who care more about maintaining their internal purity than about winning public office by pleasing the people.

This is not to suggest that the president and vice-president must be worlds apart in their policy preferences in order to please everyone (or no one). There is obvious good sense in providing for a basic continuity in policy in case a president should die or be disabled. But this need not mean that the two should be identical in every respect, even if that were possible. Within the broad outlines of agreement on the basic principles of the nation's foreign policy and of the government's role in the economy, for example, a president would have no great difficulty in finding a variety of running mates who were somewhat more or less liberal than himself, who appealed to somewhat different groups, or who differed in other salient ways. To go this far to promote party unity, factional conciliation, and popular preference should not discomfort anyone who realizes the costs of failing to balance the ticket in some important way.

Actually there is no evidence whatsoever to suggest that vice-presidents add or detract from the popularity of presidential candidates with the voters. By helping unite the party, however, and by giving diverse party leaders another focus of identification with the ticket, a vice-presidential nominee with the right characteristics can help assurè greater effort by party workers, and this may bring results at election time.

Even if balancing the ticket does not help the party at the polls, it may indirectly help the people. It may aid our political parties in maintaining unity within diversity and thereby in performing their historic function of bringing our varied population closer together rather than pulling it farther apart.

The Future of National Conventions

One of the lessons of recent presidential elections may be that national conventions are declining in importance as decision-making bodies.[38] They are not now taken seriously as decision-making instruments of the party of an incumbent president. The turnover of delegates from convention to convention is very high, averaging about 64 percent.[39] This suggests the introduction of large numbers of delegates who are recruited by national candidates rather than by local parties. The success of Senator Kennedy in 1960, Senator Goldwater in 1964, Richard Nixon in 1968, and Senator McGovern in 1972, as well as the new rules in the Democratic party, make it plausible to argue that increasingly commitments are being made earlier and earlier in the nomination process, even when the nomination of the out party is being contested among several factions.

The large number of first-ballot nominations in recent years suggests that important things are happening in the out party before the convention meets. Nationwide television coverage of the primaries gives early-bird candidates a head start on the free publicity of the election year.[40] Private polls (as well as those published in the newspapers) put more information about the comparative popularity of candidates in the hands of party leaders earlier than before. Thus the pressures upon state party leaders to decide what they want to do seem to be urging them to make decisions earlier in the election year—before national publicity creates a rush of sentiment in one direction or another that takes matters wholly out of their hands. When one or a few party leaders come to feel the need for early decisions, soon the others must follow suit or lose their own room for maneuvering. These early decisions must, perforce, take place at widely separate places on the map, thus enhancing the bargaining power of candidates who can deal with party leaders piecemeal under these circumstances, rather than having to face them en masse at a convention where they can wheel and deal with one another.

Number of Presidential Ballots in National Party Conventions
1928–1972*

Year	Democrats	Republicans
1928	1	1
1932	4	①
1936	①	1
1940	①	8
1944	①	1
1948	①	3
1952	3	1
1956	1	①
1960	1	1
1964	①	1
1968	1	1
1972	1	①
First-ballot total:	10/12	10/12
	(5 incumbents)	(3 incumbents)

Combined (Democrats and Republicans) first-ballot nominations:
Nonincumbents: 12/16
Incumbents: 8/8

* Nominations won by incumbents are circled.

If this tendency is correctly identified, it leads to the further conclusion that over the long run, as mass communications media continue or possibly increase their saturation coverage of early events in the election year, successful candidates (at least of the party out of office) increasingly will have to have access to large sums of money apart from the resources generally available to the party, a large personal organization, and an extra measure of skill and attractiveness on the hustings and over television. In these circumstances, other resources—such as the high regard of party leaders—would come to be less important. Thus, early candidacy, opulent private financing (preferably gathered by a mail campaign that pulls in small contributions), and strong personal organizations such as characterized the Kennedy, Goldwater, Nixon, and Mc-Govern preconvention campaigns can overcome strong misgivings on the part of party leaders whose main concern is winning elections. If out-party candidates in the future follow similar strategies, the national convention as a decision-making body may go into eclipse.

But there are also counteracting tendencies. The predominance of proportional and districting rules in Democratic party primaries plus the federal financial incentives that will surely entice candidates of middling promise into the primaries decrease the probability that one candidate will have a clear majority before the convention. If a candidate does not win big and early, the chances are he will not make it large and late. A bare victory in the last big primary that produces a bumper crop of delegates under a winner-take-all rule, like the one that carried McGovern in, will no longer be possible.

The same trends that make it harder to win decisively before the convention also serve to make bargaining difficult once there. Proportional and district primaries give the advantage to the more extreme tendencies because they place a premium on the intense commitments of candidate enthusiasts; so does the weakness of party organization and the proclivity of educated activists with time on their hands to be stylistically purist and ideologically distant from voters.

The dilemmas of a centrist candidate were well exemplified in 1972 by Senator Muskie of Maine, who had to compete for the votes of party moderates with Senators Humphrey and Jackson. Because Wallace and McGovern supporters were more intense in their convictions earlier on, they were able to build grass roots organizations. (Had Wallace's people caught on to the rules of the primary process in time they would have done a lot better.) When Wallace became active, he took the right with him. When former New York Mayor John Lindsay dropped out after the Florida primary and former Senator McCarthy after the Illinois primary, McGovern had the left pretty much to himself. He could count on a plurality over his rivals. By the time Humphrey emerged as the strongest center candidate, McGovern was barely able to beat him out. And that may have been appropriate. Within the Democratic party, the left liberals may have a small majority among those who turn out at primaries. But that is not the same, as McGovern discovered, as a national majority.

A healthy political party requires activists as well as voters. So long as the policy preferences and group identifications of these two populations are reasonably compatible, their differing interests can be reconciled by bargaining. Once they grow far apart, however, the tension between them may become unbearable until one or another leaves its ancestral party. In Europe this tension takes the form of a clash between the militant party cadres and the moderate parliamentarians interested in winning elections. Since it is the parliamentarians who elect the party leaders, including the prime minister, they have real resources with which to combat the militants. The separate elections of senators and congressmen and the federal system in the United States, however, take the presidential nomination outside of normal politics. Congressional and gubernatorial candidates rarely run on as radical or conservative a basis as the rhetoric of their activist supporters might suggest. But these elected officials have much less of a stake in the presidency. And the party leaders who used to guard that stake are increasingly weak or absent.

Notes

1. This is the number that White, *The Making of the President, 1968*, p. 259, estimates that the Democrats need for their convention.

2. Material on the Kennedy organization in 1960 is drawn from Fred G. Burke, "Senator Kennedy's Convention Organization," in *Inside Politics*, ed. Tillett, pp. 25–39.

3. Ibid., p. 39.

4. Recognizing the importance of communication at the Republican convention of 1860, a supporter of Abraham Lincoln carefully seated all the solid Seward states

close together and as far as possible from the states whose delegates were in some doubt about whom to support. Glyndon G. Van Deusen, *Thurlow Weed: Wizard of the Lobby* (Boston, 1947), p. 253. Mayor Daley arranged for something similar at the Democratic National Convention in 1968, but the level of protest about excessive security procedures and the lack of communications facilities reached such a pitch that whatever strategic advantages Daley might have hoped for evaporated.

5. See David, Moos, and Goldman, *Presidential Nominating Politics in 1952*, vol. 1; Robert Elson, "A Question for Democrats: If Not Truman, Who?" *Life*, March 24, 1952; Albert Votaw, "The Pros Put Adlai Over," *New Leader*, August 4, 1952; Douglass Cater, "How the Democrats Got Together," *The Reporter*, August 19, 1952; Arvey and Madigan, "The Reluctant Candidate: An Inside Story"; and Walter Johnson, *How We Drafted Adlai Stevenson* (New York, 1955).

6. Democratic National Committee, *Mandate for Reform*, p. 40. The Republican party has also adopted language encouraging the participation of women, young people, and black people in the next convention, but it has stopped short of requiring quotas.

7. Cavala, "Changing the Rules Changes the Game," p. 37.

8. Ibid.

9. See Sullivan, Pressman, Page, and Lyons, *The Politics of Representation*, pp. 41–70.

10. This account and the paragraphs that follow are taken from the important study by Jeane J. Kirkpatrick, "Representation in National Political Conventions: The Case of 1972," paper delivered at the annual meeting of the American Political Science Association, 1974, p. 22.

11. Kirkpatrick, "Representation in National Political Conventions," p. 23.

12. McClosky, Hoffman, and O'Hara, "Issue Conflict and Consensus Among Party Leaders and Followers," pp. 406–27.

13. Kirkpatrick, "Representation in National Political Conventions," p. 40.

14. For extensive documentation, see Everett Carll Ladd, Jr. (with Charles D. Hadley), *Transformation of the Party System: Political Coalitions from the New Deal to the 1970's* (New York, 1975). See also their "Political Parties and Political Issues: Patterns in Differentiation since the New Deal," a Sage Professional Paper, *American Politics Series* (Beverly Hills, 1973), pp. 4–11.

15. William R. Shafer, Romano E. Weber, and Robert S. Montjoy, "Mass and Political Elite Beliefs about the Policies of the Regime," paper delivered at the annual meeting of the American Political Science Association, 1973.

16. Thomas Roback, "Political Attitudes among Republican Leaders: The Case of Delegates to the 1972 National Convention," paper delivered at the annual meeting of the American Political Science Association, 1974. See also Roback, "Amateurs and Professionals: Delegates to the 1972 Republican National Convention," *Journal of Politics* 37 (May 1975), p. 462.

17. Austin Ranney, *Curing the Mischiefs of Faction* (Berkeley, 1975), p. 153. The italics are Ranney's.

18. Presidents Andrew Johnson and Chester Arthur are the only clear exceptions to this since the Civil War. Coolidge and Wilson may also have had vague hopes of renomination.

19. See Ostrogorski, *Democracy and the Party System in the United States*, pp. 145–60, for excellent descriptions of convention confusion. Tillett, ed., *Inside Politics*, contains more up-to-date material in the same vein. White, *The Making of the President, 1964*, in contrast, describes the order and efficiency of conventions, like those in 1964, when there was no real contest for the nomination; see especially pp. 201–2. See also Ralph G. Martin, *Ballots and Bandwagons* (Chicago, 1964).

20. See Roy V. Peel and Thomas C. Donnelly, *The 1932 Campaign: An Analysis* (New York, 1935), pp. 92–93. Arthur Schlesinger, Jr., writes that strategist James Farley opposed the attempt to attack the two-thirds rule, "knowing well that not all delegates who were for Roosevelt were against the rule, and fearing that a defeat on this issue might set back the whole Roosevelt drive." Roosevelt backed down just in time. *The Crisis of the Old Order, 1919–1933* (Boston, 1957), pp. 299–300. See also Robert Morss Lovett, "Big Wind at Chicago," *The New Republic*, July 13, 1932, p. 228.

21. Wesley Bagby, "The 'Smoke-Filled Room' and the Nomination of Warren G. Harding," *Mississippi Valley Historical Review* 41 (March 1955), pp. 657–74.

22. Caroline T. Harnsberger, *A Man of Courage—Robert A. Taft* (Chicago, 1952), p. 146. See also Joseph Martin's memoirs, *My First 50 Years in Politics*.

23. Peel and Donnelly, *The 1932 Campaign: An Analysis*, pp. 95–96.

24. For instance, on the Roosevelt election of 1932: "Farley had held a few votes in reserve for the second ballot, knowing the importance of showing an increase each time round." Schlesinger, *The Crisis of the Old Order, 1919–1933*, p. 306.

25. Eugene B. McGregor, Jr., "Rationality and Uncertainty at National Nominating Conventions," *The Journal of Politics* 35 (1973), pp. 472–77.

26. Harry Daugherty, *The Inside Story of the Harding Tragedy* (New York, 1932), pp. 36, 46; and Mark Sullivan, *Our Times* (New York, 1926–35), vol. 2, p. 54. See also, Bagby, "The 'Smoke-Filled Room' and the Nomination of Warren G. Harding," pp. 657–74.

27. Arthur Vandenberg, Jr., ed., *The Private Papers of Senator Vandenberg* (Boston, 1952), p. 6.

28. Frank R. Kent, *The Democratic Party* (New York, 1928), p. 493.

29. See Jules Abels, *Out of the Jaws of Victory* (New York, 1959), pp. 65–68.

30. See Aaron Wildavsky, "What Can I Do? Ohio Delegates View the Democratic Convention," in *Inside Politics*, ed. Tillett, pp. 112–30.

31. See Edward Stanwood, *A History of the Presidency from 1788 to 1897* (Boston, 1898), pp. 206–25.

32. Mark Sullivan, *Our Times*, vol. 6, 35–67. See also Daugherty, *The Inside Story of the Harding Tragedy*, pp. 41–55.

33. See Kent, *The Democratic Party*, pp. 483–505.

34. Ferdinand Lundberg, *Imperial Hearst* (New York, 1936), pp. 273–75, and Schlesinger, *The Crisis of the Old Order, 1919–1933*, pp. 304–8.

35. See Irving G. Williams, *The American Vice-Presidency: New Look* (New York, 1954).

36. The best accounts of the selection of Spiro Agnew are in White, *The Making of the President, 1968*, pp. 244–53, and Witcover, *The Resurrection of Richard Nixon*, pp. 349–55. See also Richard Cohen and Jules Witcover, *A Heartbeat Away* (New York, 1974).

37. Most of the 130-odd Goldwater delegates we interviewed at the 1964 Republican convention were prepared to sacrifice victory if victory meant becoming a "me-too" party or "going against principles" by adopting what they termed the "devious and corrupt" balanced tickets of the past.

38. William Carleton, "The Revolution in the Presidential Nominating Convention," *Political Science Quarterly* 72 (June 1957), pp. 224–40.

39. Loch K. Johnson and Harlan Hahn, "Delegate Turnover at National Party Conventions, 1944–68," in *Perspectives on Presidential Selection,* ed. Donald R. Matthews (Washington, D.C., 1973), p. 148.

40. Obviously this entails risks as well as opportunities. George Romney was the first serious Republican candidate in the field in 1968, and the early exposure before he could put together a fully coherent position on the Vietnam issue almost certainly caused his downfall. See White, *The Making of the President, 1968*, pp. 54–61, and Witcover, *The Resurrection of Richard Nixon*, pp. 171–91.

CHAPTER FIVE

The
Campaign

❧〰❧

Once the conventions are over, the two presidential candidates traditionally "relax" for a few weeks until Labor Day when they ordinarily begin their official campaigning. From that day onward they confront the voters directly, each carrying the banner of his political party. How do the candidates behave? Why do they act the way they do? And what kind of impact do their activities have on the electorate?

For the small minority of people who are party workers, campaigns serve as a signal to get to work. How hard they work depends in part on whether the candidates' political opinions, slogans, personalities, and visits spark their enthusiasm. The workers may "sit on their hands," or they may pursue their generally unrewarding jobs—checking voting lists, mailing campaign flyers, ringing doorbells—with something approaching fervor. They cannot be taken for granted; activating them and imbuing them with purpose and ardor is perhaps the first task of the candidate.

For the rest of the population, most of whom are normally uninterested in politics, campaigns call attention to the advent of an

157

election. Some excitement may be generated and some diversion (as well as annoyance) provided for those who were not aware, until they turned on the TV, that their favorite program had been preempted by a political speech. The campaign is a great spectacle. Talk about politics increases, and a small percentage of citizens may even become intensely involved as they get caught up in campaign oratory.

For the vast majority of citizens in America, campaigns do not function so much to change minds as to reinforce previous convictions. As the campaign wears on, the underlying party identification of most people rises ever more powerfully to the surface. Republican and Democratic identifiers are split further apart (polarized) as their increased awareness of party strife emphasizes the things that divide them.[1]

The Center for Political Studies at the University of Michigan has found repeatedly that about three-quarters of those in its samples eligible to vote claimed a party identification; of these, three-fifths were Democrats.[2] Thus, the outstanding strategic problem for Democratic politicians is to get their adherents to turn out and to vote for Democratic candidates. No need to worry about Republicans or independents if Democrats can do their basic job. Thus Democrats stress appeals to the faithful. They try to raise in their supporters the old party spirit. One of their major problems, as we have seen, is that most citizens who identify with them are found at the lower end of the socioeconomic scale and are less likely to turn out to vote than those with Republican leanings. So the Democrats put on mobilization drives and seek in every way to get as large a turnout as possible. If they are well organized, they scour the lower-income areas. They try to provide cars for the elderly and infirm, baby-sitters for mothers, and, occasionally, inducements of a less savory kind to reinforce the party loyalty of the faithful. The seemingly neutral campaigns put on by radio, TV, and newspapers to stress the civic obligation to vote, if they have any effect at all, probably help the Democrats more than the Republicans.[3]

For Republicans involved in presidential nominating politics, the most important fact of life is that their party is without question the minority party in the United States. What is more, the Republicans can claim the allegiance of what seems to be a minority of citizens that has shrunk somewhat over the last twenty-five years.

In presidential elections in which considerations of party are foremost and allowing for the greater propensity of Republicans to turn out to vote, it has been plausibly argued that the Democrats could expect to win with around 53 or 54 percent of the vote.[4]

Percentage of adults identifying themselves as:

	Republican	Democratic	Other
1940	38	42	20
1950	33	45	22
1960	30	47	23
1964	25	53	22
1968	27	46	27
1972	28	43	29
1974	23	44	33

SOURCE: *Gallup Monthly Index*, July 1974.

This is close enough to kindle justifiable hope in Republican breasts; despite the clear Democratic majority in this country, it must be assumed that either major party can win a presidential election. But over the last thirty years it has generally been necessary for the Republicans to devise a strategy that could not only make them win, but win from behind.

The decline in party identification from something over three-quarters to just above two-thirds of the adult population may lead to questions about the continuing importance of party identification. Perhaps independent voters are or will soon become the decisive ones in presidential elections. This is possible but doubtful. For one thing, most independents have leanings; scratch an independent and underneath you are likely to find an almost-Republican or a near-Democrat. And those who are left are least likely to turn out. For another, it is hard to mobilize independents except under the banner of one or the other of the major parties. Independents are fair game; so are more weakly identified Democrats and Republicans. Capturing them is what elections are about, especially for Republicans who begin with a handicap.

Three Underdog Strategies

With the handwriting so plainly on the wall, the strategic alternatives available to Republicans can hardly be regarded as secret. They can be boiled down to three possibilities. First, Republicans can attempt to deemphasize the impact of party habit as a component of electoral choice by capitalizing upon a more compelling cue to action. The nomination of General Eisenhower, the most popular hero of the Second World War, overrode party considerations and is a clear example of the efficacy of this strategy.[5] Efforts to play upon popular dissatisfaction in a variety of issue areas also exemplify this strategy, but these dissatisfactions must preexist in the population and must be widespread and intense before they will produce the desired effect. When issues do come to the fore in a compelling way, the payoff to the advantaged party is sometimes enormous, because these are the circumstances under which new party loyalties can be created.

Another possible Republican strategy, similar in some ways to the first, also seeks to depress the salience of party in the minds of voters by blurring the differences between the parties, by seeking to efface certain of the stigmata that have been attached to the party over the years as stereotypes having general currency (e.g., "party of the rich").[6] This strategy gives full recognition to the arithmetic of Democratic superiority and also to the unit rule of the Electoral College, which weighs disproportionately votes cast in the large states that so often contain the heaviest concentrations of traditional allies of the Democratic party.[7] It has been used by Republican nominees such as Willkie, Dewey, and Nixon, with results that have often fallen short—sometimes barely short—of victory; in consequence this "me-too" strategy has over the years become increasingly controversial among Republicans. The fact that no Republican candidate has actually been able to gain a majority vote with it has created doubts about its efficacy.[8] The "me-too" strategy may entail the advocacy of policies generally favored by most American voters, but this approach apparently does not correctly mirror the political sentiments of Republican activists.[9] Critics of the "me-too" approach have argued that this strategy merely alienates potential Republican voters while failing to attract sufficient Democrats. Alienated Republicans, so goes this argument, seeing no difference between the policies espoused by the major parties, withdraw from politics into apathy.[10]

Thus, a third strategy, whose claim of victory is based upon the presupposition of a hidden Republican vote, can be identified. This was the strategy pursued by the Goldwater forces in 1964. Its main characteristic is the attempt to sharpen rather than blur party lines on matters of substantive policy. Goldwater supporters argued that he could win, basing their case upon the possibility that he could put together a coalition in the Electoral College of southern and western states and, in particular, upon the notion of a hidden vote. But did this hidden vote exist—or was this argument an instance of misperception on the part of those who believed it and supported Goldwater, thinking he could win?

The resulting disastrous consequences for the Republican party at the congressional and state levels[11] invite the exercise of hindsight on the question of the hidden Republican vote. But, for once, hindsight merely confirms foresight. It was apparent before the election of 1964 as well as afterwards that there are only very weak factual grounds supporting the notion of a hidden Republican vote, waiting to be tapped by an unequivocally conservative candidate.

In examining the evidence we must first ask where the Republican vote could be hidden that this strategy seeks to tap. Presumably not among Democrats, at least outside the South, since this approach relies so heavily upon sharpening the cleavage between the two parties. Nor can there be much of a hidden vote among disaffected conservative Republicans who fail to turn out, since the best knowledge we have of Republicans is that they do turn out and vote Republican.[12]

The only other possible location for the hidden vote is among those who profess no regular party affiliation—roughly 33 percent of the potential electorate. What do we know about these people that might lead us to conclude that they can be moved to vote Republican by a highly ideological appeal based on conservative and right-wing doctrines?

There is, in fact, no reason at all to suspect that these people can be reached in this way. All the information we have on party neutrals indicates that they are much less interested, less informed, less likely to seek information about politics, and less likely to vote than are regular partisans. Nonaffiliates are relatively unconcerned about issues and are only dimly aware of political events.[13] Efforts to reach this population, to attract their attention, are likely to fail. Attempts to outline issue positions to them, to engage their support in behalf of any self-consistent philosophical and political position, seem on a par with the famous campaign to sell refrigerators to Eskimos.

There is a well-known suspicion, voiced from time to time by imaginative writers, that conservative elements of the population are in fact alienated from politics and sit in the wings, frustrated, immobilized, and without party loyalties, until someone pursuing a Goldwater-like strategy gives them the "choice" they are looking for. This is probably a canard. What fragments of evidence we have point to the probability that the dedicated conservatives and right-wing ideologues who are sufficiently interested in politics to hold strong opinions about public policy do in fact belong to political parties and participate actively in them. These people are almost all Republicans. Thus, the hidden vote that Goldwater hoped to attract was probably hidden inside the vote Richard Nixon received in 1960.[14]

Another assumption underlying the hidden vote theory is that in 1964 it would have been possible to attract this mythical vote in substantial numbers without losing the allegiance of large numbers of more moderate people who supported the almost-successful candidacy of Richard Nixon in 1960.

In fact, this proved impossible to accomplish. An enormous number—probably around 20 percent—of Nixon's 1960 supporters voted for Lyndon Johnson in 1964.[15] But this outcome might have been extrapolated from poll and primary election data in the preconvention period which showed that, even among Republican voters, Goldwater enjoyed far from overwhelming support.[16]

In addition, he aroused great antipathy among the general population. According to the Gallup poll in mid-September, 38.3 percent of respondents expressed definite hostility to Goldwater (including 14.7 percent expressing the most extreme hostility on an eleven-point scale) while only 8.1 percent expressed any antipathy at all toward President Johnson.[17] Likewise, on a number of issues, Louis Harris surveys found that sizable majorities in the general population defined themselves as opposed to positions that they believed Senator Goldwater held.[18]

The election of 1964, as a result of the Goldwater nomination and the campaign strategy he pursued, was an extremely good test of the hidden vote hypothesis and also, by indirection, of the "me-too" Republican strategy, which was closer to the strategy of Richard Nixon in 1968. Nixon's main tactic was to avoid antagonizing voters, to avoid direct confrontations with the opposition or with the press, and to avoid saying anything controversial about Vietnam.[19]

Because of Nixon's hairbreadth plurality over Humphrey, a conclusive explanation for his victory cannot be given. It is clear, though, that he won back almost all of the Republicans who had deserted their party in the Goldwater election four years before. He also won over many Democrats who had voted for Johnson. Indeed, "a full 40 percent of Nixon's vote came from citizens who had supported Lyndon Johnson in 1964!" [20] Votes received by the Democratic party dropped from 61 percent in 1964 to something less than 43 percent in 1968, a total loss of 19 percent. The vote for the Republican presidential candidate rose a comparatively small 4 percent from 39 to 43. Naturally, the third-party candidacy of George Wallace made up the difference. Insofar as the matter can be determined at all, almost all of Wallace's votes came from people who nominally considered themselves Democrats but who, in his absence, would have given more of their votes to Nixon than to Humphrey. The primary effect of the Wallace candidacy, therefore, was to decrease slightly Nixon's margin of victory.[21]

Despite the unusually severe defections in 1968 from the Democratic party at the presidential level, the party label continued to exert its customary force at state and local levels. The result in elections for the House of Representatives was virtually a standoff. The *Congressional Quarterly* shows that where the Democrats had occupied 57.7 percent of the legislative seats in the state capitols throughout the nation before the election, afterwards they retained virtually the same proportion despite the fact that there were contests of some kind in forty-three states.[22] While there is ample evidence that people defected from the Democratic candidate in large numbers, it was premature—and in fact probably incorrect—to say that they had abandoned their party for good.

The strong Democratic recovery in the 1970 election bore this out. In the Senate, the very large Democratic class of 1958—first elected in a Republican recession and reelected in the Goldwater landslide —finally faced a reasonably normal electoral situation. They sustained a net loss of only two seats. Meanwhile, in the House, the Democrats picked up nine seats. They might have done better, but Nixon's 1968 coattails were nonexistent and it is presidential coattail victories every four years that more than any other factor produce the decline in House seats held by the president's party in the midterm election. In 1970 Democrats also registered dramatic gains in state elections, gaining a net of eleven governors.

In the face of a Republican presidential victory of overwhelming proportions in 1972, the Democrats nearly held their own in Congress, actually gaining two Senate seats and losing only twelve House seats—including six in the South, where party alignments have been changing. In the 1974 midterm election, with the Watergate scandals of the Nixon administration much in the air, and without McGovern at the top of the ticket to stave off a landslide, Democrats won an enormous victory, gaining forty-three seats in the House, five governor's seats, and four Senate seats. The Democratic party has won victories of this range and depth fairly frequently over the last two decades: in 1958, 1964, and 1974. Democratic landslides defeat Republicans all up and down the ticket; Republican landslides, on the other hand, when they occur, appear to be more highly particularized to a single race. Eisenhower can overwhelm Stevenson as in 1956, Nixon can defeat McGovern as in 1972, but these results do not carry over in a way that helps the Republican party generally, and their mildly pro-Republican results are frequently obliterated by the very next election. This is a chronic difficulty of the minority party, even in a reasonably competitive two-party system.

Theory and Action

The contents of election campaigns appear to be largely opportunistic. The swiftly changing nature of events makes it unwise for candidates to lay down all-embracing rules for campaigning which cannot meet special situations as they arise. A candidate may prepare for battle on one front and discover that the movement of events forces him to fight on another. Yet on closer examination, it is evident that the political strategist has to rely on some sort of theory about the probable behavior of large groups of voters under a few likely conditions. For there are too many millions of voters and too many thousands of possible events to deal with each as a separate category. Keynes pointed out years ago, quite rightly, that those among us, including politicians, who most loudly proclaim their avoidance of theory are generally the victims of some long-dead economist or philosopher whose assumptions they have unknowingly assimilated. The candidates must simplify their picture of the political world or its full complexity will paralyze them; the only question is whether or not their theories, both explicit and implicit, will prove helpful to them.

What kind of organization shall they use or construct? How shall they raise money? Where shall they campaign? How much time shall they allocate to the various regions and states? What kinds of appeals shall they make to what voting groups? How specific or general shall they be in their policy proposals? What kind of personal impression shall they seek to create or reinforce? How far should they go in castigating the opposition? These are the kinds of strategic questions for which presidential candidates need answers— answers that necessarily vary depending on their party affiliations, their personal attributes, whether they are in or out of office, and on targets of opportunity that come up in the course of current events. Let us take up each of these questions in turn, taking care to specify the different problems faced by "ins" and "outs" and by Democrats and Republicans. For purposes of illustration, we shall turn often to the last few elections.

Ins and Outs

While the incumbent may have disadvantages to offset some of his advantages, as we saw in Chapter 1, the challenger faces his own set of problems. He may not be well known and may find that much of his effort must be devoted to publicizing himself. All the while, the president is getting reams of free publicity and is in a position to create major news by the things he does—a tariff on imported oil, proposals for lowering taxes, impounding and/or releasing billions for highways and public works.

The candidate aspiring to office may find that he lacks information, which puts him at a disadvantage in discussing foreign policy and defense issues. On the other hand, he may deliberately forbear from finding out too much for fear that he be restrained in his criticism by an implied pledge not to use information the president has furnished to him. Perhaps the major advantage the challenger possesses is his ability to criticize policies freely and sometimes in exaggerated terms, whereas the incumbent is often restrained by his current official responsibilities from talking too much about them. Obligations to other nations, for example, may restrain a president from talking about changes in foreign policy or from tipping his hand in a case like Vietnam or the Middle East.

Friends, Volunteers, and Professionals

While the incumbent has a going organization, molded and tested through his years in office, the challenger has to build one piecemeal as he goes along in the frantic days of the campaign when there is never enough time to do everything that has to be done. Should he have a man of his own run the show without much of a nod to the professionals? They may resist, if not sabotage, his efforts. And, if he gets into trouble later, as Nixon discovered, they may abandon him who scorned them. Should he enlist the cooperation of the old party men, knowing that he may thereby lose some control over his campaign? Should there be two centers of campaigning with the inevitable duplication and problems of coordination? There is apparently no costless solution to this problem. There always seems to be grumbling from party professionals and the candidate's own people about their relationship.

All candidates seek special volunteer organizations to help attract voters who prefer not to associate themselves with the party organizations. The distaste with which some middle- and upper-class people regard party organizations is difficult to overcome. It is easier to construct new organizations in which they can feel ennobled by attachment to an Eisenhower or a Stevenson rather than (as they may feel) associating with a group of vulgar politicians. The danger here is that the volunteer organizations will take on lives of their own and attempt to dictate strategy and policy to the candidates. The candidates need the volunteers, but it is advisable for them to follow the lead set by John Kennedy in keeping tight reins on them, thus assuring reasonable coordination of efforts and avoiding the possibility of capture.

The mechanics of electioneering are no simple matter; they cannot be entrusted wholly to amateurs. Not only must the candidate get to his various speaking engagements on time, but he also needs to have some good idea of to whom he is speaking and what kind of approach to take. In the hurly-burly of the campaign, where issues and plans may change from day to day, where yesterday's ideas may have to end up in the wastebasket to make room for today's problems, where changes of schedule are made in response to the opportunities and dangers suggested by private and public polls, a poor organization can be severely damaging. The troubles of Adlai

Stevenson present a case in point. His apparent distaste for the niceties of organization in 1956 hurt him badly. He was excessively rushed going from one place to another so that he lost the valuable assets of composure and thoughtfulness which should have been his stock-in-trade. If he continually made speeches that were inappropriate for his audiences, it may have been because he was badly informed about who his audience would be, not because he was talking "over people's heads." For instance, he once went to New Haven during the 1956 campaign and made a speech redolent with allusions to Yale and Princeton, with punch lines depending on knowledge of what the "subjunctive" was, to an audience that happened to be composed largely of old-time Democratic party workers from around Connecticut.[23] In 1972, because George McGovern and his staff were tired, worn out, and preparing for the challenge to their California delegates, they did not check as carefully as they might have into their vice-presidential nominee's background. To be sure, some mix-ups, if not a few outright fiascoes, are inevitable given the frantic pace and the pressure of time. Resilience is not the least qualification of a presidential candidate.

An example of the risks and rewards of a special campaign organization are illustrated by President Nixon's decision in 1972 to bypass entirely the Republican party in setting up his Committee to Reelect the President. This comported with Nixon's desire to insulate himself as much as possible from the fortunes of the Republican party. In behalf of an incumbent president, Maurice Stans, Herbert Kalmbach, and others had no difficulty raising enormous amounts of money. Some estimates of the total take range up to $60 million.[24]

Since 1972, businessmen whose firms are in regulated industries have testified that they gave campaign contributions in part to protect themselves and their companies against adverse decisions of the government, and some of them have pleaded guilty to charges of illegally contributing to Nixon's campaign chest as an ordinary corporate expense.

At the Committee to Reelect the President, meanwhile, persons of low character and no common sense devised plans to spend the gross surpluses the president's fund-raisers were supplying. One such plan has become famous, since it entailed bugging the headquarters of the Democratic National Committee, the botching of which led to the president's near-impeachment and to the unraveling of the Nixon presidency.

Two little-noticed facts about the CREEP operation deserve mention here: the first is that by raising money in this fashion, President Nixon starved many other Republican candidates who had to rely on many of the same sources for cash. And the second is that apparently the president and his employees had no intention of sharing the take with other Republicans.

Yet when Nixon's downfall came, he dragged numerous Republicans with him at a minimum by spoiling the party's chances at the next election. This illustrates the profound stake political parties have in the caliber of their presidential candidates.

In deciding where to campaign, the candidates are aided by distinctive features of the national political structure which go a long way toward giving them guidance. They know that it is not votes as such that matter but rather electoral votes which are counted on a state-by-state basis. The candidate who wins by a small plurality in a state gains all the electoral votes there are for that state. The candidates realize that a huge margin of victory in a state with a handful of electoral votes will not do them nearly as much good as a bare plurality in states like New York and California with large numbers of electoral votes. So their first guideline is evident: Campaign in states with large electoral votes. There is, however, not much point in campaigning in states where they know they are bound to win or to lose. Thus, states that almost always go for a particular party receive only perfunctory attention. Hence, the original guideline may be modified to read: Campaign in states with large electoral votes which are doubtful. In practice, a "doubtful" state is one where there is a good chance for either party to capture the state. Politicians usually gauge this chance by the extent to which the state has delivered victories to both parties within recent memory. Republicans and Democrats thus spend more time in New York, Ohio, Illinois, Pennsylvania, Texas, and California than they do elsewhere. Even if one or two one-party states should change in one election, the likelihood of such an event is too slim and the payoff in terms of electoral votes too meager to justify extensive campaigning when time might better be spent elsewhere. As the campaign wears on, the candidates take soundings from the opinion polls and are likely to redouble their efforts in states where they believe a personal visit might turn the tide.

Here we once again come across the pervasive problem of uncertainty. No one really knows how much value in changed votes or turnout is gained by personal visits to a particular state. By the time the campaign is under way, most voters have made up their minds. Opponents of the candidate are unlikely to go to see him anyway and one wonders what a glimpse in a motorcade will do to influence a potential voter. Yet no one is certain that whistle-stop methods produce no useful result. Visiting localities may serve to increase publicity because many of the media of communication are geared to "local" events. It also provides an opportunity to stress issues like energy or unemployment which may be of special significance to citizens in a given region. Party activists may be energized by a look at, or a handshake with, the candidate. New alliances, such as the one that emerged in 1964 between Goldwater and many longtime Democratic sectors of the Deep South, can be solidified. And so rather than let the opportunity pass, the candidates usually decide to take no chances and get out on the hustings. They hedge against uncertainty by doing all they can.

Consider the case of John Kennedy in Ohio. He traversed that pivotal state several times in the 1960 campaign and exerted great physical effort in getting himself seen traveling there. But when the votes were counted, he found himself on the short end. The future president professed to be annoyed and stumped at why this happened. An analysis of the voting returns showed that Kennedy's vote was correlated with the percentage of Catholic population in the various counties.[25] Kennedy made a considerable improvement over the Democratic showing in 1956, but that was not enough to win. Despite evidence of this kind, which suggests that personal appearances may well be overwhelmed by other factors, visits to localities will undoubtedly continue. Who can say, to take a contrary instance, that Kennedy's visit to Illinois did not provide the bare margin of a few thousand votes necessary for victory?

There was a time when presidential nominees faced the serious choice of whether to conduct a "front porch" campaign or to get out and meet the people. A candidate like Warren Harding, whom his sponsors felt would put his foot in his mouth every time he spoke, was well advised to stay home. More hardy souls like William Jennings Bryan took off in all directions only to discover that to be seen was not necessarily to be loved. An underdog, like Harry Truman in 1948, goes out to meet the people because he is so far behind. A favored candidate, like Thomas Dewey in 1948, goes out to meet the people to avoid being accused of complacency. Everybody does it because it is the fashion, and the spectacle of seeing one's opponent run around the country at a furious pace without following suit is too nerve-wracking to contemplate. It is beside the point that no one knows whether all this does any good. Richard Nixon seems to have learned from his enervating experience in 1960, when he pledged to visit each and every state and then had to follow through, despite a severe illness. In 1968, he ran a different kind of campaign, taking account of the fact that radio and television made it possible to reach millions, without leaving the big metropolitan areas. Nixon did a small amount of traditional campaigning, which was faithfully chronicled by the press corps that followed him around the country. But more basic to his strategy was the technique of fixing upon regional centers and making major appearances and speeches in these places, followed by elaborate, regionally oriented television commercials that reached the voters directly—"over the heads," so to speak, of the news media that were covering and interpreting only the part of the campaign they could see—which did not include Nixon's television programs.[26]

In 1972 Nixon had even more reason to pursue the same tactics. As the incumbent, he did not have to worry about establishing personal visibility or name recognition. And he was blessed with an opponent who made well-publicized mistakes. Among the worst of these was announcing a series of detailed policy proposals early in the campaign. For a time it almost seemed as if McGovern were the incumbent and that Nixon was running against his "record."

Domestic Issues

On the broad range of domestic affairs and "pocketbook" issues, the Democrats are highly favored as the party most voters believe will best meet their needs. Statements like "The Democrats are best for the workingman" and "We have better times under the Democrats" abound when people are asked to state how they feel about the Democratic party. The Republicans, on the other hand, are viewed as the party of depression under whose administration jobs are scarce and times are bad. A campaign in which the salient issues are economic, therefore, is more likely to aid the Democrats than the Republicans.[27]

Economic policy thus occasions little difficulty for the Democratic party. Its task is to be liberal in several senses of that word. It promises something for everyone. There are sizable extensions of social welfare programs financed by the federal government, increased minimum wages for the underpaid, medical insurance for new groups of people, better prices for the farmer, irrigation for arid areas, flood protection and power dams for river basins, and so on. No one is left out, not even businessmen, who are promised prosperity.

Republicans are clearly on the defensive in the realm of domestic policy, a situation stemming from the fact that they were in office when the Great Depression took place. They try to play down domestic issues. They do best when emphasizing foreign policy ("Bring the boys back from Korea"; "End the war in Vietnam"); general management of government ("We can do it better"); inflation ("We're for sound money, not like those spendthrift Democrats"); or an outstanding personality ("I like Ike"). When domestic issues are debated, a Republican candidate following the "me-too" underdog strategy takes care to stress that he is in favor of social reforms whatever else he may say. And he adds that he is in favor of helping farmers, laborers, old people, pensioners, teachers, and other worthy folk to extend their gains. That he will do this better and cheaper becomes his refrain and the major point of difference with his opponent. He is understandably upset at Democratic insinuations that he and his party have not become fully reconciled to Social Security. Over and over again such a candidate insists that he and his opponent agree on goals of domestic policy, and that the only difference separating them is the minor matter of means.[28] For if the gulf between the parties is thought to be wide on "pocketbook" issues, a majority of voters would unhesitatingly choose the Democrats.

Both parties, of course, have some difficulty in reconciling their presidential and congressional wings, but in the realm of domestic policy the Democrats have an easier task. The crucial electoral votes come from large states where the labor union and minority group interests reinforce the Democratic presidential aspirant's demand for liberal policies. Democratic conservatives, who are in any event in a minority even in Congress, can be and largely are increasingly ignored. A strong civil rights stand risks loss of southern support, but black voters are strategically placed in states with the highest number of electoral votes. Since Franklin D. Roosevelt, all Democratic presidential candidates have decided that they can win without the South but not without the large states in other sections of the country. Television and radio make the old practice of saying different things in different parts of the country rather more dangerous than it used to be.

The Republicans face much more difficult problems of internal dissension. Their congressional contingent is cohesive and generally conservative. The result is that Republican presidential candidates more often than not ignore the preferences of their congressional brethren. Party conservatives do not like the "me-too" implications of the stands taken by their conciliatory presidential candidates. In the past they have felt their candidate ought to hit harder at what they regard as Democratic statism and looseness with the public purse. But the number of strategically placed voters, or the groups from whom they take their cues, who disagree with this approach in domestic affairs is too great to forget for a Republican candidate who wants to win. Though he can talk tough at times in remarks directed to selected Republican audiences, he must usually refuse to alter the tenor of his remarks in general. With the exception of Barry Goldwater in 1964, all Republican candidates since 1936 have evidently concluded that there are not enough conservatives to elect a Republican president, that they have no place to go, and the Republican candidate would get their votes anyhow. It is permissible to send lesser lights, conservatives like Vice-President Agnew and Senator Thurmond out on the hustings to mollify the right wing. But it is ordinarily political suicide to make wholesale attacks on the Democratic party and its domestic policies.

Foreign Affairs

In the realm of foreign affairs, the Republicans have the advantage. The fact that the Democrats occupied the presidency during the First and Second World Wars, the Korean War, and the initial stages of heavy American involvement in Vietnam has apparently convinced most voters that Democrats tend to lead the country to war. Republicans have on the whole escaped this stigma and are known as the party of peace.[29] Whether this impression of Democrats is any more useful or valid than that of Republicans as the party of depression is beside the point for present purposes. We are after the strategic implications, which are interesting. For if foreign affairs issues can be made sufficiently important to enough voters, the Republicans stand a better chance of winning. Republicans generally do best by building up foreign affairs and playing on the fear that Democrats are not competent in this field. Democrats have the choice of deemphasizing foreign policy, something that has become increasingly difficult to do, or trying to show somehow that they are more peace-loving than Republicans, though also at least as tough on communism.

How this used to work in practice can be seen in Richard Nixon's 1960 campaign, as the lamb of domestic controversy turned into the lion of foreign affairs. Nixon sought to differentiate himself as much as possible from Kennedy in the field of foreign policy. He suggested that he was uniquely capable of securing peace without surrender and that Kennedy was not. He tried to strengthen the prevailing impression of the Democratic party as the party of war. He implied alternatively that Kennedy would permit the Communists to make unwarranted advances (for example, in Matsu and Quemoy), and that the Democrats would make rash moves (Cuba). Even Nixon's espousal of an aggressive line such as he took regarding Matsu and Quemoy helped him because in foreign affairs voters trust the Republicans. On the other hand, Kennedy's equally aggressive stand toward Cuba in his speeches did not correspondingly help him.[30]

All this may appear paradoxical, but it is perfectly understandable in the light of our knowledge of voting behavior. Kennedy did not succeed in convincing most voters that issues of foreign policy were more important than domestic concerns. He won on his party affiliation, on domestic issues, and on his appeal to Catholics.[31] Had he accomplished his purpose of alerting voters to the importance of foreign affairs, there is every reason to believe he would have lost support, since voters, in line with their previous inclinations, would have decided that the perilous times called for a Republican in the White House.

The television debates reflected this. Those viewers of the debates who were especially attentive to foreign policy issues were more likely to be pro-Nixon than pro-Kennedy, just the reverse of the situation in domestic affairs. A summary of public opinion surveys on the debates concludes, "The evidence suggests that foreign affairs was the paramount issue during the entire campaign and . . . since Nixon was generally conceded to be the more expert and experienced in foreign affairs—he was far ahead of Kennedy in perceived ability at 'handling the Russians' and 'keeping the peace'—the focus on foreign affairs was clearly to Nixon's advantage." [32]

Foreign affairs was also an area that helped Nixon in the 1968 campaign. He managed to combine peace with toughness without saying exactly how he would bring peace or where he would get tough. Democratic dissension on the war issue did not hide the fact that Democratic presidents were in office when the war expanded and were unable to end it. Nothing Nixon said could have added to that, and anything more specific would have gotten him into trouble with one side or the other in a campaign in which his major strategy was to anger as few people as possible.

In 1972, foreign policy proved to be a sizable problem to Senator McGovern. It was, no doubt, his strong dovelike position on American participation in the Vietnam war that especially commended him to the vocal, active Democrats who did so much to help him win the nomination. But once he faced President Nixon in the general election, McGovern's avowed willingness to sponsor a quick withdrawal of American troops, to cut defense spending, to "beg" Hanoi for the release of American prisoners, and to refuse future military aid to South Vietnam all were seen in a context where voters were used to trusting Republicans, not Democrats. Thus the issue that may have been McGovern's trump card in winning the nomination could only do him harm if it remained salient in the general election.[33]

Will Republicans maintain their preeminence in foreign policy in the light of a series of difficulties for U.S. foreign policy in Cambodia, Vietnam, the Middle East, Cyprus, the United Nations, Portugal, India, and so on? That depends. If public opinion feels ashamed of American weakness, President Ford and Secretary of State Kissinger may yet convince people that the refusal of Democratic congressional majorities to provide support is to blame. If the nation feels that inept leadership made a bad situation worse, it may conclude that Democrats like Senator McGovern were right in urging a more decisive break with past policies earlier on. It will be interesting not only to see who gets the blame but also whether anyone gets credit, for it is not impossible that both major parties should be discredited.

Law and Order

If, on the whole, foreign affairs and war and peace are Republican issues, and domestic welfare and the economy are Democratic issues, what about the third great cluster of problems, variously labeled (and understood) as law and order, domestic violence, and race relations? As Richard Scammon and Ben Wattenberg point out, this issue has grown enormously in prominence to voters over the last few years: "Suddenly, some time in the 1960s, 'crime' and 'race' and 'lawlessness' and 'civil rights' became the most important domestic issues in America." [34] It is too early to tell whether this cluster of issues works consistently for or against a particular political party. More likely, over the short run, it works against incumbents. After all, everyone is against crime. Since crime is always increasing, incumbents must have failed to do whatever ought to be done to make things better. The officeholder may, as Governor Reagan of California did in 1970, say he is needed even more because of the very fact that conditions are deteriorating. But this argument is unlikely to carry much weight.

Presentation of Self

Another set of strategic problems concerns the personal impression made by the candidates. A candidate is helped by being thought of as trustworthy, reliable, mature, kind but firm, a devoted family man, and in every way normal and presentable. No amount of expostulation about the irrelevance of all this ordinariness as qualification for an extraordinary office wipes out the fact that candidates must try to conform to the public stereotype of goodness, a standard that is typically far more demanding of politicians than of ordinary mortals. It would be an excruciating process for a candidate to remodel his entire personality along the indicated lines. And, to be fair, most candidates are not so far from the mark as to make this drastic expedient necessary or they would not have been nominated in the first place. What the candidates actually try to do is to smooth off the rough edges, that is, to counter the most unfavorable impressions of specific aspects of their public image to which they believe they are susceptible. Kennedy, who was accused of being young and immature, hardly cracked a smile in his debates with Nixon, while the latter, who was said to be stiff and frightening, beamed with friendliness. Kennedy restyled his youthful shock of hair, and Nixon thinned his eyebrows to look less threatening.

The little things that some people don't like may be interpreted favorably by other people. Hubert Humphrey was alleged to be a man who could not stop talking; his garrulousness, however, is just another side of his encyclopedic and detailed knowledge of the widest variety of public policies. He might talk too much to suit some, but the fact that he knew a lot pleased others. Was George McGovern kindly and compassionate? Or just wishy-washy?

The political folklore of previous campaigns provides candidates with helpful homilies about how to conduct themselves. Typical bits of advice include the following: Always carry the attack to your opponent; the best defense is offense; separate the other candidate from his party; when in doubt as to the course that will produce the most votes, do what you believe is right; guard against acts that can hurt you because they are more significant than acts that can help you; avoid making personal attacks that may gain sympathy for the opposition. Unfortunately for the politicians in search of a guide, these bits of folk wisdom do not contain detailed instructions about the conditions under which they should be applied.

The case of Adlai Stevenson suggests a familiar dilemma for candidates. Shall they write (or have written) new speeches for most occasions or shall they rest content to hammer home a few themes, embroidering just a little here and there? No one really knows which is better. Stevenson is famous for the care he took with his speeches and the originality he sought to impart to his efforts. Had he won office he might have established a trend. As it is, most candidates are likely to follow Kennedy, Nixon, Johnson, and Goldwater in using just a few set speeches. In view of the pervasive inattention to public affairs and political talk in our society, this approach may have the advantage of driving points home (as well as driving mad the newsmen who must listen to the same thing all the time).[35] Newspaper people and television journalists who cover the campaigns complain quite a lot about the repetitiousness of presidential candidates, as though the campaign should be designed mostly to amuse them. This ranks high on the list of unsolved (and no doubt unsolvable) problems of American democracy: how to appeal to the relatively inattentive American people without totally alienating the superattentive mandarins of the news media through whom a candidate must reach the rank-and-file voter.

More important, perhaps, is the desirability of appearing comfortable in delivery. Televised speeches may establish the major opportunity for a candidate to be seen and evaluated by large numbers of people. Eisenhower's ability to project a radiant appearance helped him; Stevenson's obvious discomfort before the camera hurt him. On this point we have evidence that those who listened to Stevenson's delivery over radio were more favorably impressed with him than those who watched him on TV.[36] In 1968, Richard Nixon used regional television appearances as a means of reaching voters directly and making an end run around what he feared would be hostile press coverage of his campaign.[37] With television occupying an important place in American life, ability to make a good appearance is not a trivial matter. If people are judged by the company they keep, the appearance of delegates to the 1972 Democratic convention did not help their nominee. The reaction throughout the nation was negative—these were not "folks like us." Viewers were uneasy with what, on the tube, seemed like visible evidence of a culture that was indeed counter to their own.

The major difficulty with the strategic principles we have been discussing is not that they are too theoretical, but that they do not really tell the candidates what to do in case they are mutually incompatible. Like proverbs, one can often find principles to justify opposing courses of action. ("Look before you leap," but "He who hesitates is lost.") Nixon in 1960 could not take full advantage of international affairs without hitting so hard as to reinforce the unfavorable impression of himself as being harsh and unprincipled. Kennedy could hardly capitalize on the Rooseveltian image of the vigorous leader without attacking the foreign policy of a popular president. The result is that the candidates must take calculated risks when existing knowledge about the consequences of alternative courses of action is inadequate. Hunch, intuition, and temperament necessarily play an important role in choosing among competing alternatives.

The Television Debates

The famous TV debates of 1960 between Nixon and Kennedy provide an excellent illustration of the difficulty of choosing between competing considerations in the absence of knowledge of the most likely results. With the benefit of hindsight, many observers now suggest that Nixon was obviously foolish to engage in the debates. Let us try to look at the situation from the perspective of each of the presidential aspirants at the time.

Kennedy issued a challenge to debate on television. The possible advantages from his point of view were many. He could use a refusal to debate to accuse Nixon of running away and depriving the people of a unique opportunity to judge the candidates. Among Kennedy's greatest handicaps in the campaign were his youth and the inevitable charges of inexperience. Television debates could and did help to overcome these difficulties by showing the audience not so much that Kennedy was superior in knowledge but that there was not that much difference in the information, age, and general stature of the two men. Whatever administrative skills or inside information Nixon might have had would not and did not show up on the screen as the candidates necessarily confined themselves to broad discussions of issues known to all politically literate people. Kennedy could only guess but he could not know that Nixon would not stump him in an embarrassing way in front of millions of viewers. But Kennedy was in a position to know that despite the reams of publicity he had received, he was unknown to many voters, much less known than the vice-president. Here was a golden opportunity to increase his visibility in a sudden and dramatic way. And his good looks were not calculated to hurt him with those who like to judge the appearance of a man.[38]

Nixon was in a more difficult position. To say no would not have been a neutral decision; it would have subjected him to being called a man who was afraid to face his opposition. Saying yes had a number of possible advantages. One stemmed from the numerical disadvantage of the Republican party. Normally, most people do not pay very much attention to the opposition candidate, making it difficult to win them over. They avoid contact with his statements and screen out his messages. Televised debates would provide a unique instance in which huge numbers of people attracted to both parties could be expected to tune in attentively. Nixon had good reason for believing that if he made a favorable impression he would be in a position to convince more of the people (the Democratic identifiers) he needed to convince than would Kennedy. The risk that Kennedy might use the opportunity to solidify the support of those attracted to a Democrat simply had to be taken. Another potential advantage that might have accrued to Nixon arose from the heritage of his previous political life. He had been labeled by some people as "tricky Dick," an immoral and vindictive man. This picture might have been supplanted on television by the new Nixon of smiling visage and magnanimous gesture who had it all over his opponent in knowledge of public affairs. Nixon had to judge whether his handicap was serious or whether it was confined to convinced liberals whose numbers were insignificant and who would never have voted for him in any event. He also had to guess whether it would be worthwhile to overcome this handicap, even if it also meant giving Kennedy an opportunity to overcome his own disabilities.[39] Perhaps a record of success in debate situations going back to high school was not irrelevant in guiding Nixon to his eventual decision to go on television with his opponent.[40] Surveys taken after the event suggest that Nixon miscalculated.[41] But if he had won the election instead of losing it by a wafer-thin margin, he would hardly have been reminded of any error on his part, and there would probably have been discussions of what a brilliant move it was for him to go on TV.

The election of 1964 presented an entirely different set of circumstances. President Johnson, an incumbent enjoying enormous personal popularity at the head of the majority party, had nothing to gain and everything to lose by debating his rival. And so, despite strenuous efforts by Senator Goldwater and his allies to involve the president in debates, none were held.

By 1968, observers were beginning to question whether candidates would ever again seek an epic confrontation with one another on the 1960 model. What seems to be required before the likely occurrence of such a debate is two major candidates equally eager for such a battle. If one is an incumbent, or feels himself securely in the lead, there is little incentive to debate. Hubert Humphrey pursued Richard Nixon fiercely on this point in 1968, but Nixon prudently refrained from a debate that would needlessly have risked his chances of victory. His excuse in 1972 was that a president in office could not tell all he knew. Had John Kennedy lived to debate again, in 1964, he might have established a "tradition" that would have been difficult for future candidates to break. Now, however, inertia has established a trend in the other direction.

Getting a Good Press

Although we have seen that newspapers themselves—whether in editorials or news stories—do not markedly influence reader opinion, it is still important for a candidate to get the most favorable coverage possible. It usually does not pay to try to line up support from publishers who have already made up their minds before the campaign has officially started. But the candidates can and do assiduously court the newspapermen assigned to them.[42]

The space a candidate gets and the slant of the story may depend to some extent on how the reporters regard him. If they find it difficult to get material, if they find the candidate suspicious and uncommunicative, this too may have its effect on how much and what gets published. Little things like phasing news to meet the requirements of both morning and afternoon newspapers or supplying reporters with human interest material are helpful to the candidate. Thus, the personality of the candidate, his ability to command the respect of the rather cynical men and women assigned to cover him, may count heavily. Democratic candidates probably have to work a little harder at cultivating good relations in order to help counteract the editorial slant in most papers. They also must make the most of their opportunities in public appearances or radio and TV speeches to counteract the impression given in segments of the press. If what they say and do "makes news," and their press secretaries help promote the stories, they may get space through the desire of the newspapers to sell copies.

Thus far, we have spoken of the press as if it were a monolithic entity. For the most part this is how the candidates regard it. But they also recognize that there are all sorts of papers with differing biases, needs, and audiences. A great deal of a candidate's attention is devoted to stories destined for the racial, religious, and ethnic interest group press. The circulations of these publications may not be huge but it is assumed that they have readers who are concerned with topics of special interest to smaller and more attentive constituencies. A story on religion in a Protestant journal may do more to convince people than much greater coverage in the daily press.

Mud-Slinging and Heckling

In the closing days of what appears to be a close race, there may be a temptation for the parties, now thoroughly engrossed in the heat of battle, to loose a stream of invective directly at the other side. How much of this they do and how often they do it is partially determined by the kind of people they are. In the long run, however, the standards of the voting population determine the standards of the candidates. Should it happen that vituperation is rewarded, we can expect to see it occur again. Should it prove to be the case, however, as in the Scandinavian countries, that departures from proper deportment are severely punished at the polls, candidates can be expected to take the hint. One of the results of the Watergate scandals is said to be the advent in the populace at large of a "post-Watergate morality" in which failure to abide by rules of common decency can be expected to be strongly disfavored. This does not necessarily provide much in the way of guidance to candidates, however. It may, in fact, be a gross violation of common decency, as elites understand such matters, to hurl an accusation of immorality at an opponent that forces him into a complex explanation which few people will understand. Yet it may be winning politics to indulge in such smear tactics under the incentives set up by post-Watergate morality.

For example, there are frequently adequate and legitimate reasons of public policy for congressmen to travel abroad on public funds, even if they have a good time doing it. But woe betide the congressman who for one reason or another is forced to defend his case before an aroused electorate.

Many observers claim that Senator Edmund Muskie fatally injured his campaign for the 1972 Democratic nomination by showing too much emotion in response to a Republican smear, concocted for the purpose of branding him a racist. Muskie, it is true, had in many prior campaigns managed with enormous success to show indignation at the moral lapses of opponents who attacked him,[43] but this time something went wrong, and he was widely criticized for showing the wrong sort of demeanor as the victim of that sort of thing.

Perhaps on this one occasion he should have taken a leaf from the book of Franklin Delano Roosevelt, who paid no attention to most accusations about him but seized on an attack involving his dog, Fala, to rib his opponents unmercifully for impugning a dog that could not reply.[44] If all else fails, it is always possible to take the advice attributed to a Chicago politician who said that in politics, as in poker, the way to meet scandalous charges is to "call 'em and raise 'em. If you are denounced as a fool, call your opponent a damned fool; if he says you are a crook, call him a robber; if he intimates that you are careless with the truth, tell your audience that he is a pathological liar."

Why, we may wonder, are men supposed to behave in a more exalted fashion in politics and in the midst of a passionately fought contest than we would expect of them in other areas of life? Successful public officials, like successful businessmen and union leaders, deal with people as they are, not as they would wish them to be. Campaigning is concerned primarily with winning support; any secondary effects it may have, such as educating the public, are incidental. If we wonder at the level of appeals made to us in elections we need only look as far as our own qualities to get the answer. There are occasions when we might be thankful that our politicians do not fully reflect the ethical standards actually practiced (not preached) in society. Knowledge of our own character may explain the wish (and expose the fallacy) of expecting politicians to be better than we are.[45]

However, the standards of the voting population do not necessarily determine the actions of organized hecklers and mischief makers. Heckling has probably always been a part of any politics in which votes are publicly solicited, though Americans have never indulged in the practice to the degree that it exists in Great Britain.

The heckling in the 1968 campaign was different from that of recent American politics in its scope. Both Hubert Humphrey and George Wallace had to face frequent, deliberate, disruptive activities on the part of groups of young people whose aim was to prohibit them from speaking at all, rather than to "score points" on them through clever interruptions. If a rule of thumb were to be developed from this, it would seem to be that extreme conservatives and moderate liberals were most likely to face such activity, while moderate conservatives (e.g., Richard Nixon) and extreme liberals (e.g., various peace-and-freedom types) would escape. To the degree that such heckling had any impact, in the end it probably gained a little sympathy for the candidate under fire. Unlike mud-slinging, however, when a campaign that boomerangs is usually quickly squelched by party leaders, the disruptive forms of heckling in 1968 were less easy to control. The hecklers had no candidate who might have lost votes by being identified with them and, in any event, their purpose was to show contempt for the electoral process rather than for any single candidate.

It is ironic that President Nixon and his campaign managers should have sought, in 1972, to adapt the tactics they attributed to the far-out left to their own uses. The contempt of insiders for a political system that nurtures them is a far more serious phenomenon than the antics of dissidents. Yet it appears that the Nixon campaign hired people to fake evidence tending to discredit former Democratic presidents and to harass Democratic presidential candidates by playing "dirty tricks" on them (such as ordering huge numbers of pizzas in their name). Presumably the passage of laws prohibiting such behavior in the future will be of some help, but the fact that the reelection campaign of a president of the United States sheltered such disgusting behavior is a shameful blot upon our history.[46]

In the United States we seem to be in a middle position in regard to mud-slinging. It is not everyday practice but neither is it a rarity. A glance at the history of presidential campaigns suggests that vituperation is largely irrelevant to the outcomes of campaigns and that its benefits are problematical.

Thomas Jefferson was accused of seducing a highborn Virginia maiden, fathering a brood of mulattoes, and being an atheist. Andrew Jackson was called a murderer, a gambler, and an adulterer. Lincoln was charged with being a vulgar village politician and fourth-rate lawyer. President Grover Cleveland was accused of fathering an illegitimate child and, though he was not certain of its paternity, he admitted responsibility. His opponents taunted him with the chant:

> Ma, Ma, where's my Pa?
> Gone to the White House
> Ha! Ha! Ha! [47]

The point is, however, that all these men won office, as have many others who have been subject to similar aspersions.

Even more instructive is the case of William Henry Harrison whom Democratic politicians derogated with the remark that he would be content to spend the rest of his life in a log cabin drinking hard cider. His party seized on this to make him into a symbol of the common man and drowned out all attempts to discuss issues with cries about humble living in log cabins. Van Buren, the Democratic candidate, was crushed with doggerel like this:

> Let Van from his coolers of silver drink wine
> And lounge on his cushioned settee;
> Our man on his buckeye bench can recline
> Content with hard cider is he.

Feedback

As the campaign progresses, the candidates attempt to take soundings from various sources and to modify their behavior as seems best suited to make the most of opportunities as they arise. But this process presents tremendous problems in the chaotic atmosphere of a campaign. Even under conditions of comparative tranquillity, who knows what the world is like? In our everyday lives we make assumptions that simplify reality tremendously in order to make decisions. Consider, then, the poor candidate who must try to take hold of a complicated universe in which the actions and the reactions of millions of voters, his own staff, his opponents, party workers, the press, and other relevant publics have to be taken into account under widely varying conditions. There is, of course, hardly any time to think about these matters. The strategies adopted by the candidates surely depend on some notions about what the consequences of these strategies will be. In turn, it is necessary to make assumptions about how people are going to act in response to one's own actions. Yet, no one can be certain that the simple picture of the world in his mind corresponds to the complex reality.

The candidate evolves an organization and a staff whose purpose in part is to inform him of the state of the political world. But he comes to know soon enough that it is unwise to trust his closest associates completely. Their fortunes are identified with his, their future prospects may depend on his, and their very battles for him may warp their judgment. Will they come to think that bad news should be withheld lest it sap his will to win? Will their hopes and fears color their judgment? Will the fact that they, in turn, depend upon other "loyalists" mean that those they trust are also unreliable? It is clear that the candidate has to place some sort of discount on the reports of his advisers. But it is not clear how much of a discount should be taken.

In trying to get a more objective estimate of the political situation, a candidate has a number of devices available—polls, the mass media, audience reaction—which are better than nothing but which are ambiguous and difficult to interpret. The first question about a poll is whether or not to believe it. Perhaps the apparent findings are more an artifact of the way the questions are phrased and the kind of people who administer them than of any objective reality. When in doubt candidates may have two polls taken, though this is terribly expensive, especially if their results do not correspond. Then the candidates, who have some reason to fancy themselves political experts, may cast the polls to the winds and rely on their own observations. Moreover, conditions may change more rapidly than a polling organization can find out. The questions asked may be the important ones in the mind of the pollster but not necessarily in that of the voter. And if the results seem intolerably pessimistic, the candidate may decide that there is no point in listening to the voice of doom anyhow. So he may turn next to the mass media. If newspapers happen to be on his side, he risks the distortions of favoritism; if they are against him, he risks the distortions of malice. If they are neutral he may wonder if they know any more about what is going on than he does. Yet he ignores what they say at his peril. The candidate cannot possibly read all the papers or listen to all the commentators; he requires summaries. Here again appears the risk of unconscious distortion by his eager staff.

Closest to the candidate's experience in the mad rush of the campaign are the audiences he addresses, and he may anxiously scan their response. At the beginning of the campaign, he is likely to try out different approaches on audiences composed of the party faithful. As a result, he may discover that what the "people" want are the kinds of traditional cries that rally those who are already disposed to vote for him; but this, at least for a Republican, may not reach the voters he needs to convince. The Republican candidate discovers that the people want an end to disastrous government spending, and the Democratic standard-bearer learns that they want more welfare programs. As the campaign progresses, candidates begin to believe that the crowds are no longer so one-sided, and their varying size and enthusiasm may be read as significant portents. There are, however, many possible reasons to explain why crowds turn out: curiosity, desire to heckle, nothing else to do, a look at a glamorous figure, as well as the desire to support a particular candidate. A large crowd may mean many things. It may mean that the candidate's managers have picked their spot wisely (such as market day at a farm distribution center) and have brought their man to a crowd rather than a crowd to him. Or a large crowd may mean that the candidate has succeeded in gaining intense support from the strongest party identifiers, but their enthusiasm may tell him nothing about his general prospects or the appeals he needs to make. In 1960, the disparity between the roaring crowds and the vote in a state like Ohio may have brought home the reality of this kind of misperception to the Kennedy forces.[48]

The feedback a candidate gets can hurt him if it reinforces and amplifies negative soundings that lead to pessimistic interpretations of his chances. Consider the plight of Vice-President Humphrey in 1968. He emerged from the Democratic convention with his party in disarray and his own image tarnished because he could not condemn, condone, or control events in the streets of Chicago or on the convention floor. Before he could pull his party together, he received indications that his campaign was falling apart. In the first few weeks the crowds (compared with those for Nixon) were poor wherever he went. Although a candidate normally rises in the estimation of the people after he has received exposure during his nomination, Humphrey's public opinion poll rating dropped precipitously after the convention. All at once his chances seemed pitifully small. An immediate result was that financial contributions did not come in as expected. Consequently he did not have enough money to go on TV in the early days of his campaign when it might have helped him most, and he had to spend a considerable portion of his first month raising the necessary funds. In those days Humphrey was pyramiding his liabilities and discovering why it is hard to start on your way up when everyone tells you you are already too far down.

While the candidate is making his assessment as best he can, others in his organization are doing the same. The party organizer, for example, may gauge the trend of the campaign by the number of people who show up at party headquarters willing to do some work. This may be as good an index as any. Like the mass meeting, however, attendance at headquarters may be an unreliable indicator of success. Party headquarters may be attracting an influx of a special, limited segment of the public attracted to a man like Adlai

Stevenson or lonely people who find this a good way to meet others. The reports of workers in the various states may or may not be more useful. Although they may be wholly accurate, they are subject to the usual biases and may be representative only of narrow portions of the public rather than a good sample of the electorate.

After an election it may be amusing to note than an activity like Les Biffle's nationwide tour masquerading as a chicken farmer proved more reliable for Harry Truman than the polls of 1948;[49] during the campaign, however, this was just one among a number of cues. The candidates are always in the dark because they can never be sure which cues to believe or whether to believe any of them. If they had lots of time, they might pore over the various signals and arrive at a composite estimate that might make some sense. Time is in terribly short supply, however, and so the presidential candidate is reduced to a haphazard savoring of some of the relevant signs. He may add some credence to one hint, subtract from another, and ultimately rely on his own intuition. The conduct of a campaign is far from being an established science; at best it is a shaky art.

One hears much about campaign blunders as if there really were objective assurance that another course of action would have turned out better for the unfortunate candidate. The most famous of these in recent years was Thomas E. Dewey's decision in 1948 to mute the issues, which was said to have snatched defeat from the jaws of victory.[50] A vigorous campaign on his part, it was said, would have taken steam out of Harry Truman's charges and would thus have brought victory to Dewey. Perhaps. What we know of the 1948 election suggests that it provoked a higher degree of voting on the basis of economic class than any of the elections that have succeeded it.[51] A slashing attack by Dewey, therefore, might have polarized the voters even further. This would have increased Truman's margin since there are many more people with low than with high incomes. Had the election gone the other way—and a handful of votes in a few states would have done it—we would have heard much less about Dewey's blunder and much more about how unpopular Truman was supposed to have been in 1948.

A whole series of "mistakes" have been attributed to Richard Nixon in 1960, the year he lost the election by such a small margin. Here are two, culled from a best-selling book on the 1960 campaign. On the civil rights plank of the Republican platform: "The original draft plank prepared by the Platform Committee was a moderate one. . . . This plank, as written, would almost certainly have carried the Southern states for Nixon and, it seems in retrospect, might have given him victory. . . . On Monday, July 25th, it is almost certain, it lay in Nixon's power to reorient the Republican Party toward an axis of Northern-Southern conservatives. His alone was the choice. . . . Nixon insisted that the Platform Committee substitute for the moderate position on civil rights (which probably would have won him the election) the advanced Rockefeller position on civil rights. . . ." [52] On Nixon's failure to protest the imprisonment of Martin Luther King during the campaign: "He had made the political decision at Chicago to court the Negro vote in the North, only now, apparently, he felt it quite possible that Texas, South Carolina, and Louisiana might all be won to him by the white vote and he did not wish to offend that vote. So he did not act—there was no whole philosophy of politics to instruct him." [53]

Apparently, there are times when hindsight converts every act of a losing candidate into a blunder. Victory can have the same effect in reverse. Consider the situation of Richard Nixon, 1968 version, as he dealt with the same southern white–northern black dilemma—in the same way. Theodore White reports:

> Nixon had laid it down, at the Mission Bay gathering, that none of his people, North or South, were to out-Wallace Wallace. He insisted, as he was to insist to the end of the campaign, that he would not divide the country; he wanted a campaign that would unify a nation so he could govern it. To compete with Wallace in the South on any civilized level was impossible. . . . Instead, Nixon would challenge Wallace in the peripheral states—Florida, North Carolina, Virginia, Tennessee, South Carolina. . . . It was only later that the trap within this strategy became evident—for, to enlarge his base in the Northern industrial states, Nixon would have to reach across from the rock-solid Republican base there, across center, to the independents, the disenchanted Democrats, to the ghettos. But to do that would be to shake the peripheral strategy in the new South. And to hold to the course he had set for the peripheral strategy limited his call in the North.[54]

Nixon's strategy was aimed, in both years, at chipping off the "peripheral" southern states while not taking such a strong anti–civil rights position as to bring northern black voters to the polls in great numbers and to turn northern suburban whites against him.

In 1968, of course, he won; his margin over 1960 consisted of North Carolina, South Carolina, Illinois, and New Jersey. Would it have been a gain for him to "out-Wallace Wallace"? Not likely, in view of the heavy margins Wallace piled up in the states he did carry and his inability to do very well elsewhere. Would it have been a gain for Nixon to repudiate all possible anti–civil rights votes? Not likely, in view of the near-unanimity against him of the black vote and probably of most strongly pro–civil rights white liberals. In short, did his strategy of equivocation almost win or almost lose the presidency for Richard M. Nixon in 1960 and/or 1968?

We have previously dealt with Nixon's decision to engage in television debates with Kennedy. Let us take a look at his decision on timing the 1960 campaign. Nixon calculated that the election was going to be very close because the Democrats were the majority party in the country and the Republicans lacked Eisenhower. Nixon reasoned, therefore, that the candidate who closed his campaign with the strongest spurt would be the winner.[55] Consequently, he held his fire somewhat until the latter part of October, hoping thereby to peak his campaign while Kennedy's was falling off. This is precisely what he did, and Kennedy's supporters were worried that he had lost and Nixon had gained impetus in the last two weeks. Nevertheless, Kennedy won. What lesson might a future candidate derive from this experience? Nixon's strategy of timing has a common-sense ring to it. Yet it is really difficult to say whether it had meaning. Would he have done better to come to a peak earlier? Might the general public not have gotten tired of a full-blast effort straight through? There is no way of knowing. It is possible that Nixon lost because of his strategy, that he gained though not enough, or that the strategy had no effect whatsoever. It would have been possible to use a successive survey of the same voters to check on whether votes were changed in his favor during the period he put on the steam, but other factors could also affect the outcome of such a study. Furthermore, there is no way of measuring how well he might have done had he pursued a different strategy.

How should George McGovern have treated the Eagleton affair? Had he failed to remove Senator Eagleton as vice-presidential nominee, the campaign might have revolved around charges, ill-founded or not, that Eagleton was psychologically unfit to succeed to the presidency if and when that became necessary. McGovern, moreover, felt that he had been taken in by Eagleton's failure to mention his past psychiatric treatment. Had McGovern kept Eagleton on the Democratic ticket, however, as the ideology of the mental health movement (past illness should not disqualify for future activity) would suggest, positive use might have been made of the events. If the Democrats were indeed the party of the people who needed help, this was certainly a good time to demonstrate it. Punitive Republicans might have been compared with compassionate Democrats. But there is reason to believe that McGovern activists threatened to abandon his campaign if he did not dump his running mate. These activists were apparently outraged at the thought that their issue preferences would be subordinated to discussion of mental illness. They were, of course, beaten before the race began, so they had nothing to lose by sticking to principle; but they did not know that then.

Should the candidate arrive at a coherent strategy that fits reasonably well with what is known of the political world, he still will find that the party organization has an inertia in favor of its accustomed ways of doing things. The party workers, upon whom he is dependent to some extent, have their own ways of interpreting the world, and he disregards their point of view at some risk. Should the candidate fail to appear in a particular locality as others have done, the party workers may feel slighted. More important, they may interpret this as a sign that the candidate has written off that area and they may slacken their own efforts. Suppose the candidate decides to divert funds from campaign buttons and stickers to polls and television or to transportation? He may be right in his belief that the campaign methods he prefers may bring more return from the funds that are spent. But let the party faithful interpret this as a sign that he is losing—where, oh where, are those familiar signs of his popularity?—and their low morale may encourage a result that bears out this dire prophecy. An innovation in policy may shock the loyal followers of the party. It may seem to go against time-honored precepts which are not easily unlearned. Could a Republican convince his party that a balanced budget is not sacred? Obviously, Gerald Ford will have to do so in 1976. A selling job may have to be done on the rank and file; otherwise they may sit on their hands during the campaign. It may make better political sense (if less intellectual sense) to phrase the new in old terms and make the departure seem less extreme than it might actually be. The value of the issue in the campaign may thus be blunted. The forces of inertia and tradition may be overcome by strong and persuasive candidates; the parties are greatly dependent on their candidates and have little choice but to follow them even if haltingly. But in the absence of a special effort, in the presence of enormous uncertainties and the inevitable insecurities, the forces of tradition may do more to shape a campaign than the overt decisions of the candidates possibly can.

APPENDIX

Predicting Elections

As the time for voting draws closer, more and more interest focuses on attempts to forecast the outcome. This process of forecasting elections is not at all mysterious; it depends on well-settled findings about the behavior of American electorates, many of which have already been discussed. But it may be useful for citizens to understand how the "experts" go about picking the winner.

There are several ways to do it. One way, popularized by journalists Joseph Alsop and Samuel Lubell, is to interview the residents of neighborhoods where there are people who in the past have voted with great stability in one pattern or another. There are neighborhoods, for example, that always vote for the Republicans by a margin of 90 percent or better. Let us say that the interviewer finds that only 50 percent of the people he talks to tell him they are going to vote for the Republicans this time, but when he visits areas voting heavily Democratic, respondents continue to support the Democratic nominee heavily. A finding such as this permits the reporter to make a forecast, even though it is only based on a very small number of interviews, which may represent not at all the opinions of most voters.

Reporters who use this technique very rarely make firm predictions about election outcomes. Instead, they concentrate on telling about the clues they have picked up: what they learned in heavily black areas, what the people in Catholic areas said, what Midwest farmers say, what people from localities that always vote with the winner report, and so on.[56] This technique is impressive insofar as it digs into some of the dynamic properties of what goes into voting decisions. It reports what the issues are that seem to be on people's minds. It examines the different ways in which members of different subgroups see the candidates and the campaign. It is also a technique that can be executed at relatively low cost. But it is unsystematic, in that people are not polled in proportions reflecting the distributions of their characteristics in the population (so many men, so many women, so many white, so many black, and so forth) and thus the results of this technique would be regarded as unreliable in a scientific sense, even though they may enhance people's intuitive grasp of what is going on. The results are also unreliable in the sense that two different journalists using this method may come to drastically different conclusions, and there is no certain way of resolving the disagreement; nor is there any prescribed method for choosing between their conflicting interpretations.

A second technique has been used most extensively by the economist and statistician Louis Bean and does not rely on interviews at all.[57] Bean, it will be remembered, contradicted all the polls and predicted that President Truman would be reelected in 1948. The Bean method relies principally upon assumptions about (1) the stability of voting habits, (2) the stability of the relationship between turnout and the two-party vote, (3) the stability of the relationship between the two-party distribution of the vote in one area and the two-party distribution of the vote in another, and (4) the continuation of trends in voting in whatever direction they may be heading. Some of these assumptions are quite dubious, as we shall see, and Bean customarily hedges his predictions by claiming that they will hold unless some issue or another intercedes to upset them. His method does not provide a way for the impact of issues to be examined, and, in fact, Bean does not demonstrate how the effects of issues have sustained or failed to sustain his predictions.

The basic material out of which Bean constructs his forecasts is a historical record of two-party voting. Let us suppose the Democratic percentage of the two-party vote has risen in each of the last five elections. The Bean technique continues the line on the graph in a simple extrapolation. Even when the percentage of the two-party vote does not describe a straight line on a graph, it is possible to make an extrapolation by assuming that the historical pattern of fluctuation will be followed in the future.

Another type of analysis done by Bean made use of the September election results in Maine. This became unusable when Maine moved its Election Day from September to November, thus bringing it into line with practice in the rest of the country. But for many years it was possible to make a forecast based on the Maine results. Maine's distribution of the two-party vote, Bean said, bore a historically consistent relation to the national two-party vote distribution, rising and falling at about the same rate (but always somewhat below the nation on the Democratic graph and above the nation on the Republican graph). And so it was possible to forecast the outcome nationwide, or in any state, by noting the two-party ratio in the early Maine results and correcting it for two-party voting habits in the area whose result he wanted to predict.

The strength of forecasting from historical voting statistics arises out of the marvelous stability of American voting habits. But the weakness of such a technique is also manifest. Sometimes gross changes in population, through immigration, or changes in the appeals of the parties to different voting groups will throw the historical two-party vote ratios in the sample area out of joint. When a forecast made with this technique is wrong, it is usually quite difficult to tell whether transitory or lasting causes are at the root of it. This limits the usefulness of the forecast greatly, since, in the end, it rests on assumptions that have only partial validity in any one election, and nobody can say precisely how or where or to what extent they may be valid.

A third technique is a variant of the two foregoing types of analyses and is used by electronic computers at the radio and television networks on Election Night. The basic principle of these machines, for our purposes, can be described simply. They are given information about the past voting history of various locales. As these locales report their returns on Election Night, the machine compares this year's result with the information about previous years and arrives at a prediction of how this year's election will turn out, when all the votes are counted. The system is exactly the same as we have already described for Alsop and Lubell, only the machine can be loaded with historical information about many localities—precincts, wards, and so on—and then the machine compares this historical information, not with voting *intentions* as expressed by a few interviewees, but by voting *results* as expressed by the whole voting population of the area. The method the machine uses to predict the outcome early in the evening is roughly the same as Louis Bean's technique, only, once again, instead of the Maine election, the machine has results from a great many early reporting areas and can therefore correct discrepancies arising out of one or two purely local situations.

Interestingly enough, at least one of the network machines on election night in 1960 was not programmed in this way. The IBM system set up for CBS began election night in 1960 with the erroneous prediction that Richard Nixon would win the presidency—a prediction that was later corrected as more and more returns came in.[58] It is useful to pause for a moment to look at this mistake, because it demonstrates clearly that these machines, like any other tools, are only as good as the people who use them.

The IBM computer was fed information based not on the geographic locale of the vote, but rather on the order in which the vote was reported to election headquarters. Thus, all the machine knew in 1960 was how many Democratic votes and how many Republican votes had been reported at 7:00 P.M. in previous elections, at 7:15, and so on. But it did not know *where* these votes had come from. The introduction of a faster method of vote-counting in Kansas between 1956 and 1960 was the reason for the IBM computer's early mistake. A flood of Kansas Republican votes arrived earlier than ever before. The computer, not knowing where they came from, compared them with the early returns in 1956, which were from the "swing" state of Connecticut, and drew a false conclusion.

Since the order in which states report their vote varies quite a bit more than the voting habits of people living in specific early-reporting places, all the computers seem likely in the future to be working on geographic assumptions. It will, in all probability, be almost impossible to find out what assumptions the computers are using during Election Night coverage, however, because of the network reporters' dislike of imparting "complicated" information. It is so much friendlier to give the machine a nickname and ask it to "do tricks" and to bat one's eyelashes helplessly at the TV camera while the "mysterious" machine does its prosaic work.

The final method for predicting elections is the most controversial and by all odds the most famous: polls. These are based on a few simple assumptions that have been found to be quite correct over the years. One is that people will generally tell you the truth if you ask them how they are going to vote. Another is that it is not necessary to ask everyone what he is going to do in order to get as accurate a forecast as if you had asked nearly everyone.

The polls are commercial operations and, these days, they are big businesses. In addition to the publicly available polls, such as the Gallup and Harris newspaper reports, politicians commission private polls. They are expensive. They entail writing up a list of questions and asking them all, and all in the same way, to several thousand people, spread all over the country; collecting the answers; and figuring out what it all means. Each of these phases of the operation—writing questions, selecting the sample of the total population to be interviewed, interviewing, organizing the answers, and interpreting the results—is a job requiring skill and training. It is this that commercial polling organizations provide.

In the past, regrettably, some of these organizations have treated the technical aspects of their operation as trade secrets (which they are not) and have left the impression that their forecasts are the result of a particularly efficacious kind of witchcraft. Since the fiasco of 1948, when pollsters were so sure of the result that they became professionally careless, there has been less ballyhoo. But the general reader will do well to keep a sharp eye on the following points as the polls begin reporting early in the campaign.[59]

1. How big is the population that is reported to be "undecided"? There are some elections in which members of this group cast the crucial ballots. In reporting their results pollsters have a rule that goes this way: "If the undecided people were to cast their ballots in the same proportion as those

who have made up their minds . . ." But wait. If those people *were* like the decided, they too would have made up their minds. Sometimes they *do* vote like early deciders. But sometimes they don't. Unfortunately, not enough is known about when they do and when they don't; the best advice we can give is to pay close attention to what the pollster says he is doing about them, and if they are more than 10 to 15 percent of the population sampled, then place little confidence in the poll report. Until these people make up their minds, it is too early to tell about the outcome.

2. What is the stability of general sentiment in the population? Very often, the polls will report wide swings of sentiment from week to week. In 1960, the Gallup organization began averaging one week's totals with the previous week's part way through the campaign—without telling its readers.[60] This tended to depress the extent of an apparent shift of sympathy from Nixon to Kennedy, and it also tended to make the figures appear a great deal more stable and settled than they actually were. In general, wide swings of sentiment from week to week mean that opinions have not crystallized sufficiently for a reliable prediction to be made.

3. Remember that the polls are based on a gross, overall, nationwide sample, but that presidential elections are decided by the distribution of votes in the Electoral College. Thus a really reliable prediction would have to include a state-by-state breakdown. This is prohibitively expensive, and so it is not done. If it were done, it would be possible to detect situations like the following: Candidate A has 49 percent of the popular vote in polls taken in all the populous states and 75 percent of the popular vote in sparsely settled states. He loses badly to Candidate B in the Electoral College, although it looks like a close election. Pollsters generally caution that they are trying only to forecast the percentage distributions in the popular vote. Here again, if the result is closely divided around 50 percent, then the poll may be quite close to being perfectly accurate, but still forecast the wrong winner.

4. Some people never show up to vote on Election Day; these tend to be undecideds and Democrats (in that order) more often than Republicans, but in any event some sort of grain of salt has to be taken with results in order to account for the phenomenon of differential turnout. Most experienced polling organizations do build some sort of correction into their results based on assumptions about how many people in their sample will actually vote. It is important to know precisely what this assumption is and what the resulting corrections are.

5. Many people are plagued with the feeling that the samples used by pollsters—of 2,000 to 5,000 people—are inadequate to represent the feelings of the millions of Americans whose voting they are supposed to represent. This, by and large, is a false issue. Experience has shown that very few of the errors one makes with a sample of 3,000 are correctable with a sample

of 15,000 or 20,000, although the expense of polling such a population rises steeply.[61]

Generally, it is not a sampling error that is at fault nowadays when pollsters' predictions go awry, but illicit "cooking" of the data or incompetent interpretations of findings. There is one famous instance of a sampling error, when polling was in its most rudimentary stages. In 1936 the *Literary Digest* predicted a landslide victory for the Republican Alfred Landon.[62] When Franklin D. Roosevelt won overwhelmingly, the *Digest* became a laughingstock and soon thereafter went out of business. What had happened was simple enough. The magazine had sent out millions of postcards to telephone subscribers asking them how they intended to vote. The returns showed a huge Republican triumph. Surely, the *Digest* must have thought, we cannot possibly be wrong when our total response is so large and so one-sided. But, of course, something was terribly wrong. And that stemmed from the fact that in the depression years only the relatively wealthy had telephones. So the *Digest* got its returns from that group in the population most likely to vote Republican and completely ignored the much larger number of poorer people who were going to vote Democratic. Moreover, there is a much greater tendency for people of wealth and education to return mail questionnaires so that the bias in favor of people likely to vote Republican was further enhanced.[63]

In 1948, a whole series of errors were made, but none of them seem to have been connected with the size of the sample. In that year, the Gallup, Roper, and Crossley polls all predicted that Governor Dewey would unseat President Truman. Among the problems with the polls that year, the following were uncovered by a committee of social scientists after the event.[64]

1. The pollsters were so sure of the outcome that they stopped taking polls early in the campaign, assuming that the large population of undecideds would vote, if they voted, in the same way as those who had made up their minds early in the campaign.

2. The undecideds voted in just the reverse proportions.

3. Many instances were revealed where polling organization analysts, disbelieving pro-Truman results, arbitrarily "corrected" them in favor of Dewey. The methods of analysis employed were not traced in any systematic way, however, because they could not systematically be reconstructed from records of the polling organizations.

4. Sampling error occurred not because of the size of the samples, but because respondents were selected by methods that gave interviewers too much leeway to introduce biases into the sample. The so-called quota-control method (which instructs interviewers, for example, out of twenty interviews to pick ten men, ten women; fifteen Protestants, four Catholics, one Jew; seventeen whites and three blacks, and so on) has been replaced

with "stratified random samples" in which geographic areas are picked randomly, and neighborhoods and houses within neighborhoods are selected randomly with controls so that areas representing a variety of economic levels are sure to be selected. This gives the people in charge of the poll greater control over who is going to be in their sample and prevents interviewers from asking only people who live near them or who are conveniently accessible in some other way and are likely to be similar to them in social standing and political outlook.

Predicting presidential elections is largely a matter of satisfying curiosity. It is a great game to guess who will win, and we look to the polls for indications of the signs of the times. But the importance of this kind of prediction is not great. After all, we do get to know who has won very soon after Election Day with much greater detail and accuracy than the polls can supply. The bare prediction of the outcome, even if it is reasonably correct, tells us little about how the result came to occur. More may be learned if it is possible to break down the figures to see what kind of groups—ethnic, racial, economic, regional—voted to what degree for which candidates. Yet our enlightenment at this point is still not great. Suppose we know that in one election Catholics voted Democratic 60 percent of the time and in another election this percentage was reduced to 53. Surely this is interesting; but unless we have some good idea about why Catholics have switched their allegiance, our knowledge has hardly advanced. The polls often tell us "what" but seldom "why." There is, however, no reason why polling techniques in the future cannot be used to answer "why" questions.

The usual polling technique consists of talking to samples of the population at various points in time. The samples may be perfectly adequate but different people constitute each successive sample as the interviewers seek out people who meet their specifications. It is difficult to discover with any reliability why particular individuals or classes of people are changing their minds because interviewers ordinarily do not go back to the same people who gave their original preferences. A panel survey is used to overcome this difficulty.[65] In a panel survey, a sample of the voting population is obtained and the very same people are interviewed at various intervals before Election Day and perhaps afterwards. This technique makes it possible to isolate the people who make up their minds early and those who decide late. These groups can be reinterviewed and examined for other distinguishing characteristics. More important, perhaps, those voters who change their minds during the campaign can be identified and studied. If a panel of respondents can be reinterviewed over a number of years and a series of elections, it may become possible to discover directly why some people change their voting habits from election to election.

Notes

1. See Lipset, Lazarsfeld, Barton, and Linz, "The Psychology of Voting: An Analysis of Political Behavior," pp. 1124–75; Lazarsfeld, Berelson, and Gaudet, *The People's Choice*, pp. 87–93; Berelson, Lazarsfeld, and McPhee, *Voting*, pp. 16–17; and Richard A. Brody, "Change and Stability in Partisan Identification: A Note of Caution," unpublished manuscript, 1974.

2. See Campbell, Converse, Miller, and Stokes, *The American Voter*, pp. 124, 532–53. Table 6–1 on p. 124 summarizes the highly consistent results of seven separate national sample surveys taken by the Center for Political Studies Survey Research Center for October 1952 to October 1958. Here are C.P.S./S.R.C. figures for October 1958, November 1968, and November 1974 (the latter figures taken from unpublished C.P.S./S.R.C. tables).

Party Affiliations Are Stable

	October 1958	November 1968	November 1974
	(percent)	*(percent)*	*(percent)*
Strong Republicans	13	10	8
Weak Republicans	16	14	14
Independent Republicans	4	9	9
Independents	8	11	15
Independent Democrats	7	10	13
Weak Democrats	24	25	21
Strong Democrats	23	20	17
Apolitical, don't know	5	1	3

3. There is another possibility: that voters who turn out only by being dinned at by the media are likely to be less stable in their political orientations and will therefore vote less for the party and more for the candidate whose name or personality seems more familiar to them. This, in a year when an Eisenhower is on the ticket, might well mean Republican votes.

4. See Philip E. Converse, Angus Campbell, Warren E. Miller, and Donald E. Stokes, "Stability and Change in 1960: A Reinstating Election," *American Political Science Review* 55 (June 1961), pp. 269–80, especially p. 274.

5. See Campbell, Converse, Miller, and Stokes, *The American Voter,* pp. 537–38, and Hyman and Sheatsley, "The Political Appeal of President Eisenhower," pp. 26–39.

6. For indications that this strategy is feasible despite the existence of general stereotypes, see Campbell, Converse, Miller, and Stokes, *The American Voter*, pp. 44–59, 179–87. See also American Institute of Public Opinion News Releases, February 6, 1963; October 9, 1964; and October 25, 1964.

7. For a striking demonstration of this, see Ithiel de Sola Pool, Robert P. Abelson, and Samuel Popkin, *Candidates, Issues and Strategies* (Cambridge, Mass., 1964), pp. 117–18.

8. Recall Senator Dirksen's famous castigation of Thomas E. Dewey at the Republican convention of 1952: "We followed you before, and you took us down the path to defeat." Richard Nixon in 1968 did pursue a modified "me-too" strategy.

The main thrust of his campaign, however, was more like the first strategy we discussed: emphasizing dissatisfaction with a new issue, "law and order." Furthermore, there is some reason to suppose that rather than scoring a clear win what Nixon really did was sneak through to victory because the Democrats tore themselves apart. In 1972, running as an incumbent against the very controversial choice of only a minority of Democrats, Nixon's strategy strongly deemphasized party. "Reelect the President" was his slogan, thus ignoring not only the Republican party but even Mr. Nixon's own name.

9. For indications that this is so, see in particular McClosky, Hoffman, and O'Hara, "Issue Conflicts and Consensus among Party Leaders and Followers," pp. 406–27.

10. Good accounts of debates over strategy among Republicans can be found in such sources as Charles O. Jones, *The Republican Party in American Politics* (New York, 1965); Robert Donovan, *The Future of the Republican Party* (New York, 1964); Moos, *The Republicans*; Novak, *The Agony of the G.O.P. 1964*; and Conrad Joyner, *The Republican Dilemma* (Tucson, 1964).

11. The *Congressional Quarterly*, November 20, 1964, p. 2709, estimated that Republicans lost more than 500 seats in state legislatures in the 1964 election. Republicans gained one governor (for a total of 17), lost two United States senators (reducing their senatorial representation to 32), and sustained a net loss in the House of Representatives of 38 seats, reducing their strength to 140 members, the lowest since the Roosevelt landslide of 1936.

12. See, for example, Jones, *The Republican Party in American Politics*, pp. 66–71. The Michigan Survey Research Center estimates that an overwhelming 96 to 98 percent of such Republicans typically vote. Philip E. Converse, Aage R. Clausen, and Warren E. Miller, "Electoral Myth and Reality: The 1964 Election," *American Political Science Review* 59 (June 1965), pp. 322–23.

13. As the number of "independents" increases, it seems likely that students will discover differences among them on these and other dimensions. Nevertheless, see Berelson, Lazarsfeld, and McPhee, *Voting*, pp. 333–47, e.g., propositions 39, 50, 51, 66, 68, 69, 70, 71, 78, 79; Campbell, Converse, Miller, and Stokes, *The American Voter*, pp. 142–45.

14. The study of right-wing ideologues and their supporters is more speculative than empirical. Nevertheless, there are a few straws in the wind, and all blow in the same direction. In 1962, Raymond E. Wolfinger and his associates administered a questionnaire to 308 "students" at an anticommunism school conducted by Dr. Fred Schwarz's Christian Anti-Communism Crusade in Oakland, California. Among the findings of this study were that 278 of the 302 persons in this sample who voted in 1960 (or 92 percent of those who voted) had voted for Nixon, and that 58 percent of those who answered the question chose Goldwater over Nixon for 1964. At about the same time, a nationwide Gallup poll showed Goldwater the choice of only 13 percent of Republicans. Raymond E. Wolfinger, Barbara Kaye Wolfinger, Kenneth Prewitt, and Sheilah Rosenhack, "America's Radical Right: Politics and Ideology," in *Ideology and Discontent*, ed. David Apter (New York, 1964), pp. 267–69. Analysis of various election returns and of a 1954 Gallup poll suggests that support for the late Senator Joseph McCarthy was importantly

determined by party affiliation, with Republicans far exceeding Democrats or independents in the ranks of his supporters. See Nelson W. Polsby, "Towards an Explanation of McCarthyism," *Political Studies* 8 (October 1960), pp. 250–71.

15. AIPO News Releases of September 6, 1964, and October 16, 1964, suggested that Republican defections would run as high as 30 percent, but the release of December 11 indicated that a 20 percent defection figure was more accurate. This compares with defections by Republican voters of 5 percent, 4 percent, and 8 percent in the three previous elections. Democratic defections in this election were also high—13 percent of those calling themselves Democrats voted for Goldwater—but these were confined mostly to the southern states.

16. In early July, the Gallup poll (AIPO News Release, November 11, 1964) showed the following figures among Republican voters:

Preferring

Goldwater	22 percent	Scranton	20 percent
Lodge	21 percent	Rockefeller	6 percent

Just before the Republican convention, the figures among Republicans were:

Scranton	60 percent	Undecided	6 percent
Goldwater	34 percent		

Goldwater received 23 percent of the vote in the New Hampshire primary; 18 percent in Oregon; 8 percent in Pennsylvania (fourth in a field of five write-ins); 10.5 percent in Massachusetts; 71 percent in Indiana, where Harold Stassen received the remainder; only 49 percent in Nebraska, where Goldwater's name alone was on the ballot; 51.4 percent in California; 76 percent in Texas, running in a trial heat with only Rockefeller; 31.9 percent in South Dakota; and a bit better than 60 percent in Illinois, where he was opposed on the ballot only by Margaret Chase Smith and where there is no law requiring election officials to tabulate write-in votes.

Gallup trial heats (AIPO News Release, July 1, 1964) before the Republican convention showed Goldwater running a poorer race against President Johnson than either Scranton or Nixon:

Goldwater	18 percent	Scranton	26 percent	Nixon	27 percent
Johnson	77 percent	Johnson	69 percent	Johnson	70 percent
Undecided	5 percent	Undecided	5 percent	Undecided	3 percent

17. AIPO News Release, September 13, 1964.

18. Louis Harris Survey News Releases, July 13, 1964, and September 14, 1964. Some of the Harris survey findings on foreign affairs were:

Issue		Voters Describe Goldwater Position		Describe Own Position	
		July *(percent)*	Sept. *(percent)*	July *(percent)*	Sept. *(percent)*
Go to war over	For	78	71	29	29
Cuba	Against	22	29	71	71
Use atomic bombs	For	72	58	18	18
in Asia	Against	28	42	82	82
United Nations	For	42	50	82	83
	Against	58	50	18	17

19. Witcover, *The Resurrection of Richard Nixon*, Chapter 8.

20. Philip E. Converse, Warren E. Miller, General Jerrold G. Rusk, and Arthur C. Wolfe, "Continuity and Change in American Politics: Parties and Issues in the 1968 Election," *American Political Science Review* 63 (December 1969), p. 1084.

21. See the discussion in ibid., pp. 1090–1104.

22. *Congressional Quarterly*, November 22, 1968, p. 3177.

23. The report of the speech in the *New York Times*, October 6, 1956, gives no indication of how it was received. The authors heard it delivered.

24. "The records . . . revealed that the 1972 Nixon campaign effort raised a record total of $60.2 million, $8 million more than the previously acknowledged total. The committee said that $56.1 million of this amount had been spent." *Congressional Quarterly*, October 6, 1973, p. 2659.

25. Thomas Flinn, "How Nixon Took Ohio," *Western Political Quarterly* 15 (June 1962), pp. 276–79.

26. Witcover, *The Resurrection of Richard Nixon*, pp. 237–39.

27. See, for example, the American Institute of Public Opinion News Release of September 3, 1964, in which 53 percent of a national sample said that the Democrats were the party best able to keep the country prosperous. Only 21 percent picked the Republicans. *Gallup Opinion Index*, April 1974. See graph page 202. See also Campbell, Converse, Miller, and Stokes, *The American Voter*, pp. 44–59.

28. See, for example, *The Joint Appearances of Senator John F. Kennedy and Vice-President Richard M. Nixon, Presidential Campaign of 1960*, Report 994, Part 3, 87th Congress, 1st Session, U.S. Senate (Washington, D.C., 1961). Especially see Mr. Nixon's opening remarks in the first joint television debate, pp. 75–78.

29. See, for example, Campbell, Converse, Miller, and Stokes, *The American Voter*, pp. 44–59, and Angus Campbell, Gerald Gurin, and Warren E. Miller, *The Voter Decides* (Evanston, Ill., 1954), pp. 44–45, especially Table 4–3, p. 45.

AIPO surveys show the twenty-year trend on this issue indicated in the graph on page 203. The graph is remarkably consistent in several ways. First, it testifies to the continuing perception (with ten of these years under Republican presidents and ten under Democrats) that the Republican party is more "the party of peace"; there may have been a slight erosion of the Republican position and a gain by the Democrats over this period as a whole, although in March 1970 the Democrats were only one percentage point above where they had been twenty years earlier, while the Republicans were only four points below their 1951 reading. Second, and very revealing, is the clear periodicity of the relationship; there is a sharp peak and maximum difference between the parties as November of every presidential election year approaches, followed by a convergence over the next two years, followed by divergence toward the presidential election peak again. Just before elections we would expect voters' expressions of their accustomed stereotypes to be at their strongest, because of the polarization in the attitudes of voters that normally takes place during the heat of a campaign. Senator Goldwater's extreme foreign policy positions caused the lone reversal in the positions of the two parties, but, despite the

Which Party Best to Keep U.S. Prosperous?

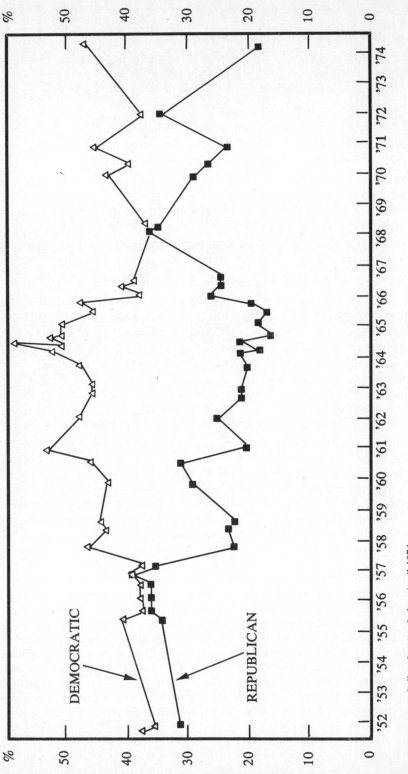

SOURCE: *Gallup Opinion Index*, April 1974.

Which Party Best to Keep U.S. Out of World War III?

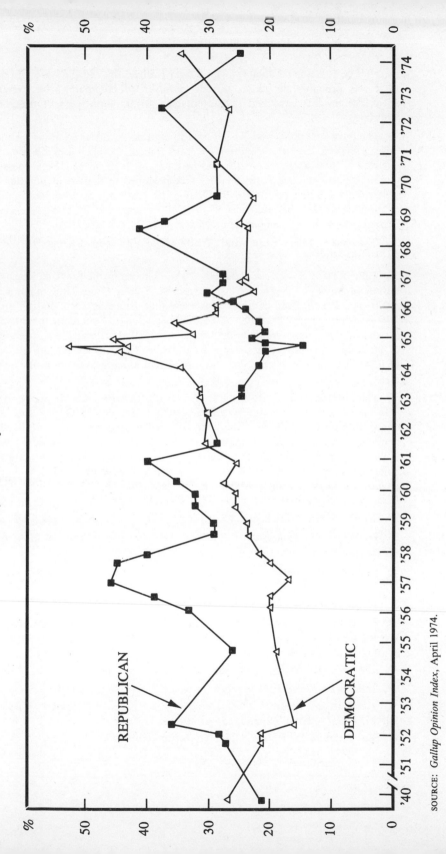

SOURCE: *Gallup Opinion Index*, April 1974.

204 • Presidential Elections

fact that both major candidates in 1968 were pledged to "end the war" and despite what was probably the more "dovish" position of Humphrey, the Republican advantage on this issue had reasserted itself within four years of the Johnson landslide.

30. The most well-publicized clashes over foreign policy occurred in the second and third television debates; see the *New York Times*, October 8, 1960, pp. 1, 12; October 9, 1960, Section 4, p. 10; and October 14, 1960, p. 22. The impression of journalists and political observers that Nixon gained in these confrontations (see, for example, the *New York Times* for October 17, 1960) was corroborated by surveys of the viewers (see the references in n. 32, following) and by Pool, Abelson, and Popkin, *Candidates, Issues and Strategies*, p. 118.

31. Converse, Miller, Rusk, and Wolfe, "Stability and Change in 1960: A Reinstating Election," pp. 269–80.

32. Elihu Katz and Jacob J. Feldman, "The Debates in the Light of Research: A Survey of Surveys," in *The Great Debates*, ed. Sidney Kraus (Bloomington, Ind., 1962), pp. 201–2. Bear in mind, however, that *issues* as such do not strongly influence voting behavior. Katz and Feldman conclude: "First of all, it seems safe to say that the debates—especially the first one—resulted primarily in a strengthening of commitment to one's own party and candidate. This was much more the case for Democrats than Republicans, but the former had much greater room for improvement" (p. 208).

33. This disability of McGovern's is vividly portrayed in the Michigan analysis: "On Vietnam, the issue most decidedly associated with him, McGovern was capable of securing only slightly more than his expected proportion of the two-party vote from the 29 percent of the population that most intensely favored immediate withdrawal from Vietnam. The remaining 71 percent displayed extremely high defection rates, ranging from 20 to 30 and 35 percent below the expected Democratic vote." Miller, Miller, Raine, and Brown, "A Majority Party in Disarray: Policy Polarization in the 1972 Elections," pp. 19, 20.

34. Scammon and Wattenberg, *The Real Majority*, p. 39. See also pp. 37–43.

35. See White, *The Making of the President, 1960*, pp. 269–75, and *The Making of the President, 1964*, passim.

36. Department of Marketing, Miami University, Oxford Research Associates, *The Influence of Television on the Election of 1952* (Oxford, Ohio, 1954), pp. 151–60.

37. Witcover, *The Resurrection of Richard Nixon*, pp. 237–39.

38. See White, *The Making of the President, 1960*, pp. 282–83, and Herbert A. Selz and Richard D. Yoakum, "Production Diary of the Debates," in *The Great Debates*, ed. Kraus, pp. 73–126.

39. Ibid.; see also Nixon, *Six Crises*.

40. Earl Mazo, *Richard Nixon* (New York, 1959), pp. 21–22, 362–69.

41. See Katz and Feldman, "The Debates in the Light of Research: A Survey of Surveys," in *The Great Debates*, ed. Kraus, pp. 173–223.

42. See William L. Rivers, "The Correspondents after 25 Years," *Columbia*

Journalism Review 1 (Spring 1962); Nixon, *Six Crises*; and especially White, *The Making of the President, 1960,* for a discussion of two candidates' contrasting attitudes toward their "camp" of reporters. For the 1964 election, see White, *The Making of the President, 1964.* For 1968, see White, *The Making of the President, 1968,* pp. 327 ff. For 1972, see Crouse, *The Boys on the Bus.*

43. "In elections at home, which Muskie contests vigorously and wins by handsome margins despite the state's strong Republican orientation, he rarely mentions his opponent's name, let alone attack him. He dwells instead on his own positive (and pragmatic) approach to problems. . . . Throughout the campaign he waits hopefully for his opponent to strike, in desperation, some more or less low blow in response to which Muskie can become magnificently outraged. Then, voice trembling with indignation but still without mentioning his opponent's name, he chastises the opposition for stooping to such levels, and thus manages to introduce a little color into the campaign. Usually the opposition obliges him: 'I can always count on the Republicans doing something stupid,' he once said with satisfaction." David Nevin, *Muskie of Maine* (New York, 1972), p. 27.

44. Robert E. Sherwood, *Roosevelt and Hopkins* (New York, 1948), p. 821.

45. The effectiveness of underhanded tactics remains unknown. Dan Nimmo argues that deviating from a vague sense of "fairness" that exists in the electorate may backfire. *The Political Persuaders* (Englewood Cliffs, N.J., 1970), p. 50. There is plenty of evidence on the other side as well. For a treasure trove of such material, see Stanley Kelley, *Professional Public Relations and Political Power* (Baltimore, 1956).

46. See Carl Bernstein and Bob Woodward, *All The President's Men* (New York, 1974), pp. 112–62, 197, 199, 251–53, 273–74, 285–86, 328; and Senate Select Committee on Presidential Campaign Activities, *The Senate Watergate Report* (Washington, D.C., 1974).

47. For further examples see Bone, *American Politics and the Party System,* pp. 457–69. Readers may not be aware that Al Smith had thought of moving the Vatican to Washington or that Herbert Hoover had a black concubine, yet these ridiculous allegations were made (p. 458).

48. See Flinn, "How Nixon Took Ohio."

49. *New York Times,* August 1, 1948, p. 49.

50. See Abels, *Out of the Jaws of Victory.*

51. Robert Alford, "The Role of Social Class in American Voting Behavior," *Western Political Quarterly* 16 (March 1963), pp. 180–94; Campbell, Converse, Miller, and Stokes, *The American Voter,* Chapter 13.

52. White, *The Making of the President, 1960,* pp. 203–4.

53. Ibid., p. 315.

54. White, *The Making of the President, 1968,* p. 331.

55. See Nixon, *Six Crises,* pp. 315–461.

56. See, for example, Lubell, *The Future of American Politics;* his "Personalities and

Issues," in *The Great Debates*, ed. Kraus, pp. 151–62; and Joseph Alsop, "The Negro Vote and New York," *New York Herald-Tribune* (and elsewhere) August 8, 1960. Reporting of this sort has become a feature of the election year coverage of the *Washington Post*.

57. Louis H. Bean, *Ballot Behavior* (Washington, D.C., 1940).

58. IBM published a pamphlet, *The Fastest Reported Election*, in 1961 describing their operations.

59. These suggestions are drawn in part from a reading of the Report of a Committee of the Social Science Research Council, Frederick Mosteller et al., *The Pre-Election Polls of 1948*, Social Science Research Council Bulletin 60 (New York, 1949). The misfortunes of the British polls in the 1970 general election underscores the usefulness of these suggestions.

60. Joseph Alsop, "The Wayward Press: Dissection of a Poll," *The New Yorker*, September 24, 1960, pp. 170–84.

61. There are several sources about the technology and tactics of polling. George Gallup has published *A Guide to Public Opinion Polls* (Princeton, 1948). More recently, see *Opinion Polls, Interviews by Donald McDonald with Elmo Roper and George Gallup* (Santa Barbara, 1962). In 1972, Representative Lucien Nedzi held congressional hearings on the possible effects of information about polls on subsequent voting. See *Public Opinion Polls*, Hearings before the Subcommittee on Library and Memorials, Committee on House Administration, House of Representatives, 93rd Congress on H.R. 5003 (September 19, 20, 21, October 5, 1972).

62. Sherwood, *Roosevelt and Hopkins*, p. 86. See also "Straw Polls in 1936," by Archibald M. Crossley, and a survey of the literature existing at that time, "Technical Research," by Hadley Cantril, both in *The Public Opinion Quarterly* 1 (January 1937), pp. 24–36 and 97–110, respectively.

63. As a matter of fact, this method produced a correct prediction in 1932, when the *Literary Digest* said that Roosevelt would win. Sampling error is tricky; an atypical sample may still give the correct prediction—by luck; but sooner or later, the law of averages is bound to catch up with it.

64. Mosteller et al., *The Pre-Election Polls of 1948*.

65. See Paul F. Lazarsfeld, "The Use of Panels in Social Research," *Proceedings of the American Philosophical Society* 92 (November 1948), pp. 405–10.

CHAPTER SIX

More Reform?

Previous chapters have concentrated on features of the presidential nomination process as it presently exists, and on the political consequences that flow from our system as it is now organized. Some of these features have been part of the landscape of American politics for a generation or more; others are new, and the changes they may bring about lie mostly in the future. Nevertheless, if there is one certainty about presidential elections, it is that this process is subject to continuous pressure to change.

In this chapter we review a number of proposals for future change of the American party system and its nomination and election processes. Because of the rapid reforms of the last few years, some of the impetus behind suggestions for further reform has no doubt slackened. Nevertheless, many proposals remain on the agenda.

These stem on the whole from two camps which for purposes of discussion we wish to treat as distinct. One camp urges "openness" and "participation" in the political process and has focused upon weakening party organizations in favor of ideological concerns. The other group urges strengthened parties, but not as the focus of organizational loyalties so much as vehicles for the promulgation of policy. Thus, while both sets of reformers ostensibly disagree about whether they want parties strong or weak, this in the end comes down to a difference in predictions about the outcome of the application of the same remedy, for both in the end prescribe the same thing: more ideology as the tie that binds voters to elected officials, and less organizational loyalty.

The Political Theory of Policy Government

The first branch of the party reform movement has its antecedents in the writings of Woodrow Wilson, James Bryce, and other passionate constitutional tinkerers who founded and breathed life into the academic study of political science. The descendants of these thinkers have through the years elaborated a series of proposals that are embodied in a coherent general political theory, a theory that contains a conception of the proper function of the political party, that evaluates the legitimacy and the roles of Congress and the president, and that enshrines a particular definition of the public interest. Different advocates of reform have stated this theory with greater or less elaboration; some reformers leave out certain features of it, and some are disinclined to face squarely the implications of the measures they espouse. We shall try here to reproduce correctly a style of argument that, though it ignores the slight differences separating these party reformers one from another, gives a coherent statement of their party reform theory and contrasts it with the political theory that critics of their position appear to advance.[1]

This group of party reformers suggests that democratic government requires political parties which (1) make policy commitments to the electorate, (2) are willing and able to carry them out when in office, (3) develop alternatives to government policies when out of office, and (4) differ sufficiently to "provide the electorate with a proper range of choice between alternatives of action."[2] They thus come to define a political party as "an association of broadly like-minded voters seeking to carry out common objectives through their elected representatives."[3] In a word, party is based on policy.

Virtually all significant party relationships are, for these reformers, mediated by policy considerations. The electorate is assumed to be policy motivated and mandate conscious. Policy discussion among party members is expected to create widespread agreement upon which party discipline will then be based. Pressure groups are to be resisted and accommodated only as the overall policy commitments of the party permit. The weaknesses of parties and the disabilities of governments are seen as stemming from failure to develop and support satisfactory policy programs. Hence it seems sensible to refer to this theory of party reform as a theory of "policy government." This theory suggests "that the choices provided by the two-party system are valuable to the American people in proportion to their definition in terms of public policy." [4] It differs from the participatory brand of party reform in that policy reformers believe they are revitalizing party organizations, whereas participatory democrats are likely to be indifferent to party organization.

Opponents of party reform believe that democratic government in the United States requires the minimization of conflict between contending interests and social forces.[5] Their ideal political party is one that serves as a mechanism for accomplishing and reinforcing adjustment and compromise among the various interests in society to prevent severe social conflict. Where reformers desire parties that operate "not as mere brokers between different groups and interests but as agencies of the electorate," their critics see the party as an "agency for compromise." Opponents of party reform and policy government hold that "the general welfare is achieved by harmonizing and adjusting group interests." [6] In fact, they sometimes go so far as to suggest that "the contribution that parties make to policy is inconsequential so long as they maintain conditions for adjustment." [7] Thus, the theory of the political party upheld by critics of the party reform position is rooted in a notion of "consensus government."

A basic cleavage between advocates of policy government and consensus government may be observed in their radically opposed conceptions of the public interest. For advocates of consensus government, the public interest is defined as whatever emerges from the negotiations, adjustments, and compromises made among conflicting interest groups. They suggest no external criteria by which policies can be measured in order to determine whether or not they are in the public interest. So long as the process by which decisions are made consists of intergroup bargaining, within certain specified democratic "rules of the game," they regard the outcomes as being in the public interest.

For advocates of policy government, the public interest is held to be a discoverable set of policies which represents "something more than the mathematical result of the claims of all the pressure groups." [8] While they suggest that there are, in principle, ways of judging whether a policy is in the public interest, apart from the procedural test applied by supporters of consensus government, these methods are never identified. This lack of concrete criteria spelling out the public interest would not present great difficulties if it were not for the fact that policy government advocates demand that an authoritative determination of party policy be made and that party members be held to it. Information about the policy preferences of members is supposed to flow upward and orders establishing and enforcing final policy decisions are supposed to flow downward in a greatly strengthened pyramid of party authority. Without criteria of the public interest clearly in mind, however, party leaders are in a position to define the public interest in any terms they find convenient.

If we were to have parties that resembled the ideal of the party reformers, what would they be like? They would be coherent in their policies, reliable in carrying them out and accountable to the people, sharply differentiated and in conflict with each other, disciplined and hierarchical internally. Let us see, then, what it would take to create a party system of this kind.

For the parties to carry out the promises they make, the people responsible for making promises would have to be the same as (or in control of) the people responsible for carrying them out. This means, logically, one of two alternatives. Either the people who controlled party performance all year round would have to write the party platforms at the national conventions; or the people who wrote the platforms would have to be put in charge of party performance. In the first case, the party platforms would have to be written by leaders such as the congressmen who at present refrain from enacting laws favored by both national conventions. State and local political leaders would write their respective platforms. Under such an arrangement, very little formal, overall coordination or policy coherence seems likely to emerge. Since logically coherent, unified policy is the main point of policy government, we must reject the first alternative as a possible way to fulfill the demands of party reformers.

In fact, it is the second alternative that is most often recommended by advocates of policy government. National conventions must make policy that will be enforced on national, state, and local levels by means of party discipline, and the people who write the convention platforms must be put in charge. This arrangement also has a fatal defect: it ignores the power of the people who do not write the platforms. How are independently elected congressmen to be bypassed? Will present-day sectional and state party leaders acquiesce in this rearrangement of power and subject themselves to discipline from a newly constituted outside source? Generally, we assume they will not. Getting politicians to exchange some political power for none is a task the magnitude of which has surely been underestimated. When reforms have to be carried out by those who would stand to lose the most from them, their practicality is dubious.

One reformer says: "As for the clash of personal political ambitions in the United States, they are being completely submerged by the international and domestic concerns of the American public. War and peace, inflation and depression are both personal and universal issues; tariffs, taxes, foreign aid, military spending, federal reserve policies, and hosts of other national policies affect local economic activities across the land. Politicians who wish to become statesmen must be able to talk intelligently about issues that concern people in all constituencies. . . ." [9]

But is it necessarily the case, as party reformers suggest, that the increasing importance of national issues will inevitably lead to placing greater power in the hands of party leaders with national (that is to say, presidential) constituencies? There is no necessary connection between political power in the national arena and the national scope of issues. National political power may rest upon local control of nomination, alliances with locally based interest groups, and many other bases. Even if national issues become more important, this may only enhance the powers of the local interests best able to influence national policy—such as, for example, the people in the congressional districts that elect powerful House committee chairmen.

The people who have the most to lose from reforms leading to policy government are, of course, the leaders of Congress. As of now, the major electoral risks facing national legislators are local. This does not mean that they will necessarily be parochial in their attitudes and policy commitments. But it does mean that they are not necessarily bound to support the president or national party leadership on issues of high local saliency. In order to impose discipline successfully, the national party must be able either to control sanctions presently important to legislators, such as nomination to office, or to impose still more severe ones upon them. At the moment, our system provides for control of congressional, state, and local nominations and elections by geographically localized electorates and party leaders. Presidents are not totally helpless in affecting the outcomes of these local decisions, but their influence is in most cases quite marginal.

In the light of this, one obvious electoral prerequisite of disciplined parties is that the local voters must be so strongly tied to national party issues that they will reward rather than penalize their local representatives for supporting national policy pronouncements, even at the expense of local advantage. To a certain extent, with the growing influence of national news media and the rising educational level of the electorate, as well as some increase in its general propensity to be ideologically purist, this condition is being met. The issues on which the national party makes its appeal must either unify a large number of constituencies in favor of the party or appeal at the least to some substantial segment of opinion everywhere. But even if this could be accomplished, it would be strategically unwise for parties to attempt to discipline their members who lived in areas that are strongly against national party policy. This would mean reading the offending area out of the party. Therefore, reformers must show how they intend to contribute to the national character of political parties by enforcing national policies upon members of Congress whose local constituencies are drastically opposed to national party policy, or whose constituents do not pay attention to issues but care more for the personality or the services of the congressman.[10] Insofar as leeway exists, let us say, for Republicans in the Northeast to support liberal programs and for southern Democrats to oppose them, the parties shall, in fact, have retained their old, "undisciplined," "irresponsible" shapes. Insofar as this leeway does not exist, splinter groups of various kinds are encouraged to split off from the established parties, which happens to be a consequence regarded as undesirable by most party reformers.

A second method for reducing the independent power over policy outcomes of independently elected congressional leaders has begun to have an effect in national politics. This method addresses not the prospects for nomination and election of congressional leaders but rather their capacity to lead in Congress. Adherence to the conservatism of the majority of Republicans in Congress has in general been a prerequisite of leadership within the Republican party. Among congressional Democrats, however, consistently the majority party in Congress and in the nation, more leeway has existed for congressional leaders—at any rate committee chairmen, who in the past have been selected by seniority—to take whatever policy positions they pleased.

Since the mid-1950s, sentiment has grown in Congress that conservative Democratic committee chairmen should be more responsive to the policy preferences of the majority of the majority party, and in recent years the Democratic caucus of the House of Representatives has acted to remove committee chairmen they have regarded as unresponsive. This has not, however, proceeded strictly along ideological lines. One of the first chairmen to be removed, Wright Patman of Texas, was as liberal as any Democrat in the House. Another chairman, Edward Hebert of the Armed Services Committee, was replaced by a leader ideologically indistinguishable from him on matters coming before the committee. So, despite the unlimbering of a new weapon which has the potential of encouraging party responsibility in Congress, it has not been used quite in this way, and concerns related to the management of Congress itself have thus far been more significant than the shaping or enforcement of party policy in the activities of the reactivated Democratic caucus.

The Evolution of a Second Branch of Party Reform

It should be obvious that party reforms are generally not politically neutral. They are designed almost entirely to strengthen the president and to weaken Congress, especially as Congress is presently constituted. Reforms of the party system are in general also designed to help Democrats and weaken Republicans. The reasoning is this: Republican presidents represent a party generally unsympathetic to increased activity by the federal government. Hence, they will be inclined to ask less of Congress, and thus they run less risk of being stymied on matters of policy by a recalcitrant Congress. Democratic presidents, on the other hand, in behalf of the more liberal, more activist, and more innovative party, ask much more of Congress and customarily have to settle for much less of what they ask for.

It seems to us quite understandable that agitation for party reform, which during the late 1940s so excited the liberal academicians who are its chief proponents, died away to a whisper during the Eisenhower decade. In the early 1960s frustrated liberals took up their cudgels in the cause of righteousness, "responsibility," and presidential prerogative. The underlying aim, it seems to us, was to speed up social changes that they desired by trying to rig the rules of the game more in favor of that political institution, the presidency, which shared their policy preferences.

The close connection between the desire for party reform and the policy preferences of reformers was again illustrated in the late 1960s. Reformers could no longer complain about the failure of a conservative Congress to enact New Deal–type welfare measures; the 89th Congress had taken care of that. Their attention now became focused on foreign policy because they were outraged by America's continued involvement in the war in Vietnam. It turned out that presidents were, if anything, more in favor of this policy than were many congressmen. The frustrations of reformers were centered on the inability of senators who favored an antiwar policy to persuade the president to withdraw American troops and commitments as fast as they would have liked. Hence, it was no longer feasible to advocate reforms that would enable presidents to pursue presidential foreign policies despite the reluctance of congressmen. Instead, reformers began to entertain notions of limitations on presidential prerogatives. It is, unfortunately, exceedingly difficult to stop presidents from doing things one doesn't like (such as, for example, in Indochina) without also preventing them from taking actions of which one approves (such as, for instance, with respect to the economy).

Since it is not feasible to limit the damage presidents can do without also limiting the good they can do, the attention of many current party reformers has focused on making the presidential selection procedure more responsive to their preferences. They believe that if the nomination procedure were opened up to more party voters in primaries and to party activists in district and state conventions, they would have a better chance of nominating a man they prefer. Their immediate cause célèbre was the 1968 Democratic convention in which they believed the fortunes of nominees like Eugene McCarthy and George McGovern were damaged by undemocratic modes of delegate selection. In view of the commanding margin of victory at the convention for Hubert Humphrey it seems doubtful that different procedures, even if they had been enforced at the time, would have changed enough delegate votes to make a difference in the 1968 outcome. But it was strongly thought so at the time, and at that convention rules changes were begun that have changed the face of politics in the Democratic party. The assumption behind the views of new reformers, who represent generally left-wing policy positions within the Democratic party, is that if the people are given a choice they will support candidates with policy preferences more like their own.

Reform by Means of Participatory Democracy: An Appraisal

In earlier chapters we discussed the considerable successes that have attended the efforts of purists who advocate participatory democracy and who have attempted to make the Democratic party the vehicle of this approach to government. Here we wish to contemplate the theory of politics that underlies this position. Ordinarily, participatory democrats criticize the American political system in two respects. First, they argue that elections have insufficient impact on the policy outcomes of the government. These critics see no direct link between public policy and the desires of electoral majorities. Second, there is the critique of the electoral process itself which argues that policy does not represent what majorities want because elected representatives are not responsive to majority desires. These criticisms are simpleminded in one sense and cogent in another: simpleminded, in that they ignore the immense problems that would have to be overcome if we were truly serious about transforming America or any large diverse population into a participatory democracy; cogent, in that responsiveness to majorities on questions of policy is a fundamental value that gives legitimacy to democratic government. The connection between such criticism and the legitimacy of government makes it important to deal at least briefly with some of the issues and problems that should be raised (and usually are not) by judgments of this fundamental nature.

The first and obvious question to ask is whether the criticisms are based on fact. Is the American system unresponsive to the policy desires of a majority of its citizens? Unfortunately, there is no unambiguous way to answer this question. If we focus our attention, for example, on the mechanics of the policy process, we find what appears to be government by minorities. In some policy areas a great number of people and interests, organized and unorganized, may have both a say in open hearings and some influence on the final product. But fewer individuals may be involved in areas dealing with other problems and policies, some of which will be of a specialized nature, of limited interest, and so on. Certainly it is true that even members of Congress do not have equal or high influence over every decision: committee jurisdictions, seniority, special knowledge, party, individual reputation—all combine to weigh the influence of each member on a different scale for each issue.

So we must conclude that if we adopt direct participation in and equal influence over the policy decisions of our government (the decisions that "affect our lives") as *the* single criterion of democracy, then our system surely fails the test. So, we might note, does every government known to us—possibly excepting two or three rural Swiss cantons.

Another approach might focus on public opinion as an index of majority desires. Using this standard a quite different picture emerges. The vast majority of policy decisions made by the government have the support of popular majorities. In cases where this is not true, the lack of "responsiveness" may have several causes, not all of them curable: (1) conflicts between majority desires and intractable situations in the world (for example, the desire to transform, peaceably, the Soviet Union into a liberal democratic ally); or (2) public attitudes favoring certain sets of policies that are mutually incompatible (such as the desires for a very high rate of employment and very low rates of inflation); or (3) finally, majority desires are clear, consistent, and feasible, yet ignored by the government because the desires are unconstitutional or antithetical to enduring values of the political system to which leaders are more sensitive than popular majorities. Surveys, for example, have from time to time revealed majorities in favor of constitutionally questionable repressive measures against dissenters and the press.

Criticisms of presidential elections are more difficult to assess. American politics *does* respond to the application of resources which are arguably nondemocratic, that is, which cause the influence of different actors to be weighed unequally. In a truly democratic system, it could be argued, each person would count for one and no person would count for more than one: the system would respond to numbers and only numbers. As we have indicated, however, money, energy and enthusiasm, popularity, ability, and experience are all valuable assets within the structure of American politics. Should the system be condemned for this? Should we attempt to eradicate the influence these resources presently command? Before joining a campaign in behalf of this cause, it may be wise to consider for a moment why these nondemocratic resources are useful.

Possession of the relevant political resources could increase the influence of an individual because candidates seek the support of such individuals. Why do they do so? Because a contender needs money to publicize himself and his cause; because he needs experienced and able allies to aid him get his image effectively delivered to the voter. Political resources and the people who possess them are important, in short, because campaigns are important. And campaigns are important because the general public needs to be roused and alerted to the fact that an election is near. Partisans must be mobilized, the uncommitted convinced, perhaps even a few minds changed. Resources other than votes are important because—and only because—numerical majorities must be mobilized.

American politics responds to nondemocratic resources because many, if not most, citizens are politically apathetic. If nearly everyone participated, no other resources would be necessary. Why is political apathy widespread? There are several alternative explanations. Perhaps it is because the system presents the citizenry with no real alternatives from which to choose. However, in the election of 1964, there was at least a partial test of this "hidden vote" theory, and the evidence is negative. And in 1972, another year when there was an unambiguous choice, nonvoting hit a high for recent elections. Perhaps it is because the public has been imbued with a "false consciousness" that blinds them to their "real" desires and interests. This is an explanation traditionally seized upon by the enlightened few to deny value to the preferences of the ignorant many. The people, we are told, are easily fooled; this testifies to their credulity. They do not know what is good for them; this makes them childlike. But when the people cannot trust their own feelings, when their desires are alleged to be unworthy, when their policy preferences should be ignored because they are not "genuine" or "authentic," they are being deprived of their humanity as well. What is left for the people if they are deprived of judgment, wisdom, feeling, desire, and preference? Such an argument would offer little hope for democracy of any sort, for it introduces the most blatant form of inegalitarianism as a political "given": a structured, ascribed difference between those who know what is "good" for themselves and those who must be "told." But, then, persons who make this argument do not believe in democracy.

A more hopeful and less self-contradictory explanation of political apathy might note that throughout American history a substantial number of American citizens have not wished to concern themselves continually with the problems and actions of government. Many citizens prefer to participate on their own terms, involving themselves with a particular issue area or a specific problem. The participation of these citizens is necessarily sporadic and more narrow than that of the voter interested in all public problems and actively involved in general political life. Many other citizens (surely a majority) are more interested in the problems of their own personal life than they are in any issue of public policy.[11] This, we would suggest, is the real "silent majority": citizens who meet their public obligations by going to the polls at fairly regular intervals, making their selections on the basis of their own criteria, and then supporting the actions and policies of the winners—whether their first choice or not. In the intervals, unless they themselves are personally affected by some policy proposal, most of these citizens simply wish to be left alone. Most citizens, that is, do not participate because they are concerned with other things important to them, like earning a living or painting a picture or cultivating a garden, not because they feel it is so difficult to influence outcomes.

Imagine for a moment a situation where these conditions did not hold. Consider a society in which all citizens were as concerned about public matters as the most active of our party volunteers. Such a society would not require mobilization: all who were able would vote. The hoopla and gimmickry associated with our contemporary (and past) political campaigns would have little effect: this citizenry would know the record of the party and the candidate and, presumably, would make their reasoned choice on this basis. Should such an active society be the goal of those whose political philosophy is democratic? This question should not and cannot be answered without first addressing the problem of how such a society could be achieved and what the achievement would require.

Without attempting to be comprehensive, a few difficulties do merit some specific comment. First and foremost, political participation—as Aristotle made clear several thousand years ago—takes a great deal of time. For this reason (among others) a large population of slaves was felt to be a necessary concomitant of participatory government: it freed Athenian citizens from the cares of maintaining life and thus provided them the leisure time that made their political activity possible. But having rejected this ingenious solution to the problems related to relatively large-scale participation some hundred years ago, we must deal with the fact that the vast majority of our citizens must work for a living. Most Americans lack the disposable time that permits professionals and students to choose their working hours. Most citizens lack the time, even if they had the temperament and training, to engage continually in politics. To the degree that mass representative institutions—political parties, legislatures, elected executives—are denigrated in favor of more direct modes of activity, the majority of the people will be without the means of participation through which they can most effectively make their will felt. In short, to impose requirements of direct participation on those desiring a voice in decisions would be to ensure that the incessant few rather than the sporadic many would rule: thus the slogan "power to the people" really proposes to replace a representative few, who are elected, with an unrepresentative few, who are self-appointed. And this, as we have indicated, is precisely the effect that changes in the rules governing nominations in the Democratic party will have.

We raise this issue not because we are opposed in principle to the idea of an active, participatory, democratic society. By persuasion and political education the majority of our citizens might indeed be convinced that the quality of our shared existence could and should be improved through more continuous devotion to public activity. But to argue this is quite a different matter than to argue that the rules of the game should be changed to disenfranchise those who presently lack the opportunity or desire to be active in this sense. We do not favor efforts to implement ideal goals when the preconditions and the means of achieving these goals do not exist. More importantly, we do not favor actions that in the name of democracy (or under any other guise) restrict the ability of most of the people to have their political say.

Three Specific Reforms

Comprehensive reform of the party system rides in on tides of strong feeling. Until such feelings exist among party activists, rational advocacy looking toward reform is wasted; once such feeling exists, rational advocacy is superfluous. So the type of analysis we undertake here is bound to be uninfluential. We attempt it only because thoughtful citizens outside the mainstream of political life may find it instructive to consider the consequences of the best-laid plans. Once these consequences have had an opportunity to manifest themselves, however, a new generation of reform may be in order. After all, practically everything that reformers object to now was once somebody's favorite reform.

We suspect that achievement of many of the specific objectives of party reformers would be detrimental to their aims and to those of most thoughtful citizens. Let us consider, for example, three specific reforms of governmental machinery, commonly advocated to make the parties more responsive to popular will and more democratic. Party reformers often advocate a variety of changes in the nomination process, simplification of the process of registering voters, and modification or abolition of the Electoral College. Two of these reforms might well have the exactly opposite effects.

An Appraisal of the Nomination Process

In order to evaluate the nominating process, it would be helpful to suggest a set of goals which most Americans would accept as desirable and important.[12] The following six standards appear to meet this test: any method for nominating presidents should (1) aid in preserving the two-party system, (2) help secure vigorous competition between the parties, (3) maintain some degree of cohesion and agreement within the parties, (4) produce candidates who have a likelihood of winning voter support, (5) lead to the choice of candidates who are reasonably well qualified, (6) result in the acceptance of candidates as legitimate. We may first look at some suggested alternatives to a system that relies heavily upon decision-making by party leaders at national conventions.

A national direct primary has often been suggested. Many people took heart in 1968 from the way in which the piecemeal primaries around the country facilitated the expression of antiwar sentiment, and they noted that nonprimary states were less responsive to persons whose participation in party activities was largely precipitated by strong feelings about the war. This led to a conclusion that primaries were rather a good thing and that, therefore, a national primary was in order.

We believe this would have serious disadvantages. First of all, it would have been self-defeating as far as the professed goals of many antiwar people who advocated it were concerned. By contesting primaries one at a time in 1968, Senator McCarthy, and later Senator Kennedy, were able to construct "test cases." We doubt that McCarthy, given the limitations of his resources before New Hampshire, could have even entered a national primary.

This merely points to a more general problem of financing national primary elections. It is quite probable that many candidates—perhaps as many as ten of them—might obtain enough signatures on nominating petitions to get on the ballot. Imagine a crowd of challengers hustling all over the United States, campaigning in a national primary. It would take, of course, enormous amounts of money. The parties could hardly be expected to show favoritism. Although government financing might be made available, this would have to depend upon demonstrated ability to raise money previously in order to discourage frivolous candidates. The pre-primary campaign, therefore, would assume enormous importance and would be exceedingly expensive. Nationwide challengers would have to have access to very large amounts of money. It would also help if they were already well known in some connection or other. They would also have to be quite sturdy physically. It is not hard to forecast that nobody would win a clear majority in a primary with a large number of contenders. Since all contenders would be wearing the same party label, it is hard to see how voters could differentiate among candidates except by already knowing one or two of their names in favorable or unfavorable contexts, by liking or not liking their looks, by identifying or not identifying with their ethnic or racial characteristics, or by some other means of differentiation having nothing whatever to do with ability or inclination to do the job, or even with their policy positions. Since patents on policy positions are not available, it is reasonable to suppose that more than one candidate would adopt roughly the same set of positions. The intellectual content of the campaign thereafter would consist of quibbling about who proposed what first and, more relevantly, who could deliver better.

Suppose, then, that the primary vote was divided among several candidates. Suppose, as is the case for gubernatorial elections in some southern states, that ten or twelve aspirants divided the votes. One possibility is that the party nominee would be the man with the highest number of votes, say, 19 percent of those cast, a much less democratic choice than we now have. Another possibility would be for the two highest candidates to contest a fifty-state runoff after the first primary and before the general election in a campaign that would begin to remind observers who can remember that far back of a marathon jitterbug contest. The party might end up with a good candidate, of course, if there was anything left of him to give to his party in the *real* election campaign, which would follow. Then if the poor fellow was elected he would have to find the energy to govern. By following this procedure, the United States might have to restrict its presidential candidates to wealthy athletes.

It is also possible that the parties would emerge with candidates no better on the average than those currently being picked to run for high office. And perhaps they would be worse on the average, because the national primary provides for no consideration of the criteria of fitness to hold office that can best be applied by those who actually know the candidates, who have themselves a heavy invest-ment of time and energy in making the government work, and who know that they may have to live at close quarters with the results of their deliberations. It is difficult to persuade those who participate only casually in politics, and those who tend to do so when moved by a great issue of the day, that the intensity of their feelings does not confer a sweeping mandate. These feelings, no matter how worthy, do not make occasional participants more worthy than steady participants. They do not confer a special moral status upon latecomers to politics as compared with people who are already active. Party activists or even party leaders are not necessarily excludable on grounds of moral inferiority from decision-making in the presidential nomination process. The great virtue of primaries is, of course, that they provide a means—increasingly supplemented by polls—of gauging the popularity of various candidates and their effectiveness in public speaking under adverse circumstances. On the other hand, the virtue of conventions and state caucus systems (when, that is, they are allowed to operate) is that by living at closer quarters than ordinary citizens with the results of the collective choice, party leaders may bring to the choosing greater knowledge and even, sometimes, a higher sense of responsibility.

It is generally conceded that Adlai Stevenson would have made a rather better president than Estes Kefauver, who ran and won in most of the primaries in 1952. Stevenson, for his entire career in elective office, was the product of selection by party leaders—in some cases even by "bosses"—who were knowledgeable and continuously involved in the political process, acquainted with what governing demanded and with the personal capabilities of the men among whom they chose.

This is not per se an evil system. Unchecked by the ultimate necessity to appeal for votes it would no doubt deteriorate. It is certainly not always a system that responds easily to short-run opinions of high intensity in the electorate, but sometimes this sort of system will pick a popular candidate over a candidate in whose personal capacities the delegates have more faith. This, we think, is what delegates to the Republican convention of 1952 did when they nominated Dwight Eisenhower over Robert A. Taft. Still, conventions and caucuses of party leaders can invoke criteria of judgment unavailable to mass electorates.

In short, we believe that as long as there are many things we demand of a president—intelligence as well as popularity, integrity as well as speaking ability, private virtue as well as public presentability—we ought to foster a selection process that provides a mixture of devices for screening according to different criteria. The mixed system we advocate is not perfect, of course, but it is greatly superior to the unmixed non-blessing of the national primary.

We are not ready to give up a substantial number of the state primaries we now have, although it is possible to argue that we have too many. It is eminently desirable that it be possible in a number of states, separated geographically and in time, for test cases to be put to voters and for trial heats to be run among aspirants for high office. But a national primary would be like a steady diet consisting exclusively of dessert.

National primaries would also lead to the weakening of the party system. It is not unusual for a party to remain in office for a long period of time. If state experience with primaries is any guide, a prolonged period of victory for one party would result in a movement of interested voters into the primary of the winning party where their votes would count for more.[13] As voters deserted the losing party, it would be largely the die-hards who were left. They would nominate candidates who pleased them but who could not win the election because they were unappealing to a majority in the nation. Eventually, the losing party would atrophy, seriously weakening the two-party system and the prospects of competition among the parties. The winning party would soon show signs of internal weakness as a consequence of the lack of opposition necessary to keep it unified. Since the long-run weakness of the Republican party in our system comes close to providing these conditions already, we believe that the institution of a national primary would in this respect be especially dangerous.

A national primary might also lead to the appearance of extremist candidates and demagogues who, unrestrained by allegiance to any permanent party organization, would have little to lose by stirring up mass hatreds or making absurd promises. On the whole, the convention system of the past has discouraged these extremists by placing responsibility in the hands of party leaders who have a permanent stake in maintaining the good name and integrity of their organization. Some insight into this problem may be had by looking at the situation in several southern states where most voters vote only in the Democratic primary and where victory in that primary is tantamount to election. The result is a chaotic factional politics in which there are few or no permanent party leaders; the distinctions between the "ins" and "outs" become blurred; it is difficult to hold anyone responsible; and demagogues sometimes arise who make use of this situation by strident appeals.[14] The fact that under some primary systems an extreme personality can take the place of party in giving a kind of minimal structure to state politics should give pause to the advocates of a national primary.

We believe, in short, that widespread use of direct primaries would weaken the party system; they would encourage prospective candidates to bypass regular party organizations in favor of campaigns stressing personal publicity, and they would throw nominations entirely into the hands of persons whose stake in the workings of the political process is not great enough to ensure that the eventual nominee would be qualified for the presidency by experience, qualities of mind, or by virtue of political alliances with others professionally engaged in political activity. The use of primaries at the state level has produced a variety of anomalous experiences: totally unqualified candidates whose names have resembled famous politicians have been nominated by innocent voters; ethnic minorities concentrated in one party have defeated attempts by party leaders to offer "balanced tickets," thus dooming to defeat their entire ticket in the general election; and palpable demagogues have defeated responsible candidates for public office. All of these consequences may not persuade reformers that an increase in the use of direct primaries is not a good idea, but they must be faced. If we value political parties, which reformers often profess to do, then we must hesitate to cut them off from the process of selecting candidates for public office, to deprive them of incentives to organize, and to set them prematurely at the mercy of masses of people whose information at the primary stage is especially poor.

This is not, we suggest, an elitist doctrine. Responsible political analysts and advocates must face the fact that party identification for most people provides the safe cognitive anchorage around which political preferences are organized. Set adrift from this anchorage as they are when faced with an intraparty primary election, most voters have little or nothing to guide their choices. Chance familiarity with a famous name or stray feelings of ethnic kinship under these circumstances seem to provide many voters with the only clues to choice.[15] Given the conditions of popular interest and participation that prevail, we would question throwing the future of the party system entirely and precipitously into the hands of primary electorates.

So long as the relevant choice is between a mixed system and a national primary, our choice lies with diversity. Suppose, however, that the number of state primaries, already overly large by our standards, grows still further. Might not a national primary be better than a series of state primaries? It might.

Stretching out primaries seriatim over the election year has the advantage of permitting knowledge of candidates to develop over time. This approach also allows candidates to get exposure who might otherwise be passed over. Money, moreover, can be raised as one goes along instead of all at once. A small band of devotees, finally, may go further and last longer if, like Antaeus, who gained strength when he touched the earth, they can replenish themselves after each primary. These virtues, however, are counterweighted by vices.

Candidates of purely local appeal and regional leaders will not do as well if there were a national primary. Corps of activists, purists and politicians alike, will matter less and the media and their managers more, for the need to reach large numbers of people in a short time will require use of the mass media in preference to individual or small-scale efforts at persuasion. The ability to capture party meetings will not matter because there will be no meetings worth capturing. Candidates of prior national reputation, whether in politics or in some less likely sphere, such as sports or the cinema, will have the advantage. As their purpose in entering the primary will be to win the election, they will cater more to the people and less to party purists. Indeed, a national primary, contested through the national media, might enable candidates to lessen their dependence on activists because they can enter directly into relationships with voters in the mass.

The great disadvantage of national primaries is that they weaken the main intermediaries between the people and their government— political parties. But if the existing and evolving presidential nominating process also weakens parties, and if it, in addition, enthrones purists over politicians, then given this unfortunate choice, a more direct relationship between candidates and their countrymen might be the lesser evil.

Regional primaries, about which there is much talk but (as yet) little action, have apparent appeal as a halfway house between a single national primary and a multitude of state primaries. The question—halfway between what and what?—is not easy to answer. Candidates would not have to campaign in as many distant places at nearly the same time; this would save them money and effort. Since each election would emcompass a larger geographic area, however, the need to campaign earlier, to be better known at the start, and to have more money with which to begin would be greater than it is now. The major advantage of regional primaries, assuming they were spaced about one month apart as in Senator Robert Packwood's plan, would be that both politicians and people could reconsider their earlier choices in the light of the latest information. Yet if delegates were pledged to candidates, the flexibility of bargainers at the national conventions would still be diminished, and if delegates were selected by congressional district, or on a proportional basis, activist voters and their candidates would still have an enormous advantage. Only if regional primaries were combined with plurality voting, thus reversing recent reforms, would outcomes be much different than they are now. It is possible that conflicts among states may doom the entire enterprise. If not, regional primaries, which create an opportunity to reconsider the rules of voting, may be more interesting as an effort to turn back in the guise of going forward than they are in and of themselves.

Another alternative is nomination by one of the branches of

Congress. This, though, would be out of the question. The caucus system of nomination has been rejected since Andrew Jackson's time, because it did not give sufficient representation to the large population groups whose votes were decisive in the election.[16] Furthermore, the large fluctuations of party membership in Congress would lead to serious difficulties. If a party happened to do very poorly for a few years in several sections of the country, the representation in Congress from those areas would be small and they would, in effect, be deprived of a voice in nominating a presidential candidate for that party. This nominating procedure could advertise itself as being national in scope, but it would be far more likely than the present system to produce candidates with a limited sectional appeal. The attempts of leaders in areas where the party is weak to strengthen themselves by nominating a candidate who might help increase their vote would be stymied.

Perhaps, it may be argued, what is required is not some radically new method of nominating candidates, but reform of some of the more obnoxious practices of the present system. High on the list of objectionable practices would be the secret gathering of party leaders in the smoke-filled room. Some liken this to a political opium den where a few irresponsible men, hidden from public view, stealthily determine the destiny of the nation.[17] Yet it is difficult to see who, other than the party's leaders, should be entrusted with the delicate task of finding a candidate to meet the majority preference. If head-on clashes of strength on the convention floor do not resolve the question, the only alternative would be continued deadlock, anarchy among scores of leaderless delegates splitting the party into rival factions, or some process of accommodation.

Let us suppose that the smoke-filled room were abolished and with it all behind-the-scenes negotiations. All parleys would then be held in public, before the delegates and millions of television viewers. As a result, the participants would spend their time scoring points against each other in order to impress the folks back home. Bargaining would not be taking place since the participants would not really be communicating with one another. No compromises would be possible; leaders would be accused by their followers of selling out to the other side. Once a stalemate existed, breaking it would be practically impossible, and the party would probably disintegrate into warring factions.

An extensive system of state primaries in which delegates are legally compelled to vote for the candidate who wins in the state has led to the eclipse of the smoke-filled room without any formal action of a convention. Since delegates cannot change their positions except by direction of the candidate to whom they are pledged, there is little point in bringing party leaders together for private conferences. Sharply increasing the number of pledged delegates introduces great rigidity into the convention because of the increased likelihood of stalemates which can not be overcome because no one is in a position to switch his support.

This more or less is coming to resemble the situation of the Democratic party today. The Democratic party, through its current rules changes, has managed to embody the following contradiction: by fragmenting delegations it has increased the chances of a contested convention, and by giving preference to purists, it has decreased the likelihood that delegates will be able to bargain with one another. Failure to arrive at a decision to nominate a candidate acceptable to all could conceivably lead to withdrawal of the defeated factions from the party. Since the national party is unified, if at all, only by the choice of a presidential candidate, inability to bargain out an agreement invites serious party fragmentation. The resulting party realignment would then depend on what happened in the Republican party.

Situational factors are of critical importance. If President Ford runs for renomination and if he is elected, these facts will override ideological suppositions. The gap between Republican activists and voters will be papered over for one more election. Should Ford be defeated in the 1976 election, conservative Republican purists will undoubtedly recapture the party. If the Republicans nominated a staunch conservative and the Democrats a near-radical, the incentives would increase for liberal Republicans and moderate Democrats to bolt their respective parties and even, conceivably, to join in a new-old Democratic-Republican party.

The old two-party system would be gone. In its place, as in France and Japan, would be a center party that usually governs with occasional challenges from right and left. The peripheral parties would be cohesive but unable to govern. The moderate center party would govern but, being heterogeneous, find agreement difficult. Instead of party competition under a two-party system, there would be factional competition within the major party of a multiparty system. We leave it to the reader to decide if the choice available to the public under such circumstances would be greater or better then than it is now.

Much criticism has been leveled at the raucousness of demonstrations that take place on the convention floor while candidates are being nominated.[18] Criticism of demonstrations on the grounds that they are unseemly and vulgar seems to us to be trivial. There is no evidence to substantiate a claim that the final decision would be better in some way if demonstrations were banned.

Undoubtedly, the demonstrations have been overdone and might be cut short. This task can safely be left to the requirements of television. As the conventions of the last few years have shown, television dictates briefer demonstrations to retain the attention of the vast audience which the party would like very much to influence in its favor.

The television coverage of the 1968 national conventions raised a number of questions concerning their future management. We wonder if all the things that went wrong at the Democratic convention were the result of willful mismanagement or whether at least some of the difficulty can be attributed to the increasing unwieldiness of the convention. Delegates complained of an inability to attract the attention of the chair. The microphones allocated to each delegation on the floor were turned on and off at the rostrum, so it was impossible to use them to get the chair's attention. Attempts to telephone the chair from the floor were often ignored. Attempts to approach the rostrum were repulsed by security guards. Attempts to signal the chair were defeated by the noise and movement in the hall.

It is hard to see how such a huge and chaotic organization can conduct itself as a parliamentary body. In fact, plenary sessions of the convention have two functions—ceremonial and business. We think it is time to consider a separation of these functions. Ceremonial activities can take place in an amphitheater or a stadium. The general public can be invited. On such occasions there are two classes of people, performers and spectators.

When the convention is conducting its business, however, a different division of labor is involved and a different decorum should prevail. If it is not possible for a convention to conduct itself as a parliamentary body when all two or three thousand members are present, perhaps some democratic and equitable means could be found to restrict the number of official delegates so as to make communication among them feasible. If, let us say, 1,000 delegates met at business meetings, much of the paraphernalia associated with meetings of 10,000 could be dispensed with. The number of guards and security officers could be cut. The business of keeping order could be placed where it belongs—in the hands of the chair who directs sergeants-at-arms publicly, rather than in the hands of an anonymous functionary who at Chicago apparently felt free to dispatch security officers to harass delegates on the floor.

A smaller number of people on the floor, the possibility of spontaneous communication with the chair and with other members, and parliamentary decorum would unquestionably facilitate and properly dignify the business of the convention. It would also provide a warrant for the reexamination of the role of television cameras at national conventions.

In fact, one effect of reforms designed to increase the representativeness of delegations has been to increase the size of each state delegation. Quotas, whether implicit or explicit, have, according to this perspective, not only increased the numbers of delegates, but also decreased the probability that they could deliberate as a body.

We believe television and other news media should continue to cover national party conventions with all the care and energy they have always used. But we question the propriety of wandering television and newspaper reporters on the floor of a convention. To be sure, so long as conventions continue in their present overblown form, reporters may as well be on the floor, since everyone else is. But if conventions were reduced in size and, for business purposes, maintained parliamentary decorum, perhaps it would be possible to consider the problems created by news media representatives at national conventions. Neither Democrats nor Republicans alone will take the lead in grappling with this problem, because both fear the wrath of the media. Thus, academic observers are ideally situated to open this discussion.

We want to increase respect for presidential nominations by having them conducted in a serious atmosphere conducive to mature deliberation. The presence of hordes of correspondents on the convention floor introduces a discordant note somewhere between individual breast-beating and mass hysteria. The very presence of numerous reporters, with their microphones and television cameras, creates a carnival atmosphere. No one would ordinarily make an important decision surrounded by people hurriedly throwing questions. No one would take seriously a decision made by people constantly distracted from the main proceedings by side conversations.

A superabundance of TV cameras on the convention floor plays up to the worst instincts of the politicians gathered there. It is hard for ordinary mortals to resist publicity; it is asking too much for politicians to forego an opportunity for national exposure. Yet the purpose of the convention is not to make the delegates look good at home, but for them to make a wise choice where they are.

The mass media not only report events; they create news. They are always after sensational stories. If conflict and controversy is not inherent in a situation, they will seek to create it. A momentary misunderstanding on the floor might be cleared up later on, but reporters will jump in immediately to widen the breach.

Imagine what football games would be like if they were reported under the same rules that prevail at national conventions. Suppose that Ken Stabler is getting clobbered in the next Super Bowl. His line is weak and defenders are pouring all over him. After the fifth interception, Stabler receives a fearful blow. Before he can pick up his shattered bones a dozen TV reporters stick their microphones and cameras in his face, shouting questions at him. "Did you get good protection today, Ken baby?" "Anybody let you down, hey?" A few answers on the spot and the team might never be able to work together again.

Is it asking too much for nominations of future presidents to be conducted with at least the same dignity as presently obtains at football games? The press, radio, and TV can broadcast the proceedings and report events from booths above the convention floor. No one but delegates and elderly, unthreatening sergeants-at-arms should be allowed on the floor while the convention is at work.

Ample interview facilities should be provided just off the floor. When a delegate is wanted for an interview, a young page should be sent to fetch him just as is done in Congress. "Mr. Smith," the page might say, "a network wants to harass you in room nine," and if he wants to be harassed he can walk off the floor to accomplish that mission.[19]

The American people deserve full reporting of the national conventions. No one wants to limit the media in any legitimate coverage. But improving the conduct of national conventions and increasing public respect for their decisions are reasons enough to ask the media to pay a small cost for a large public benefit.

The convention, as we have said, normally aids party unity in a variety of ways. It provides a forum in which initially disunited fragments of the national party can come together and find common ground as well as a common nominee. The platform aids in performing this function. In order to gain a majority of electoral votes, a party must appeal to most major population groups. Since these interests do not want the same thing in all cases, it is necessary to compromise and, sometimes, to evade issues that would lead to drastic losses of support. And since the parties must contain somewhat conflicting interests, internal accommodation is essential to avoid splits. A perfectly clear, unequivocal, consistent platform on all major issues presupposes an electorate and a party system divided neatly and more or less evenly along ideological lines, and that is not the case in this country.

The concern of reformers with party platforms stems primarily from two assumptions: first, that there is a significant demand in the electorate for more clear-cut differences on policy; second, that elections are likely to be a significant source of guidance on individual issues to policy-makers. Yet both these assumptions are either false or highly dubious. On a wide range of issues, leaders in both parties are much further apart than are ordinary citizens who, in fact, are separated by rather small differences.[20] To the degree that party platforms do spell out clear and important differences on policy, and these are quite frequently considerable, this probably results far more from a desire of party leaders to please themselves or from misinformation about what the voters desire than from any supposed demand from the electorate. It is, of course, possible for a party to meet at least three of the four prerequisites for policy government reform (making policy commitments to the electorate, developing alternatives to governmental policy when out of office, and differing sufficiently to provide "a choice, not an echo") if a large enough majority of its own activists so desire. We have argued that such activists are unlikely to be rewarded with victory if they force a unilateral movement of one of the major parties far away from the position of the other on a great number of issues at the same time and then campaign vigorously on this new position. The Republican experience of 1964 and the Democratic experience of 1972 make it clear that such a strategy can be pursued, but the outcomes of those elections stand as a warning to political activists who entertain such notions again. In any event, it is exceedingly difficult (if not impossible) to discover just what an election means in terms of the policy preferences of a majority. About all that one can expect from a platform is an indication of the general direction in which a candidate and the dominant factions in his party intend to go, and the present party platforms do reasonably well in this respect.

Some critics object to the normal convention's stress on picking a winner rather than the "best man" regardless of his popularity. This objection is not compatible with the democratic notion that voters should decide who is best for them and communicate this decision in an election. Only in dictatorial countries does a set of leaders arrogate unto themselves the right to determine who is best regardless of popular preferences. An unpopular candidate can hardly win a free election. An unpopular president can hardly secure the support he needs to accomplish his goals. Popularity can be regarded as a necessary element for obtaining consent in democratic politics.

Although popularity is normally a necessary condition for nomination, it should not be the only condition. The guideline for purposes of nomination should be to nominate the best of the popular candidates. But "best" is a slippery word. A great deal of what we mean by "best" in politics is "best for us" or "best represents our policy preferences" and this can hardly be held up as an objective criterion. What is meant by "best" in this context are certain personal qualities such as experience, intelligence, and decisiveness. Nevertheless, it is not at all clear that an extreme conservative would prefer a highly intelligent liberal to a moderately intelligent candidate who shared his conservative policy preferences. Personal qualities are clearly subject to discount based on the compatibility of interests between the voter and the candidate.

Insofar as the "best man" criterion has a residue of meaning, we believe that it is possible to argue that the criterion has largely been followed in recent times. Looking at the candidates of both parties since 1940—Roosevelt, Truman, Stevenson, Kennedy, Johnson, Humphrey, McGovern for the Democrats, and Willkie, Dewey, Eisenhower, Nixon for the Republicans—there is not one man among them who could not be said to have had some outstanding qualities or experience for the White House. Understandably, Nixon sticks in our craw. One day, perhaps, someone will invent a process that always produces good results but, until then, an occasional president is bound to prove disappointing. Actually, there is little reason to believe that the voters, who must also share the blame, would have preferred Nixon to any moderate Democrat in 1972 or that, had Democratic purists not treated Humphrey so badly in 1968, Nixon would ever have won.

As usual, Goldwater presents a special problem because in many important ways he was a candidate of extreme views, something, we have argued, the nominating process has in the past discouraged. It is unlikely that any system of nomination—total primary, total convention, mixed, or even action by Republicans in Congress—would have resulted in a different choice in 1964. For the nomination of Goldwater is, in part, the result of an underlying trend, working since the New Deal period, through which Republican activists have become separated in their preferences from Republican voters and from the electorate as a whole. It required only the temporary disarray of the moderate opposition within the Republican party for this trend to manifest itself in Senator Goldwater's visible presence on the ticket. No system of nomination, indeed no political system, can be expected forever to run counter to the desires of the activists who have the most say about running it. It is not the convention system but the desires of the activist core of the Republican party that produced an exception to the rule in 1964. The selection of the Democratic candidate in 1972 is traceable to similar factors, but the party situation is more complicated. If delegates to the Democratic convention had been like their regular county chairmen, they would still have been pretty close to their sources of support in the electorate. But, during the nomination stage, purists are activated, and purists are now preferred according to recent party rules. Thus the Democratic delegates of 1972 were like the Republicans—far from voters and idealogically extreme. What can be done about this state of affairs?

One alternative—taking the nomination away from activists and giving it directly to at least some of the voters through a national primary—has previously been considered. Another—stacking party rules against purists—has been rejected so far. In fact, the rules of the Democratic party have moved in the opposite direction. Yet things could be done to change them. Delegate seats could be awarded in greater number to party officeholders—county chairmen, state committee people, congressmen, minority and majority leaders in state legislatures. The timing of elections could be changed so that governors, mayors, and other elected officials would be up for election at the same time, thus increasing their incentive to choose a popular president. The 25 percent of each delegation that Democrats allow to escape from their usual rules could be increased to 50 percent. The national convention would then be a convocation of party leaders, tempered by primary preferences, and not a collection of activists, who appear in an election year in order to represent themselves rather than the electorate.

Whatever our preferences might be, whichever structural changes are made will not affect the social currents, such as the vast increase in formally educated people, that have produced purism. Although the present rules magnify purism, they do not create it. Purists do not have to win all intraparty battles; politicians could contest them. Why, then, are politicians of late so weak and purists so powerful?

Reform, which one might think would strengthen parties, has in recent years tended to weaken them. Once a candidate gets financial support from the government, he not only has less use for "fat cat" financiers but also for party politicians. New rules for party conferences and conventions stress expression at the expense of election.

Parties may be weak but why should their regulars be weaklings? Why should the extremes be more passionate than the middle of the party spectrum? To put the question that way is to answer it: moderate beliefs tend to be moderately pursued. But why should moderates, who are most numerous in the population, be least in evidence in party meetings and primaries? Because they are inattentive, preoccupied, or satisfied, and their opponents are not. Should conditions change so that large numbers of people feel they are suffering, as in a depression, larger numbers of moderates will appear. For this phenomenon—known to Marxists as the "over-mobilization" of the masses—to be long-lasting the nation would have to be in a constant state of turmoil, hardly a desirable prescription to cure the ills of party.

The conclusion we would draw is that the primaries, together with other methods of delegate selection that give predominance to party regulars, provide a reasonable balance between popularity and other important considerations. Without denying an element of popular participation, the decision is ultimately thrown into the hands of the people who ought to make it if we want a strong party system—the party leaders.

For some critics the defects of conventions lie not only in their poor performance in nominating candidates but also in their failure to become a sort of "superlegislature" enforcing the policy views in the platform upon party members in the executive branch and Congress. We have previously indicated that such enforcement is most unlikely to be achieved.

Let us suppose, nevertheless, for the purposes of argument, that the conventions could somehow become much more influential on matters of national policy. How could either party retain a semblance of unity if the stakes of convention deliberations were vastly increased by converting the platform into an unbreakable promise of national policy? If one believes that an increase in heated discussion necessarily increases agreement, then the problem solves itself. Experience warns us, however, that airing sharp differences, particularly when the stakes are high, is likely to decrease agreement. At the 1964 Republican convention, for example, black delegates, bitter about the defeat of Governor Scranton's proposed amendment on civil rights to the GOP education plank, held a protest march around the Cow Palace and, when Goldwater was nominated, announced that they would sit out the campaign.[21] This could not have helped Goldwater's chances of election. The fact that platforms are not binding permits a degree of unity necessary for the delegates to stay put long enough to agree on a nominee. By vastly increasing the number of delegates who would bitterly oppose platform decisions, and who would probably leave the convention, the proposed change would jeopardize the legitimacy of its nominating function. Paradoxically, in such circumstances, it would be difficult to resist the temptation to make the platform utterly innocuous in order to give offense to no one.

There are also good reasons for opposing the desires of those who love the conventions so well that they would like to see them convene once every year or two. For without a presidential candidate to nominate, they would have little to do. If the purpose of these meetings is to give free advice, there would seem to be little point to them. Congressmen are likely to pay as little attention to convention talk as they would to the pronouncements of any advisory committee that does not appreciate the context within which they operate. After all, congressmen are subject to different risks and sanctions than are most delegates, get little help from the national party in securing nomination and election, and have no reason to be beholden to it for suggesting policies that may get them into trouble. The notion of getting delegates together under circumstances where their disagreements are certain to come out into the open, merely for the purpose of making recommendations, does not seem promising.

The 1974 midterm conference of the Democratic party in Kansas City was notable, not for its accomplishments, because there weren't any, but because it barely avoided a damaging party split over demographic quotas. Party activists returned from Kansas City bathed in good feeling—or was it sweat?—because they managed to avert outright catastrophe there.

Especially now that they are an endangered species, the superiority of the traditional national conventions to the available alternatives is clear. Only the convention permits us to realize in large measure all the six goals—maintenance of the two-party system, party competition, some degree of internal cohesion, candidates attractive to voters, qualified candidates, and acceptance of nominees as legitimate—which we postulated earlier would commonly be accepted as desirable.

An Appraisal of Permanent Voting Enrollment

One reform that has received increasing attention and that would presumably have at least marginal effects on all stages of presidential elections without directly altering either the means of nominating candidates or the ways in which they campaign is universal automatic voter enrollment. One of the distinguishing features of American national elections is the low share of the potential electorate that actually gets to the polls and votes. In 1972 the number of nonvoters (61,924,000) was one and one-half times the number of votes cast for McGovern and one and one-third times the number cast for Nixon; the turnout percentage lagged ten to fifteen points behind those for other major democracies such as Britain, France, and West Germany. The most detailed study of the matter yet available traces both of these facts to the American system of voter registration; it shows that the level of voter registration is easily the greatest influence (accounting for 80 percent of the variance) on the percentage of the population that actually votes, far greater than any other single factor usually cited in studies of voting by those registered and in fact greater than all such factors put together.[22]

Unlike the citizens of foreign democracies wherein the government takes responsibility for registration, the American must prepare for the eventual vote by registering sometimes months before the election, at a time when political information and interest are at a low point.[23] Since interest and information are the important factors, the level of registration can be advanced or retarded by altering the time of year when voter registration rolls are closed or the physical ease of reaching a registration point, and practicing political leaders are well aware of the fact.[24] As Stanley Kelley and his collaborators observe, "Local differences in the turnout for elections are to a large extent related to local differences in rates of registration, and these in turn reflect to a considerable degree local differences in the rules governing, and the arrangements for handling, the registration of voters." [25]

Proposals for universal automatic voter enrollment differ according to administrative arrangements for enrollment, the time when it would occur, the duration of enrollment, and the levels of government to which it would apply. The basic idea, however, is that the United States would be divided into election districts, and deputy registrars within them would go door to door, enrolling every citizen who did not refuse to be registered.[26]

At present there are not nearly enough registration drives to enfranchise a high percentage of the electorate, and most such drives fail; a major New York City drive in 1969, for example, spent $310,000 but added only 70,000 voters, 3 percent of the electorate, for a total registered of only 35 percent of those eligible.[27] Some areas of the United States use universal automatic enrollment already. They get striking results; the state of Idaho makes an aggressive search for new registrants, and as the table on page 239 shows, the consequences for voting turnout are impressive. The table also compares U.S. national figures with those in Great Britain, and it is apparent that the percentage registered is strongly associated with the percentage of the potential electorate voting.

While the rest of the United States now lags behind the Idaho performance, there was once a time, in an era when the impact of the president was remote, mass communication absent, and electronic voting equipment unheard of, when more than 70 percent of *potential* (not just registered) voters turned out in presidential elections; in the election of 1876, 82 percent of the possible voters turned out for the nation as a whole. Soon thereafter, however, harsh registration restrictions were introduced, cloaked in rhetoric about

The Rules for Registration Are an Important Influence on the
Proportion of the Electorate That Actually Votes

	All U.S. (1968)	Idaho (1968)	Great Britain (1970)	(1966)
Persons of Voting Age (thousands)	120,773	400	40,778	36,936
Percent Registered	74.5	91.8	91.5	97.4
Percent Registered Who Vote	81.3	79.4	72.0	75.8
Percent Persons of Voting Age Who Vote	60.6	72.8	69.5	73.8

stopping corruption but aimed at keeping down the vote of "undesirable elements" (immigrants and black voters)—which they did. "In short," Kelley observes, "turnout in presidential elections in the U.S. may have declined and then risen again, not because of changes in the interest of voters in elections, but because of changes in the interest demanded of them. . . . [Not] only . . . [are] electorates . . . much more the product of political forces than many have appreciated, but also . . . to a considerable extent, they can be *political artifacts*. Within limits, they can be constructed to a size and composition deemed desirable by those in power." [28]

The effect of universal automatic enrollment on presidential politics seems relatively straightforward. We know that those who are disenfranchised by current practices are generally those with lower levels of political information and interest, and these are traditionally the young, the less well educated, those lower in income, and black citizens.[29] We also know how these groups behave politically; they are much more Democratic than Republican, but far less stable in all aspects of their participation than other groups in the electorate. Their effective entry into politics would serve to intensify the need for the parties to follow the presidential strategies we have already outlined; Democrats could afford even more to try to emphasize party identification through partisan appeals, while Republicans would be forced even more to follow "me-too" strategies, obscure party lines, claim they could better deal with the domestic problems on which the Democrats focus, and emphasize foreign affairs.

Whether this expanded electorate would have any direct effect on primaries and delegate selection would depend on the particular enrollment plan adopted. At one extreme, if enrollment were held every four years in October and provided for continuation on the rolls only if the registrant voted in each election held in the district—state and municipal elections, as well as federal—the reform would have little direct effect. If the canvass occurred in the spring, however, and registrants had to vote only once every four years to stay on the rolls, there would be a significant addition to the presidential electorate. Some have argued that this portends new strength for non-party-organization activists, since this new group would be far less tied to any political organizations than the already enfranchised groups.

Both black and white former nonvoters are likely to favor increased expenditures on policies designed to benefit lower-income people. But on questions of political style—protest, demonstrations, etc.—most newly registered voters, including young voters, will undoubtedly favor more traditional standards of seemly behavior.[30]

While universal automatic voter enrollment deals with the means by which the share of the potential electorate that gets to the polls can be changed, there are a whole series of lesser reforms that deal with changes in the size of the potential electorate itself. The major limiting factors on this potential electorate are legal requirements concerning residence, age, literacy, criminal conviction, mental incompetence, and U.S. citizenship.

The most notorious of these restrictions has been the residence requirement; in a nation noted for the geographic mobility of its population, a majority of states required, as recently as 1972, one year within the state, three months within the county, and thirty days within the precinct to vote in any election, including presidential. In 1972 the Supreme Court ruled in *Dunn* v. *Blumstein* (405 U.S. 330) that thirty days was an ample period of time for the State of Tennessee to register its voters and declared its existing six-month state residency requirement an unconstitutional denial of equal protection. In two subsequent per curiam decisions, *Marston* v. *Lewis*, 410 U.S. 759 (1973), and *Burns* v. *Forston*, 410 U.S. 686 (1972), the Court held that an extension to fifty days was permissible under certain conditions, but that this time period represented the absolute limit.

What will the consequences be of this change in the rules?

AIPO surveys suggest that those previously disenfranchised by lengthy residence requirements are disproportionately in the twenty-one-to-thirty age group.[31] We know that voters in this age group are more Democratic than Republican but less identified with any party than are older voters, that they have less political information and are less interested, and that they participate less in all forms of political activity. Thus as residence requirements for presidential voting are dropped, the potential electorate will expand by a part of the population less likely to get out to vote at all, more likely to vote Democratic in a "normal" situation if they turned out to vote, but more likely to be unstable in their preferences and to move disproportionately in any one direction if there were strong forces moving that way.

The same can, of course, be said for a group which has gotten the most recent attention—eighteen-, nineteen-, and twenty-year-olds. They could be expected to behave much as twenty-one- to thirty-year-olds, only more so. In 1970 the Supreme Court upheld the right of this group to vote in national elections, but left it for individual states to decide the age requirements in state elections.[32]

There are four other major groups currently kept out of the potential presidential electorate:

1. Travelers and the ill. William Andrews estimates that while 3,400,000 absentee ballots were cast in 1960, another 3,600,000 voters could not vote because they had departed or become ill too late to receive an absentee ballot.[33]
2. Aliens. Aliens who could not vote in 1960 totaled 2,800,000.
3. Ex-felons. Convicted felons are permanently stripped of voting rights in most states, and there were 1,400,000 such persons in 1960.[34]
4. Illiterates. Of the 3,400,000 illiterates in 1960, 1,500,000 were literate but not in English.

The analysis of whether or not such groups should be allowed to become part of the electorate must be much the same as that for nonregistrants; to the degree that voting is a means to distribute the political goods of a society, they presumably have as much (perhaps more) of a stake in its outcome as do other groups, and while they may be low in general political information, this would not be an adequate reason, in our view, to deprive them of the vote.

We write in a recession year when public service employment is being used to put people to work. At the same time questions are raised about whether useful work exists for them to do. As our small contribution, we would like to suggest that registering voters would help in two ways: by generating useful employment and by increasing respect for the electoral process.

An Appraisal of the Electoral College

Close presidential elections, where the new president has only a narrow margin in the total popular vote, always lead to renewed public discussion of the merits of the Electoral College, since close elections remind people of the mathematical possibility that the candidate with a plurality of all the votes will not necessarily be the one to become president. Reform interest surges even higher when a regionally based third party such as the party George Wallace led in 1968 becomes strong enough conceivably to prevent any candidate from having an electoral vote majority, thus threatening to drive the decision into the U.S. House of Representatives, which under the Constitution decides such matters when the Electoral College cannot.

The number of reform plans generated in the aftermath of the 1968 elections, including all their permutations and combinations, was legion. There were, however, three basic alternatives proposed to the present system, and the rest were variations. One would abolish the Electoral College outright and weigh votes equally everywhere. The net effect of such a proposal would be to undermine slightly the current strategic advantage enjoyed by populous, two-party, urbanized states; it might also have some long-run effects on the two-party system itself, but these would depend on other changes in the social situation within the country. The second proposal would retain the apportionment of the Electoral College (which gives numerical advantage to the smaller, rural states) but abolish the unit rule electoral vote (which operates strongly in favor of populous states). This proposal is quite extreme in its import, which would be to confer an additional political bonus upon states already overrepresented in positions of congressional power. A third, quite similar proposal also retains the apportionment of the Electoral College but distributes an Electoral College vote for the plurality vote winner in each congressional district and two additional electoral votes for the winner in each state. This system maximizes the strength of one-party states and of those forces that are most important in the

U.S. House of Representatives; in fact, it could realign the presidential coalition in fundamental ways.[35]

The Constitution provides that each state, regardless of its population, shall be represented in the Senate by an equal number of senators. This means that the eight largest states, with just under 50 percent of the voters in 1972, have just sixteen senators. In the course of legislative proceedings, these senators' votes can be canceled by the sixteen votes of the senators from the eight least populous states, with 2.2 percent of the voters in the 1972 presidential election. Before the series of Supreme Court decisions beginning with *Baker* v. *Carr*, and extending through *Wesberry* v. *Sanders* and *Reynolds* v. *Sims*,[36] the less populous, more rural states had been similarly favored in the distribution of seats in the House of Representatives; at one point in the early 1960s an average vote in Nevada was worth eighty-five times as much as an average vote in New York in elections for the House. The requirement that each state have at least one representative still gives the smaller states a slight edge over the big states in congressmen per capita (about 300,000 per congressman in the smaller states, and well over 400,000 in the large states), and the distribution of one-party, "safe" districts within the smaller states augments this further by tending to give House leadership positions to representatives from these areas. The imbalance is comparatively far less than it was as recently as ten years ago; it roughly corresponds to the advantage that more populous, urbanized, two-party states enjoy in the Electoral College, and thus in access to the presidency.

The present Electoral College system, with its votes apportioned according to the total of Senate and House seats a state has, and awarded on a "winner-take-all" basis, does provide a clear advantage to two groups of states. It yields a secondary advantage to the smallest states, since their overrepresentation in the Senate and the House guarantees them overrepresentation in the Electoral College; in 1968, all five states with three electoral votes each had a ratio of 150,000 or fewer citizens per electoral vote, while every state with thirteen or more electoral votes had a ratio of 350,000 or more citizens per electoral vote. But it is primarily the larger states, through the unit rule principle, who benefit from the Electoral College. A candidate who can get a narrow majority in New York State can get almost as many electoral votes (forty-one) as he could by carrying all of the sixteen smallest states (fifty-nine); he can, mathematically, carry New York by one vote and not receive any votes in those sixteen states and do just as well. This fact alone suggests that a presidential candidate should spend his energy in the larger states and tailor his programs to appeal to their voters, provided that energy expended there is nearly as likely to yield results. In fact, the larger states are usually quite close in their division of the major party vote, while the smaller states are more nearly "sure" for one party or the other. In 1968, the last close election, the average share of the vote for the winner in the sixteen smallest states was 55 percent and eight out of these sixteen states gave the winner a 10 percent margin of victory; in the eight largest states, on the other hand, the average share of the vote for the winner was 47 percent, with none of these states giving as much as 55 percent to the winner and none of them giving him as much as a 10 percent margin. The large states are the home of many organized minorities, especially racial and ethnic minorities, and this has traditionally meant that both presidential candidates have had to pitch their appeals to attract these groups, or at least not to drive off significant proportions of them. This is a major reason why U.S. presidents, Republicans as well as Democrats, have been more activist, welfare oriented, minority oriented—in a word, more liberal—than their congressional party counterparts.[37]

Some of the critics of the current system have pointed to this advantage for the larger states, and especially their urban minorities, as a drawback of that system, to be reformed out of existence,[38] but most have concentrated their fire on the possibility of "deadlock," the possibility of the "wrong winner," and the "undemocratic" nature of the unit rule.

Allowing a majority (or plurality) of voters to choose a president has a great deal to commend it. This is the simplest method of all; it would be most easily understood by the greatest number of people; it is the plan favored by the majority of Americans; and it comes closest to reflecting intuitive notions of direct popular sovereignty through majority rule. But to end the matter there would be too simpleminded. There is more than one political lesson to be learned by a closer examination of the Electoral College and available alternatives to it.

The outright abolition of the Electoral College, and the substitution of the direct election of the president, would certainly reduce the importance of the larger states. It would mean that the popular vote margin which a state could provide, not the number of electoral votes, would determine its importance; for example, under the present system a candidate who carries California by 220,000 votes (as Nixon did in 1968) has garnered about 1/7 of the support he needs to win, while under the direct vote system states like Massachusetts or Alabama can generate three and four times that much margin. In the two-party states, in which category most of the larger states fall, voters are cross-pressured in many ways, and a candidate can seldom count on defeating his opponent by a very large margin. The reason, then, that the large states lose influence is that this system switches influence from the close states to one-party states; in some states where one party's organization is weak, large majorities for the other party are easier to turn out at election time, and special rewards would be forthcoming for party leaders who could provide a large margin of victory for their candidate. As candidates currently look with favor on those who can bring them support in the large states, because this spells victory, so might they be expected to look with favor on those who can bring them large popular margins in the one-party states, should that become the criterion. The emphasis would not be on which candidate was going to win the state, already a foregone conclusion, but by how many votes he was going to win. The small states do not gain, however, because even when they are one-party, they are not large enough to generate substantial voting margins. Direct election thus changes the advantage from the biggest and the smallest two-party states to the medium-sized one-party states, and these, in the United States, happen most commonly to be located in the South.[39]

The table on page 246 lists all states having more than fourteen electoral votes and all states having more than a margin of 100,000 votes for the winner in 1968, the last close election. It shows clearly that the major gainers under a direct election system would be southern states, for six out of the eight southern states that were not "big states" on an electoral vote basis are now "big states" because of their vote margin (along with eight other randomly assorted states); conversely, three of the ten "big states" by the Electoral College standard are now "small," and all but one of the ten lag behind Alabama in their importance to a presidential candidate.

This does not, of course, settle the matter, for one of the reasons that direct election is touted is that third parties cannot deadlock the process. In fact, those southern states with the largest 1968 margins

Popular Vote Margin, 1968

	Small (less than 100,000)	Large (more than 100,000)
Large (14+)	21-Ohio-90,000 17-New Jersey-61,000 25-Texas-39,000	14-Massachusetts-702,000 43-New York-371,000 40-California-223,000 21-Michigan-222,000 14-Florida-210,000 29-Pennsylvania-169,000 26-Illinois-135,000
Small (13−)		10-Alabama-495,000 7-Mississippi-265,000 13-Indiana-261,000 10-Louisiana-221,000 10-Minnesota-199,000 7-Kansas-176,000 12-Georgia-169,000 5-Nebraska-151,000 12-Virginia-148,000 8-Oklahoma-143,000 9-Iowa-142,000 13-North Carolina-131,000 4-Rhode Island-124,000 11-Tennessee-121,000 3-D.C.-109,000

Electoral Vote Margin

were not powerful but weak, for they did not contribute to a winner but to a third-place loser. If the same chart is rearranged to show only the two-party vote and to exclude votes for Wallace, the southern influence disappears.

How one feels about this situation, however, depends on (1) how one still feels about the diminution of large-state influence and the gain by sundry other smaller states, (2) how much of a plurality one feels a newly elected president should have, and (3) how this plurality limit will affect others in the system.

Clearly, third-party votes under a direct election system are wasted if the candidate with a plurality wins, no matter how small that plurality; if this is how the system is made to work, it is quite possible that future "Dixiecrat"-type movements will disappear or

Two-Party Popular Vote Margin, 1968

Electoral Vote Margin	Small (less than 100,000)	Large (more than 100,000)
Large (14+)	21-Ohio-90,000 17-New Jersey-61,000 25-Texas-39,000	14-Massachusetts-702,000 43-New York-371,000 40-California-223,000 21-Michigan-222,000 14-Florida-210,000 29-Pennsylvania-169,000 26-Illinois-135,000
Small (13−)		13-Indiana-261,000 10-Minnesota-199,000 7-Kansas-176,000 5-Nebraska-151,000 8-Oklahoma-143,000 9-Iowa-142,000 13-North Carolina-131,000 4-Rhode Island-124,000 11-Tennessee-121,000 3-D.C.-109,000

will merge into southern Republicanism. At best, voters could express only their anger by voting for third-party candidates and this would be at the cost of foregoing the chance to decide an election. We suspect, however, that most Americans would feel uncomfortable with a president who, even though he won a plurality, was elected by, say, only 35 percent of the voters. One of the virtues of the present electoral vote system is that it magnifies the margin of a presidential victory (as, for instance, in 1960, Kennedy's .1 percent victory margin gave him 57 percent of the electoral vote), presumably conferring added legitimacy and with it acceptance of the new president's responsibility to govern in fact as well as in title. Any system of direct election would almost have to eliminate the majority principle in favor of some plurality, or it would clearly lead to much more, not less, deadlock; in three out of our last seven presidential elections the winning candidate was without an absolute majority.

Reformers have generally agreed, though, that the winner must win by at least a substantial plurality; consequently the Electoral College reform amendment that passed the House in late 1969 provided for a runoff between the top two candidates if no one secured as much as 40 percent of the popular vote in the initial election.[40] The first effect of this change would be to hand third parties back their influence; if one's candidate is going to have a second chance to win the office anyway, there is an incentive for any sizable organized minority to contest the first election on its own. That the runoff would likely be used if it were provided is suggested by the 1968 figures. A fourth candidate, perhaps a "peace" advocate, would have needed to pull only 6 or 7 percent of the national total to keep either candidate from having the required 40 percent (Nixon won with only 43.4 percent, although he had 56.2 percent of the electoral vote); a large enough minority was sufficiently concerned about this one issue to make this a real possibility.[41] Once this becomes even a plausible expectation, there is no reason for other intense minorities not to do likewise; visions of a segregationist party, a black party, a labor party, even a Catholic party, a farmers' party, etc., appear. Where one of the strong points of the present system is that it enforces a compromise by penalizing all minorities that will not come to terms, the direct election system could well approximate a continental European model, in which numerous groups contest the first election and then recombine for the second; at the very least, severe changes would be worked on the present convention system.[42] Should such a result have occurred in 1968, or should it occur in the future, the simplicity, ease of comprehension, and inherent majoritarian rightness of the direct election solution would quickly disappear.

The direct election plan passed by the House received a warmer reception in the Senate than the last time it appeared there—in 1956, when it was voted down 66 to 17—but there were, not surprisingly, two major opposition groups. The first was the bloc of the liberal senators from the biggest states, who had most to lose. The second was composed of some of the conservative senators from the smallest states, whom we have named as the group deriving second-greatest benefits from the current system. They argued that direct election would be a complete breach of the federalism underlying our Constitution, since it would de facto abolish state boundaries for presidential elections.[43]

Another proposal, once embodied in the unsuccessful Lodge-Gossett Resolution, is seen by some reformers as an acceptable "compromise" between outright abolition of the Electoral College and its retention.[44] In this scheme, the electoral vote in each state is split between the candidates according to their proportion of the state's popular vote. This may seem to be a procedural compromise, but it is a rather extreme reform in political terms. As the table on page 250 shows, the large, urban, two-party states are nearly eclipsed, in a way that direct election could not do; four out of the ten largest states would not in 1968 have been able to provide their winner with even one full electoral vote margin, while fifteen other states *would* have been able to do so.

The bargaining position of the large states at national conventions would be drastically reduced, and presidential nominees would have to follow a different strategy in their campaigns, giving special attention to those states in which they felt a large difference in electoral votes could be attained. Once again, the proposed reform throws the emphasis on the amount of difference within the state between the winner and the loser. In this case, however, it is the electoral votes of the states that are divided rather than the popular votes. This effectively cancels out the advantage of the large states entirely. The fact that the Electoral College underrepresents the large states in the first place even further reduces their influence. The beneficiaries are again the one-party states, as well as the smaller states, since in any particular election Idaho and Arizona, for example, may have more to contribute than Illinois, New Jersey, Ohio, or Texas.

There are two versions of this plan, one that divides electoral votes to the nearest vote and one that divides them to the nearest tenth of a vote. Most proponents favor the plan to divide them to the nearest tenth, since the nearest whole vote still in many cases would understate the closeness of the vote in a large number of states, especially those with five or fewer electoral votes to divide, and "representativeness" is the primary theoretical support for the plan. Since preventing deadlock is supposed to be one of the goals of Electoral College reform, it is interesting to note that with the majority vote victory required by proponents of both plans, either the whole or the tenth-vote system would have thrown the 1968 election into the House of Representatives (Nixon 235, Humphrey 221, Wallace 74; or, Nixon 233.8, Humphrey 223.2, Wallace 78.8, others 2.2); and the system allotting electoral votes to the nearest tenth would even have deadlocked the election of 1960 (Kennedy 264.8, Nixon 263.5, others 7.7).

The reduction in influence suffered by the large states under this

Proportional Electoral Vote Margin, 1968

	Small (1.00 −)	Large (1.00 +)
Large (14 +)	26-Illinois-0.75 21-Ohio-0.60 17-New Jersey-0.36 25-Texas-0.30	14-Massachusetts-4.22 43-New York-2.36 21-Michigan-1.41 14-Florida-1.33 29-Pennsylvania-1.30 40-California-1.21
Small (13 −)		10-Alabama-4.74 7-Mississippi-2.84 10-Louisiana-2.01 3-D.C.-1.90 12-Georgia-1.63 7-Kansas-1.41 12-Virginia-1.31 13-Indiana-1.30 4-Rhode Island-1.29 10-Minnesota-1.25 8-Oklahoma-1.21 9-Iowa-1.08 13-North Carolina-1.07 7-Idaho-1.04 5-Arizona-1.00

Electoral Vote Margin

proposal might mean, in effect, that the already overrepresented sparsely populated and one-party states in the Congress would entirely dominate the national lawmaking process, unchecked by a president obliged to cultivate urban and two-party constituencies. It is perhaps gratuitous to point out that the same plurality problem is present if the deadlock is dealt with by letting the plurality candidate win. Even with a plurality provision, splintering is facilitated under this plan because a party need only pull a fraction of a percentage point of a major state's total vote in order to get some electoral votes. The present system at least cuts off splinter groups without a strong regional base.

A third plan, the district plan, has been proposed as still another "political compromise" between the other two major reform proposals, on the grounds that since thirty-eight states must ratify a Constitutional amendment on electoral reform, the fifteen states with four or three electoral votes are not likely to support either of the first two proposals because each dilutes their current strength. The district plan would give a presidential candidate one electoral vote for every congressional district he carried, plus two more for every state. It has been pushed largely by conservative senators; it is clearly the most radical of all the reform proposals in its effect on the U.S. political system, and it is least advantageous to the big states. This system would have given Nixon victory in 1968 (289-192-57), but if it had already been in effect he probably would not have been running, since he would have won the election of 1960 (Nixon 278, Kennedy 245). Since the goal of electoral reform is supposedly to prevent the wrong man from winning, to avoid deadlock, and to do away with winner-take-all arrangements, it is hard to see what is offered by a system that would have given the less popular man victory, provides no more guarantee against deadlock than the present system (Wallace in 1968 got forty-five electoral votes under the present system, but would have received fifty-seven under this one), uses a winner-take-all principle, and has the incidental feature of ending the activist character of the American presidency and giving policy control to one-party areas for the foreseeable future.[45]

Under the present Electoral College system, there has been no time since 1876 when any splinter group has been able to make good its threat to throw the election into the House, and in fact this is quite unlikely to occur since it requires all of the Deep South (Louisiana, Arkansas, Mississippi, Alabama, Georgia, South Carolina, North Carolina) to vote for a third party, plus a very even division in nonsouthern votes. Even in 1948 Harry Truman won an Electoral College majority despite threats from both a third and a fourth party. In spite of the mathematical possibilities, not once in this century has the loser of the popular vote become president. On the other hand a direct election plan that required a 40 percent plurality might well have forced a runoff in 1968, and both the proportional and district plans would have created deadlocks in recent elections. In view of this analysis of the effect of electoral reforms, it is curious that many liberal reformers support changes in the Electoral College, presumably in order to thwart southern, racist party movements.

Underlying all of these arguments, of course, is the premise that most structural reforms "tend" to shift influence in certain ways; there may well be situations of social polarization that electoral system alternatives by themselves cannot paper over. But while we have argued that there is no better system than the current one, from the standpoint of the professed goals of most reformers, there is one minor change that would aid them. Under the present plan the electors who make up the Electoral College are in fact free to vote for whomever they wish; as an almost invariable rule, they vote for the winner in their state, but abuses are possible, and two within recent memory come to mind:

1. The unpledged electors chosen by citizens in Mississippi and Alabama in 1960 decided for whom they would vote only after the election—this clearly thwarts any popular control.
2. This liberty allowed George Wallace to hope that he could run for president, create an electoral deadlock, and then bargain with one of the other candidates for policy concessions in exchange for his electors.

An amendment making the casting of electoral votes automatic would dispel both of these possibilities.

We have argued that there is in fact no serious reason to quarrel with the major features of the present system, since in our form of government "majority rule" does not operate in a vacuum but within a system of "checks and balances." The president, for example, holds a veto power over Congress, which, if exercised, requires a two-thirds vote of each house to be overridden. Treaties must be ratified by two-thirds of the Senate, and amendments to the Constitution must be proposed by two-thirds of Congress or of the state legislatures and ratified by three-fourths of the states. Presidential appointments, in most important cases, must receive senatorial approval. The Supreme Court passes upon the constitutionality of legislative and executive actions. Involved in these political arrangements is the hope that the power of one branch of government will be counter-balanced by certain "checks" from another, the result being an approximate "balance" of forces. In our view, it is not necessarily a loss to have slightly different majorities preponderant in different institutions, but it is definitely a loss to have the same majority preponderant in several branches while other majorities are frozen out. In the past the Electoral College had its place within this system. Originally designed to check popular majorities from choosing presidents unwisely, the Electoral College provided a "check" on the overrepresentation of rural states in the legislative branch by giving extra weight to the big state constituencies of the president.

Electoral Outcomes under Various Plans

	PRESENT PLAN	DIRECT PLAN	PROPORTION PLAN	DISTRICT PLAN
1968	Nixon Wins	Nixon Wins	Nobody Wins	Nixon Wins
	Nixon 302	Nixon 43.4	Nixon 233.8	Nixon 289
	Humphrey 191	Humphrey 42.7	Humphrey 223.2	Humphrey 192
	Wallace 45	Wallace 13.5	Wallace 78.8	Wallace 57
1960	Kennedy Wins	Kennedy Wins	Nobody Wins	Nixon Wins
	Kennedy 303	Kennedy 49.7	Kennedy 264.8	Kennedy 245
	Nixon 219	Nixon 49.6	Nixon 263.5	Nixon 278
	Others 15	Others .7	Others 7.7	Others 15

Majority rule should be placed in proper perspective by considering other aspects of democratic government, such as the principle of political equality. We want majority rule, but we also want all sectors of the population to have an equal voice in government. Overrepresentation of rural interests in Congress has in the past inhibited political equality. To check this inequality we either had to alter the circumstances that promoted such inequality or provide some other means of preventing rural interests from dominating the political system. Now that the method of determining the composition of Congress is undergoing change, we can consider abolishing the Electoral College and turn to majority (or plurality) voting in electing presidents. Other things being equal, a simpler and more direct method would be preferable to a device as complex in operation and as difficult to understand as the Electoral College. But the probable defects and equivalent complexities of alternatives to the Electoral College thus far proposed make us skeptical that the day has yet arrived when we can say that other things are in fact equal.

Party Differences and Political Stability

The case for the desirability of party reform often rests on the assumption that American political parties are identical, that this is confusing and frustrating to American voters, and that it is undesirable to have a political system where parties do not disagree sharply.

We would suggest, rather, that there are enough differences

between the political parties to give voters a choice, but that many wide policy differences between the parties would be undesirable from the standpoint of the stability of the political system. The parties could well be somewhat further apart on a few issues, however, without necessarily decreasing the stability of the system. Our conceptual tools are too rough to say much about these small departures from the existing situation; let us consider only extreme changes of the kind advocated by the proponents of policy government.

Imagine for a moment that the two parties were in total and extreme disagreement on every major point of public policy. One group would appease the U.S.S.R.; the other would court nuclear war. One group would stop Social Security; the other would expand it drastically. One group would raise tariffs; the other would abolish them entirely. Obviously, one consequence of having clear-cut parties with strong policy positions would be that the costs of losing an election would skyrocket. If parties were forced to formulate coherent, full-dress programs and were forced to carry them out "responsibly," then people who did not favor these programs would have no recourse. Clearly, their confidence in a government whose policies were not to their liking would suffer, and, indeed, they might feel strongly enough about preventing these policies from being enacted to do something drastic, like leaving the country, or not complying with governmental regulations, or, in an extreme case, seeking to change the political system by force.

In fact, we have a political system that is kind to losers. Why? Because both presidential parties usually agree on a wide variety of issues; because people other than the president have to pass on policies before they are enacted into law, and these people are not bound by the presidential platform.

This is, we suggest, not necessarily a bad thing. Suppose that each major political party were composed solely of people who supported it because, and only because, it represented their views on a wide range of policies. The surface attractiveness of this idea diminishes rapidly once we consider the consequences. The most immediate results would be extraordinary instability in the party system. For as soon as people changed their minds or the party changed its position, vast numbers of its adherents would leave. Great swings in party strength might take place, leaving the minority party on occasion virtually without representation. Or, alternatively, fearing great unpopularity, parties would never change their views about anything. Who, then, would take on the burdens of party opposition? Who would take the lead in introducing rival policies to compete for public favor?

The existence of a one-party system would be the least of our troubles. What would be the point in building up a party organization if it were doomed to come tumbling down with every significant change of opinion? None at all. So the function of nominating and electing candidates would become a matter for shifting groups of individuals varying from issue to issue and place to place. Naturally, those groups with the best organizations, the most money, and the greatest interest in the policies of the day would predominate. No longer would it be possible to use party identification as a shortcut, as a means of reducing costs of acquiring information about candidates. Unless voters spent most of their time finding out precisely what officeholders were doing, they would have little idea how to vote. Nevertheless, their votes might be more important to them because the dizzying alternation of policy would have created such political chaos that normal patterns of life would be disrupted. We need go no further to make the point that the existence of a hard core of party adherents who do not easily switch party allegiance from year to year provides an element of stability for the party system and thus for the whole political system as well. Paradoxically, the attempt to make issues all-important as a means of increasing the rationality of public decisions greatly decreases the chances for making any sort of meaningful decisions at all.

Party platforms written by the presidential parties should be understood not as ends in themselves but as means to obtaining and holding public office. It would be strange indeed if one party found policies like Social Security and unemployment compensation to be enormously popular and yet refused to incorporate them into its platform.[46] This would have to be a party of ideologues who cared everything about their pet ideas and nothing about winning elections. Nor would it profit them much since they would never get elected and never be in a position to do something about their ideas. Eventually, ideologues have to make the choice between pleasing themselves and pleasing others.

Actually, party platforms do change over a period of time in a cyclical movement. The differences between the parties may be great for one or two elections until innovations made by one party are picked up by the other. The net change from one decade to the next, however, is substantial. Let us begin when platforms are more or less alike. Their similarity begins to give way as it appears that certain demands in society are not being met. The minority party of the period senses an opportunity to gain votes by articulating and promising to meet these demands. The majority party, reluctant to let go of a winning combination, resists. In one or two elections the minority party makes its bid and makes the appropriate changes in its platforms. Then, in the ensuing elections, if the party that has changed its platform loses, it drops the innovation. If it wins, however, and wins big, the other party then seeks to take over what seem to be its most popular planks, and the platforms become more and more alike again.

We can see this cycle clearly in the New Deal period. The 1932 Democratic platform, though hinting at change, was much like the Republican, especially in its emphasis on balancing the budget. A great difference in platforms could be noted in 1936 as the Democrats made a bid to consolidate the New Deal and the Republicans stood pat. The spectacular Democratic triumph signaled the end of widely divergent platforms. By 1940 the Republicans had concluded that they could not continue to oppose the welfare state wholesale if they ever wished to win again. By 1952 the parties had come much closer to each other as the Republicans adopted most of the New Deal. Though the platforms of the major parties were similar to each other in both 1932 and 1952, the differences between 1932 and 1952 for either party were enormous.[47]

Sometimes, reformers deplore what they regard as an excessive amount of mud-slinging in campaigns, but they also ask that differences among the major parties be sharply increased in order to give the voters a clear choice. The two ideas are incompatible to some extent. It would be surprising indeed if the parties disagreed more sharply about more and more subjects in an increasingly gentlemanly way. A far more likely outcome would be an increase in vituperation as the stakes of campaigns increased, passions rose, tempers flared, and the consequences of victory for the other side appeared much more threatening than had heretofore been the case. The 1936 campaign is a good case in point.

Those who claim American elections are a fraud and wish to see great things decided in these contests often point to Great Britain as a shining example of the right way to do things. There, in that wiser country, where the fires of class warfare are held (fortunately) to burn more fiercely, the voters have real choices. They vote a government in or out, and the victorious party goes about making great changes in order to carry out its mandate.

This tale may be a pretty one, according to one's taste for conflict, but it is quite exaggerated. The truth is that it occurs every once in a great while, much as American party platforms present sharp and profound differences about that often. Such was the case in 1945 when the Labour party staged its great bid to bring the full welfare state to Britain and to nationalize what it could. The overwhelming Labour victory did its work. The Conservatives soon decided to adopt all the most popular parts of the Labour party program—medicare, increased pensions—and left Labour holding the unpopular bag of nationalization. By 1955 the two major parties in Britain were presenting much the same program. By 1958 the only difference we could find was that Labour offered sixpence more on the pension. Most of the time, in fact, in Britain as in the United States, the great parties lean toward the undivided middle.[48]

Is Party Reform Relevant?

Even if reform were successful and the political system did not suffer detrimental effects such as we have outlined, many of the problems at which reform is aimed still would not be closer to solution. Thus, it can be argued that the achievement of party government is beside the point.

Can we say, for example, that the present system shows marked or widespread party incoherence in Congress? This is perhaps an overstated problem for, in fact, on roll call voting and in many other matters party allegiance is the strongest cohesive force in Congress. It has been demonstrated that party is stronger than other bases of allegiance, stronger than sectionalism, rural versus urban, native-born versus foreign-born.[49] Party cohesion depends, to be sure, on the nature of the issue. On the organization of Congress itself and on patronage matters, each party is aligned 100 percent against the other. On a significant number of issues there is widespread agreement among members of both parties, a situation that, because it limits and focuses conflict, is usually regarded as desirable. Some issues like race relations may split each of the parties down the middle. On the economic and welfare issues, where the general label of "liberal" is commonly attributed to Democrats and "conservative" to Republicans, cohesion, while not perfect, is high; the labels make sense. If we look at votes on public housing, medical care for the aged, private versus public power, and so on, we can discover that a preponderant majority of both parties takes opposing views. Cohesion does exist and it is important. Since it is not perfect, however, and one party rarely has an overwhelming advantage, it is often necessary to gain some votes from the opposing party in order to make up a majority. Party, therefore, cannot properly be viewed as a drag on unified policy-making. It is most often a force making for greater cohesion than would be the case without it. By itself, it does not supply all the agreement necessary for the making of policy, but party supplies much of the means for mobilizing lawmaking majorities. In the American context of separated and fragmented powers, based on a population divided along many lines, this is no small accomplishment.

Consider now the realm of foreign policy, where decisions made at any moment literally involve our survival and possibly that of the human race. How would policy government help us? The answer, presumably, is that the United States government would be able to follow more consistent, less internally contradictory policies and that these would lead to happier results. This assumes first that inconsistent policies are, in themselves, undesirable, a proposition that has never been convincingly demonstrated. In fact, inconsistency, "imbalance," and incoherence may in many instances be beneficial because of the necessity for satisfying a variety of diverse interests both at home and abroad through various policies of the government. By pursuing inconsistency in its policies the government often gains the legitimacy and support that are necessary to govern at all. A second assumption of the reformers is that the lack of party cohesion has been a major problem in foreign affairs. But this is simply not the case. In fact, it appears that virtually every major policy initiative of a president in the last twenty years—the blockade of Cuba, the Marshall Plan, NATO, the Eisenhower Doctrine, the Gulf of Tonkin Resolution, intervention in Korea and Vietnam, nonintervention in Indochina in 1954—has been supported by Congress, in most cases promptly and enthusiastically. When dissent appears, as it has in regard to policy toward Southeast Asia, it is a manifestation of a pervasive lack of trust between president and people, not merely between members of the same party. Dissent, moreover, comes as often from members of the president's own party as from the opposition; therefore dissent on foreign affairs is not a consequence of the party system, unless reformers seriously contemplate a system where foreign policy dissent from within the president's party is forbidden. To the contrary, it appears to us that dissent on foreign affairs—even from members of a president's own party—is not as unpopular with liberal reformers as it once was.

The difficulties facing the United States may be traced to causes for which the party system cannot be blamed. The rise of the Soviet Union and Communist China as great powers generally hostile to America, nationalist revolutions all over the world, the breakup of colonialism, the creation of weapons of unparalleled destructiveness —all these developments have neither been hastened nor delayed by the character of our party system. American makers of foreign policy have found that they could not solve problems associated with these global issues primarily because of the enormous difficulties involved, not because Congress refused to accept the correct policies. Presidents and secretaries of state today find that the world is intractable; there are so many things they can do little or nothing about. They have to deal with a worldwide range of problems, make decisions of enormous technical complexity, gain consent of allies with differing interests, take account of huge forces arrayed against them, all largely outside the help or the hindrance the party system can give them. If only they can decide what to do, if only their policies prove viable, they can expect to be strongly supported frequently on a bipartisan basis. It would be pure fantasy to claim that our presidents and their advisers have had wonderful ideas for making the world a better place only to have them frustrated by lack of ability to command support within their own party in Congress.

The chief executive has unique opportunities for leadership in foreign affairs. His is the single most commanding voice in the nation. He is visible above all others. He has the information, the opportunity to deal with foreign governments, the formal powers, and the acknowledged right to lead. Others may clamor, but in the post–Second World War environment, at least, he is the one who will be heard. All of us are dependent upon the president for guidance in a fantastically complicated world where our personal experience rarely proves a reliable guide. Perhaps this is why the president's popularity rises sharply whenever he acts in an international crisis, even in cases like the invasions of Cuba and Cambodia and the Suez crisis, which were, from our point of view, disasters.[50] Rather than seeing danger in our president's being thwarted by hostile Congresses, the more likely danger is that few, except the president, will have much to say about the most vital foreign policy decisions which may have to be made in a terribly short time.

Perhaps the most significant area with impact on foreign policy in which some contradiction among party policies appears is in the area of tariffs.[51] The United States seeks the stability of nations like Japan, on the one hand, and sets up tariff barriers which may help undermine this stability on the other. Interests that find themselves disadvantaged seek a sympathetic hearing in Congress, whose members are less attuned to global foreign policy considerations than is the president.

It would not, in any event, be surprising if governments were concerned about protecting the interests of domestic industries to some extent. Looking at nations like Britain, France, and Germany, whose governments can command automatic support in their parliaments, we find that they are also interested in protecting their domestic industries and the workers who depend on them. The negotiations on the Common Market made this abundantly clear. If party government, let us say, on the British model were suddenly to appear in the United States, there would still be the necessity of bargaining with interests within the majority party, and no one doubts that the impact of tariff levels on industry would have to be considered. The United States has, for the most part, been moving toward a tariff position more consonant with its foreign policy objectives. At least we have done no worse than other democratic nations with different party systems.

When we turn to Great Britain, where policy government has long been established, we do not find that ability to command a certain majority in the House of Commons helps prime ministers solve foreign policy problems better than presidents. In fact, the most notorious example of failure of democratic leadership in recent times comes not from the United States but from Great Britain. There, in the 1930s, Stanley Baldwin and Neville Chamberlain led their country to the brink of ruin when they failed to inform the people of the growing danger of Nazi Germany, partly because they thought their people were profoundly pacifist and would defeat them at the polls. These men were patriots who wished their country well; they had devoted their lifetimes to its service. Had they realized the full implications of their actions or failures to act, they undoubtedly would have done otherwise. Uncertain of the course of events, prone to underestimate the fury of their foes abroad, they allowed themselves to be swayed by the notion that the people would not stand for the truth, no matter how essential that truth was. Surely the existence of a cohesive party system, with sharp policy differences between the parties, did nothing to avoid this disaster. If anything, party cohesion permitted Baldwin and Chamberlain to proceed with impunity despite attacks leveled by Churchill and others who vainly sought to alert the nation. So strong was party unity that it took the calamitous events of 1940, threatening the very existence of the nation, to bring about a change in government.

Policy government is not, however, irrelevant for purposes of domestic politics, and we will want to define more precisely its likely impact. But before we proceed, it is necessary to modify the policy government proposals so that they are more defensible. For so long as proponents of policy government insist that the parties be both responsive to popular will and extremely far apart on many policies, the contradictions in this approach do grave damage to the consistency and validity of their proposals. Let us agree to modify the reformers' proposals by stating that the major presidential parties should be able to propose coherent policies to the electorate and to carry them out after they assume office, regardless of whether their policies are or are not similar.

Now we are in a position to write a sort of profit-and-loss statement on what would be involved in the realm of domestic politics if policy government were instituted. The benefits would accrue almost entirely to liberals (and the interests they represent) with superior access to the president who would have a better chance of securing the enactment of the welfare and civil rights measures they prefer. Conservatives would stand to lose their power and their policy preferences as their congressional bastions were weakened if not rendered wholly useless. Liberals in Congress would gain more of their preferred policies but their power, as congressmen, would suffer as Congress lost power. Where the present system enables them to maintain their power as congressmen while achieving some of their policies, they would have to choose between power and their other preferences under policy government. People who prefer more welfare policies and a traditionally powerful Congress would have to weigh their competing preferences carefully. Beyond this point we see dimly at best. In order to achieve somewhat greater party cohesion on domestic affairs we would risk an unspecified increase in social conflict and a somewhat greater likelihood of producing splinter parties. What the citizen has to decide is whether the benefits are worth the costs.

We think that the supporters of policy government overestimate by far the magnitude of the problem from their own viewpoint. It is not true that the parties are basically lacking in cohesion and certainly not true that no welfare legislation is passed by Congress. What is true is that medical care for the aged, aid to education, and greater attention to problems besetting urban areas have had a rough road in Congress. The recent passage of much forward-looking legislation dealing with these problems weakens the argument that there was a serious need for basic reform of the party system. It seems excessive to us to contemplate far-reaching changes in the party system which are exceedingly difficult to achieve and whose desirability is at least questionable, when there are much less drastic and much more desirable means available for securing the kinds of legislation the proponents of policy government want so badly.

A basic difficulty is that the policy government people have been so enchanted with the mystique of the presidency, and so annoyed with Congress, that they do not perceive the excellent opportunities available to them for altering the pattern of legislation. Let us consider some of the activities that have brought results:

1. Apportionment is now equitable, at least in terms of population, and consequently metropolitan areas have received greater representation in Congress.
2. Liberal strongholds in the cities have begun to supply congressional candidates who are making careers out of service in Congress, rather than regarding their service as a stepping-stone toward a judgeship or some other such position. Progress in this direction since 1958 has meant that conservatives no longer enjoy their former superiority of seniority, skill, and dedication.
3. Party leaders have paid more attention to the distribution of congressional committee positions so that liberal majorities on crucial committees may be more readily achieved. In the last decade, the start of nearly every Congress has provided important examples of this process at work.
4. Strategies have been developed which show the mass of people, especially urban people, the stake they have in legislation and which

bring home to them the importance of presenting their views to their congressmen.

No doubt it seems easier to talk blithely about a revolution in the party system than actually to do something to increase the support that the mass of people give to legislation presumed to benefit them. Action in any one or all of these directions, in our opinion, does more to secure "liberal" legislation than talking about policy government or taking actions that are bound to be futile. Knowing what we know now, we can well understand why the clamor for congressional party reform died down after the 89th Congress passed an enormous amount of the legislation that liberals had tried so hard to get in the 1940s and 1950s. The major reason these bills passed was that the Democrats were able to elect an extraordinary majority (particularly in the House) in 1964. Indirectly, of course, Barry Goldwater's candidacy was responsible for putting enough liberal Democrats in Congress to complete virtually the entire New Deal. It should also be said, however, that years of effort, begun half a decade before, that altered the composition of crucial congressional committees were also important in securing this result.

Most of the reforms suggested by students of the party system are, we believe, designed to give greater power to liberal presidents to enact their domestic programs and to diminish, correspondingly, the power of Congress. For the conduct of foreign affairs these changes would, we believe, be largely irrelevant. With respect to the stability and inclusiveness of the two major parties themselves, the reforms might well be detrimental, because of the encouragement they might well give to splinter parties. And finally, we observe that the case for party reform has certainly not been made. The enunciation of large national problems does not in and of itself demonstrate the linkage of these problems to the party system. The prescription of reforms does not in and of itself provide the strategy or the power or the inducements to carry them out.

Notes

1. There are many examples of the party reform school of thought. See, for example, Woodrow Wilson, *Congressional Government* (Boston, 1889); Henry Jones

Ford, *The Rise and Growth of American Politics* (New York, 1898); A. Lawrence Lowell, *Public Opinion and Popular Government* (New York, 1913); William MacDonald, *A New Constitution for a New America* (New York, 1921); William Y. Elliott, *The need for Constitutional Reform* (New York, 1935); Schattschneider, *Party Government*; Henry Hazlitt, *A New Constitution Now* (New York, 1942); Thomas K. Finletter, *Can Representative Government Do the Job?* (New York, 1945); James M. Burns, *Congress on Trial* (New York, 1949); Committee on Political Parties, American Political Science Association, *Toward a More Responsible Two-Party System* (New York, 1950); Stephen K. Bailey, *The Condition of Our National Political Parties* (New York, 1959); and James M. Burns, *The Deadlock of Democracy* (Englewood Cliffs, N.J., 1963). The work of the Committee on Political Parties, representing the collective judgment of a panel of distinguished political scientists in 1950, is the statement we shall refer to most often.

2. Committee on Political Parties, *Toward a More Responsible Two-Party System*, p. 1.

3. Ibid., p. 66.

4. Ibid., p. 15.

5. A sample of this literature might include Herring, *The Politics of Democracy*; Herbert Agar, *The Price of Union* (Boston, 1950); Malcolm C. Moos, *Politics, Presidents and Coattails* (Baltimore, 1952); Ranney and Kendall, *Democracy and the American Party System*; David B. Truman, *The Governmental Process* (New York, 1953); John Fischer, "Unwritten Rules of American Politics," *Harper's*, November 1948, pp. 27–36; Peter Drucker, "A Key to American Politics: Calhoun's Pluralism," *Review of Politics* 10 (October 1948), pp. 412–26; Ernest F. Griffith, *Congress: Its Contemporary Role* (New York, 1951); Murray Stedman and Herbert Sonthoff, "Party Responsibility: A Critical Inquiry," *Western Political Quarterly* 4 (September 1951), pp. 454–86; Julius Turner, "Responsible Parties: A Dissent from the Floor," *American Political Science Review* 45 (March 1951), pp. 143–52; William Goodman, "How Much Political Party Centralization Do We Want?" *The Journal of Politics* 13 (November 1961), pp. 536–61; and Austin Ranney, *The Doctrine of Responsible Party Government* (Urbana, Ill., 1954).

6. Herring, *The Politics of Democracy*, p. 327.

7. Ibid., p. 420.

8. Committee on Political Parties, *Toward a More Responsible Two-Party System*, p. 19.

9. Bailey, *The Condition of Our National Political Parties*, p. 20.

10. This is, of course, not at all uncommon. See, for instance, examples in Bauer, Pool, and Dexter, *American Business and Public Policy*, Chapters 16, 18, and 19; Donald E. Stokes and Warren E. Miller, "Party Government and the Saliency of Congress," *Public Opinion Quarterly* 26 (Winter 1962), pp. 531–46; Jacob K. Javits, "How I Used a Poll in Campaigning for Congress," *Public Opinion Quarterly* 11 (Summer 1947), pp. 222–26.

11. For strong evidence on this point, see Stouffer, *Communism, Conformity and Civil Liberties*, passim, and Woodward and Roper, "Political Activity of American Citizens," *American Political Science Review* 44 (December 1950), pp. 872–75.

12. Much of this section is adapted from Aaron B. Wildavsky, "On the Superiority of National Conventions," *Review of Politics* 24 (July 1962), pp. 307–19.

13. See V. O. Key, Jr., *American State Politics* (New York, 1956), Chapter 6.

14. Key, *Southern Politics*, e.g., Chapter 3 (Alabama) and Chapter 9 (Arkansas).

15. Key, *American State Politics*, p. 216.

16. See Stanwood, *A History of the Presidency from 1788 to 1897*, pp. 125–41.

17. A classic statement is Ostrogorski, *Democracy and the Party System in the United States*, pp. 158–60. See also Elmo Roper, "What Price Conventions?" *Saturday Review*, September 3, 1960, 26.

18. The most famous account is still Ostrogorski, *Democracy and the Party System in the United States*, pp. 141–42.

19. At least one representative of the media apparently feels as we do about this problem. Walter Cronkite argues that "it is not necessary that we be admitted to the actual floor of the convention. There is a better way (such as the use of immediate off-floor interview booths) to cover the non-podium action in order to permit a more orderly convention procedure." *The Challenges of Change* (Washington, D.C., 1971), p. 75.

20. McClosky, Hoffman, and O'Hara, "Issue Conflict and Consensus among Party Leaders and Followers," pp. 406–27. Jeane Kirkpatrick's study, "Representation in National Political Conventions," offers strong evidence of the gap between Democratic party elites and rank and file at the 1972 convention.

21. *New York Times*, July 16, 1964, p. 1.

22. Stanley Kelley, Jr., Richard E. Ayres, and William G. Bowen, "Registration and Voting: Putting First Things First," *American Political Science Review* 61 (June 1967), p. 362.

23. The general outline of this argument has been known in this country for at least fifty years. For example, in 1924, Harold G. Gosnell wrote, "In the European countries studied, a citizen who is entitled to vote does not, as a rule, have to make any effort to see that his name is on the list of eligible voters. The inconvenience of registering for voting in this country has caused many citizens to become non-voters." *Why Europe Votes* (Chicago, 1930), p. 185.

24. In *Registration 1960: Key to Democratic Victory?* (unpublished senior thesis, Princeton University, 1964), cited in Kelley, Ayres, and Bowen, "Registration and Voting: Putting First Things First," p. 375, Richard E. Ayres cites the correlation between convenience of registration and percent of the vote for the Democratic party as proof of the Daley machine's awareness of this phenomenon. By making registration extremely convenient, the State of Utah has succeeded in getting nearly total registration. See "Registration Procedures in the State of Utah," *Election Laws of the Fifty States and the District of Columbia* (Washington, D.C., Library of Congress Legislative Reference Service, June 1968), pp. 247–48. Similarly, Edmond Costantini and Willis Hawley estimate that turnout in California could be raised by more than 5 percent simply by keeping registration open until the last week before the election. "Increasing Participation in California Elections: The Need for Electoral Reform," *Public Affairs Report* 10, Bulletin of the Institute of Governmen-

tal Studies (June 1969). A 1968 registration figure of 97.8 percent was attained by holding registrations open until the Wednesday before the election (when political interest, which would stimulate the voter to register and which would stimulate the party activists to get him registered, is highest) and by having publicized locations in every district.

25. Kelley, Ayres, and Bowen, "Registration and Voting: Putting First Things First," p. 373.

26. The latest suggestions for a comprehensive program along these lines are from the Freedom to Vote Task Force of the Democratic National Committee, *That All May Vote* (Washington, D.C., 1969) and are embodied in House and Senate bills: The Universal Voter Enrollment Act of 1970 (House Resolution 19010 and Senate 4238). See the statement by Representative Morris Udall in the *Congressional Record*, August 13, 1970, pp. H8319–32.

27. Citizens Voter Registration Campaign, "Final Report" (mimeo, New York, September 3, 1969). See also Freedom to Vote Task Force, *That All May Vote*.

28. Kelley, Ayres, and Bowen, "Registration and Voting: Putting First Things First," pp. 374–75.

29. Ibid., p. 363.

30. Recent evidence shows, for example, that white youth who have not attended college are much more conservative on stylistic questions than are their peers with higher education. See the issue of *Esquire* (January 1970) devoted to this question. In general, young people divide more or less as their elders do, except more of them are neutral or undecided. See Jerald G. Bachman and Elizabeth Van Duinen, *Youth Looks at National Problems* (Ann Arbor, 1971), especially Table 3–2, p. 33, which shows the results from three surveys of teenagers conducted in 1970:

Michigan Survey 19-Year-Old Males		Purdue Study High-School Seniors		Harris Survey 15–21-Year-Old Youths	
(percent)		*(percent)*			*(percent)*
Republican	21	Republican	14	Republican	18
Democratic	32	Democratic	26	Democratic	35
Haven't Thought		Wallace A.I.P.	7	Wallace	4
About It	20	No Difference	18	Other or	
Neutral	14	Undecided	30	Not Sure	40
Other	6	Missing Data	5	Will Refuse	
Missing Data	7			to Vote	3

31. *New York Times*, "Poll Finds Residency Rules Cut Vote of Young and Democrats," December 6, 1969. Most universal automatic voter enrollment programs include a provision whereby the enrollee can at least vote for president even if he has moved within the week before election. For example, see Freedom to Vote Task Force, *That All May Vote*.

32. *U.S.* v. *Arizona*, 91 S. Ct. 260 (1970).

33. William G. Andrews, "American Voting Participation," *Western Political Quarterly* 19 (1966), p. 643.

34. Although we know of no effort to review the situation, there seems no compelling reason why felons—"ex-" or otherwise—should be denied the ballot.

Voting may be a small way of maintaining their connection with society. Their ability to vote should make politicians more interested in their welfare, including the structure and management of penal institutions. The view that loss of the right to vote penalizes would-be felons and is, therefore, a deterrent to crime is hardly worth considering.

35. There were, of course, many other plans for "reform," involving almost all possible combinations of these three alternatives. For example, President Nixon at one point recommended that the 40 percent plurality plank which usually goes with the direct election proposal be applied instead to the present Electoral College setup (*Washington Post*, March 14, 1969, p. A2). A second example is the "federal system plan" of Senators Dole and Eagleton, which states:

(1) A president would be elected if he (a) won a plurality of the national vote and (b) won *either* pluralities in more than 50 percent of the states and D.C., *or* pluralities in states with 50 percent of the voters in the election.

(2) If no candidate qualified, the election would go to an Electoral College where the states would be represented as they are today, and each candidate would automatically receive the electoral votes of the states he won.

(3) In the unlikely event that no candidate received a majority of the electoral votes, the electoral votes of states that went for third-party candidates would be divided between the two leading national candidates in proportion to their share of the popular votes in those states. (*Congressional Record*, March 5, 1970, p. S3026).

These plans have the following characteristics: (a) They are too complicated to solve any problems of public confusion or public perception that they are not "democratic." (b) They have no significant body of congressional support.

36. *Baker* v. *Carr*, 369 U.S. 186 (1962); *Wesberry* v. *Sanders*, 376 U.S. 1 (1964); and *Reynolds* v. *Sims*, 377 U.S. 533 (1964).

37. Because numbers games are such an important part of electoral reform debates, it is perhaps worth buttressing the argument about the benefits of the present system with figures. The clearest way to see who the most powerful voters are in the current system is to divide the number of electoral votes a state has into the margin of victory in that state; this is a measure of the citizen's likelihood to swing electoral votes with his vote. In 1968, the last close election, this ratio was lowest for the smallest states (Nevada, 4,300:1; Delaware, 2,700:1; and Alaska, 700:1) and the largest states (Texas, 1,600:1; Ohio, 3,500:1; California, 5,600:1). It was highest for the middle-sized states, with electoral votes in the 7 to 14 range (Louisiana, 22,100:1; Kansas, 25,000:1; Minnesota 19,900:1).

38. For example, Ed Gossett, original cosponsor of the district plan, asked, "Is it fair, is it honest, is it democratic, is it to the best interests of anyone in fact to place such a premium on a few thousand labor votes or Italian votes or Irish votes or Negro votes or Jewish votes or Polish votes, or Communist votes or big city machine votes, simply because they happen to be located in two or three industrial pivotal states? Can anything but evil come from placing such temptation and power in the hands of political parties and political bosses? Both said groups and said politicians are corrupted as a nation suffers." Cited in David Brook, "Proposed Electoral College Reforms and Urban Minorities," paper delivered at the annual meeting of the American Political Science Association, 1969, p. 6.

39. In "The South Will Not Rise Again Through Direct Election of the President, Polsby and Wildavsky Notwithstanding," *Journal of Politics* 31 (August 1969), pp. 808–11, Professor Harvey Zeidenstein shows that the winner's margin of victory in eight large northern urban states—taken together—was greater than in the eleven states of the old Confederacy—taken together—in four of the six presidential elections between 1948 and 1968. From this he concludes that the influence of northern urban states, where the votes are, is likely to be very great under a system of direct elections. We agree, but we argue in the text that direct elections do improve the strategic position of one-party states (including some southern states), as compared with the Electoral College winner-take-all system. On this issue Zeidenstein is silent.

40. On September 18, 1969, by a vote of 339 to 70, a direct election plan with a 40 percent plurality runoff provision was passed by the U.S. House of Representatives. See *Congressional Record*, September 18, 1969, pp. H8142–43; for the content of the bill, see *Congressional Record*, September 10, 1969, pp. H7745–46.

41. The Michigan Survey Research Center finds that only 1.5 percent of the voters had felt that Senator Eugene McCarthy was the best man for president in the spring and still felt that way after the election, but if all participants in the system had known that he was not going to be defeated and disappear but would be a serious candidate at least through the first election, it is at least possible to conjecture that he could have picked up an additional 4 percent or 5 percent. Converse, Miller, Rusk, and Wolfe, "Continuity and Change in American Politics: Parties and Issues in the 1968 Election," p. 1092. Cf. Richard N. Goodwin, "Reflections: Sources of the Public Unhappiness," *The New Yorker*, January 4, 1969, pp. 38–58.

42. The article that deals most clearly with the Electoral College in terms of its virtues of conciliation and of broad coalition-building is John Wildenthal, "Consensus after L.B.J.," *Southwest Review* 53 (Spring 1968). Wildenthal argues in part, "Rather than complain about being deprived of a choice when both parties wage 'me too' campaigns, the American people should be thankful that the interests of a wide variety of Americans can be reconciled by both parties with similar programs."

43. One summary of this position is given by Representative Thomas Kleppe of North Dakota in the *Congressional Record*, February 3, 1969, p. H648. An interesting sidelight, and a tribute to the change of perspective a change of office can bring, is his citation of Senator John F. Kennedy, who said, "After all, the states came into the Union as units. Electoral votes are not given out on the basis of voting numbers, but on the basis of population. The electoral votes belong to each state. The way the system works now is that we carry on a campaign in fifty states, and the electoral votes of that state belong to that party which carries each state. If we are going to change that system, it seems to me it would strike a blow at states rights in major proportions. It would probably end states rights and make this country one great unit."

44. Roscoe Drummond, "Perils of the Electoral System," *Washington Post*, November 14, 1960. An argument in some ways parallel to our own is contained in Anthony Lewis, "The Case against Electoral Reform," *The Reporter*, December 8,

1960. See also Allan P. Sindler, "Presidential Election Methods and Urban-Ethnic Interests," *Law and Contemporary Problems*, Spring 1962, pp. 213–33.

45. See Estes Kefauver, "The Electoral College: Old Reforms Take a New Look," *Law and Contemporary Problems*, Spring 1962, p. 197.

46. Despite popular misconceptions, even the 1964 Republican platform, written by supporters of Barry Goldwater, contained explicit promises to preserve these programs.

47. See Kirk H. Porter and Donald Bruce Johnson, *National Party Platforms, 1840–1956* (Urbana, Ill., 1956). There are immense differences between party platforms of both 1932 and 1952. Note, for example, the subheadings under domestic policy in the 1952 platforms dealing with a range of topics entirely missing in 1932. The Democratic 1952 platform includes subheadings on full employment, price supports, farm credit, crop insurance, rural electrification, the physically handicapped, migratory workers, river basin development, arid areas, wildlife, recreation, Social Security, unemployment insurance, public assistance, needs of our aging citizens, health, medical education, hospitals and health centers, costs of medical care, public housing, slum clearance, urban redevelopment, aid to education, school lunches, day-care facilities, specific steps under civil rights, and many other subjects completely absent in 1932. Most of these worthy causes were also supported in the 1952 Republican platform and were missing from the 1932 Republican platform. Nevertheless, there are differences *between* the parties in 1952 in regard to use of the public lands, public housing, labor legislation, farm legislation, public power, aid to education, and much more. In regard to education, for example, the 1952 Republican platform reads: "The tradition of popular education, tax-supported and free to all, is strong with our people. The responsibility for sustaining this system of popular education has always rested upon the local communities and the states. We subscribe fully to this principle." The corresponding Democratic plank reads in part: "Local, State, and Federal governments have shared responsibility to contribute appropriately to the pressing needs of our education system. . . . We pledge immediate consideration for those school systems which need further legislation to provide Federal aid for a new school construction, teachers' salaries and school maintenance and repair" (pp. 504, 485). See also Gerald M. Pomper, "If Elected, I Promise: American Party Platforms," Chapter 7 of *Elections in America* (New York, 1973), pp. 149–78.

48. This is one of the main conclusions of Arnold Rogow, *The Labour Government and British Industry* (Oxford, 1955).

49. See Julius Turner, *Party and Constituency: Pressures on Congress* (Baltimore, 1951), and David B. Truman, *The Congressional Party* (New York, 1959).

50. For a general discussion of presidential control of foreign policy, see Aaron Wildavsky, "The Two Presidencies," *Transaction* 4 (December 1966), pp. 7–14.

51. See Bauer, Pool, and Dexter, *American Business and Public Policy*, pp. 9–79.

CHAPTER SEVEN

American
Parties
and
Democracy

Because the American political system is moving toward a role for political parties that stresses their activities as policy advocates, it seems to us important to discuss at length the implications of this trend for democratic government. Our argument makes two main points. The first is that it is necessary for parties of advocacy in a democracy to receive mandates on public policy from majorities of convinced believers in their programs, but that this condition is not met in America because of the ways in which electorates actually participate in elections and conceive of public policy.

Our second point is that in view of the actual disposition of attitudes toward public policy in the electorate as compared with party elites, the fact that we are moving toward parties of advocacy poses some significant and largely unmet problems for American democracy. It is not the policy preferences of the electorate that are being advocated.

Elections and Public Policy

No doubt uncoerced and competitive elections aid in making the political system open and responsive to a great variety of people and groups in the population. But it would not be correct to say that our elections transmit unerringly the policy preferences of electorate to leaders or confer mandates upon leaders with regard to specific policies. Consider the presidential landslide of 1972, which resulted in a Republican president and a Democratic Congress. Or the Democratic landslide of 1964, when the two major presidential candidates also had divergent, sharp, and consistent policy differences. Two years later, in the election of 1966, the Republicans regained much of the ground in Congress that they had lost. Even in a landslide the mandate is at best a temporary, equivocal matter. And in any case elections that are as clear-cut as these are rare.

It is easy to be cynical and expect too little from elections or to be euphoric and expect too much from them. A cynical view would hold that the United States was ruled by a power elite—a small group outside the democratic process. Under these circumstances the ballot would be a sham and a delusion. What difference can it make how voting is carried on or who wins if the nation is actually governed by other means? On the other hand, a euphoric view, holding that the United States is ruled as a mass democracy with equal control over decisions by all or most citizens, would enormously magnify the importance of the ballot. Through the act of casting a ballot, it could be argued, a majority of citizens determine major national policies. What happens at the polls not only decides who occupies public office; it also determines the content of specific policy decisions. In a way, public office would then be a sham because the power of decision in important matters would be removed from the hands of public officials. A third type of political system in which numerous minorities compete for shares in policy-making within broad limits provided by free elections has more complex implications. It suggests that balloting is important but that it does not often determine individual policy decisions. The ballot both guides and constrains public officials who are free to act within fairly broad limits subject to anticipated responses of the voters and to the desires of the other active participants.

In fact, it is evident that the American political system is of this third type. Public officials do make major policy decisions but elections matter in that they determine which of two competing parties holds public office. In a competitive two-party situation such as exists in American presidential politics, the lively possibility of change provides an effective incentive for political leaders to remain in touch with followers.

But it would be inaccurate to suggest that voters in presidential elections transmit their policy preferences to elected officials with a high degree of reliability. There are few clear mandates in our political system because elections are fought on so many issues and in so many incompletely overlapping constituencies. Often the voters elect officials to Congress and to the presidency who disagree on public policies. Thus mandates are not only impossible to identify, but even if they could be identified they might well be impossible to enact because of inconsistency in the instructions issued to officials who must agree on legislation.[1]

Presidential elections are not referenda. The relationship between presidential elections and policies is a great deal subtler than the relations between the outcomes of referenda and the policies to which they pertain. In theory, the American political system is designed to work like this: Two teams of politicians, one in office, the other seeking office, both attempt to get enough votes to win elections. In order to win, they go to various groups of voters and, by offering to pursue policies favored by these groups, hope to attract their votes. If there were only one office-seeking team, their incentive to respond to the policy preferences of groups in the population would diminish; if there were many such teams, the chances that any one of them could achieve a sufficient number of backers to govern would diminish. Hence the two-party system is regarded as a kind of compromise between the goals of responsiveness and effectiveness.

The proponents of a different theory would say that elections give the winning party a mandate to carry out the policies proposed during the campaign. Only in this way, they maintain, is popular rule through the ballot meaningful. A basic assumption in this argument is that the voters (or at least a majority of them) approve of all or most of the policies presented by the victorious candidate. No doubt this is plausible, but not in the sense intended because as we have seen, a vote for a presidential candidate is usually merely an expression of a party habit; particular policy directions are not necessarily implied in the vote. Most voters in the United States are not ideologically oriented. That is, they do not see or make connections among issues. They do not seek to create or to adopt coherent systems of thought in which issues are related to one another in some logical pattern. If this is the case, then voters can hardly be said to transmit preferences for particular policies by electing candidates to public office.

Other basic objections to the idea that our elections are designed to confer mandates on specific public policies may also be raised. First, the issues debated in the campaign may not be the ones in which most voters are interested. These issues may be ones that interest the candidates, that they want to stress, or that interest segments of the press; but there is no clear reason to believe that any particular issue is of great concern to voters just because it gets publicity. Time and again, voting studies have demonstrated that what appear to be the major issues of a campaign turn out not to be significant for most of the electorate. In 1952, for example, three great Republican themes were communism, Korea, and corruption. It turned out that the communism issue, given perhaps the most publicity, had virtually no impact. Democrats simply would not believe that their party was the party of treason, and Republicans did not need that issue to make them vote the way they usually did. Korea and corruption were noticeable issues.[2] Yet how could anyone know, in the absence of a public opinion poll, which of the three issues were important to the voters and which constituted a mandate? There were, in any event, no significant policy differences between the parties on these issues—Democrats were also against communism and corruption and also wanted an end to the war in Korea. A broadly similar story can apparently be told, as we have seen, for more recent elections.[3]

A second reason why voting for a candidate does not necessarily signify approval of his policies is that candidates pursue many policy interests at any one time with widely varying intensity, so that they may collect support from some voters on one issue and from other voters on another. It is possible for a candidate to get 100 percent of the votes and still have every voter opposed to most of his policies, as well as having every one of his policies opposed by most of the voters.

Assume that there are four major issues in a campaign. Make the further, quite reasonable assumption that the voting population is distributed in such a way that those people who care intensely about one major issue support the victorious candidate for that reason alone, although they differ with him mildly on the other three issues. Thus, voters who are deeply concerned about the problem of nuclear defense may vote for candidate Jones who prefers a minimum deterrence position, rather than Smith, who espouses a doctrine that requires huge retaliatory forces.[4] This particular group of voters disagrees with Jones on farm price supports, on the size of government, and on national health insurance, but they do not feel strongly about any of these matters. Another group, meanwhile, believes that farmers, the noble yeomanry, are the backbone of the nation and that if they are prosperous and strong, everything else will turn out all right. So they vote for Jones, too, although they prefer a large defense budget and disagree with Jones's other policies. And so on for other groups of voters. Jones ends up with all the votes, yet each of his policies is preferred by less than a majority of the electorate. Since this is possible in any political system where many issues are debated at election time, it is hard to argue that our presidential elections give unequivocal mandates on specific policies to the candidates who win.[5]

As we have seen, people go to the polls and vote for many reasons not directly connected with issues. They may vote on the basis of party identification alone. Party habits may be joined with a general feeling that Democrats are better for the common man or that Republicans will keep us safe—feelings too diffuse to tell us much about specific issues. Some people vote on the basis of a candidate's personality, or his "image." Others follow a friend's recommendation. Still others may be thinking about policy issues but may be all wrong in their perception of where the candidates stand. It would be difficult to distinguish the votes of these people from those who know, care, and differentiate among the candidates on the basis of issues. We do know, however, that issue-oriented persons are usually in a minority while those who cast their ballots with other things in mind are generally in the majority.

Even if there is good reason to believe that a majority of voters do approve of specific policies supported by the victorious candidate, the mandate may be difficult or impossible to carry out. A candidate may get elected for a policy he pursued or preferred in the past which has no reference to present circumstances. One could have voted Republican in 1972 because Dwight Eisenhower got rid of the rascals in the Truman administration, or possibly vote Democratic in 1976 in response to Watergate; but this does not point to any future policy that is currently in the realm of presidential discretion. "Corruption" in 1952 was a kind of issue on which there was really no way of carrying out a supposed mandate other than determining to be honest, a course of action we may be pardoned for believing that Adlai Stevenson would have followed as well. John F. Kennedy promised in 1960 to get the nation moving. This was broad enough to cover a multitude of vague hopes and aspirations. More specifically, as president, Kennedy may dearly have wished to make good this promise by increasing the rate of growth in the national economy, but no one was quite sure how to do this. Lyndon Johnson was able to make good many of his 1964 campaign promises on domestic policy, but observers after the election were hard put to distinguish his subsequent Vietnam policies from those promised by Barry Goldwater.

Leaving aside all the difficulties about the content of a mandate, there is no accepted definition of what size electoral victory gives a president special popular sanction to pursue any particular policy. Would a 60 percent victory be sufficient? This is rarely achieved. Does 55 percent seem reasonable? What about 51 percent or 52 percent, however, or the cases in which the winner receives less than half of the votes cast? And is it right to ignore the multitudes who do not vote and whose preferences are not directly registered? One might ignore the nonvoters for the purpose of this analysis if they divided in their preferences between candidates in nearly the same proportions as those who do vote. But they often do not. In practice, this problem is easily solved. Whoever wins the election is allowed to pursue whatever policies he pleases, within the substantial constraints imposed by the checks and balances of the rest of the political system. This, in the end, is all that a "mandate" is in American politics.

Opinion polls may help the politician gauge policy preferences, but there are always lingering doubts as to the polls' reliability; it is not certain in any event that they tell the political leader what he needs to know. People who really have no opinion may give one just to satisfy the interviewer. People who have an opinion but who care little may be counted equally with those who are intensely concerned. Many people giving opinions may have no intention of voting for some politicians who heed them, no matter what. The result may be that the politician will get no visible support from a majority that agrees with him, but instead he will get complaints from an intense minority that disagrees. The people who agree with him may not vote while those who differ may make retribution at the ballot box. Those who are pleased may be the ones who would have voted for the public official anyway. And unless the poll is carefully done, it may leave out important groups of voters, overrepresent some, underrepresent others, and otherwise give a misleading impression.

Let us turn the question around for a moment. Suppose a candidate loses office. What does this tell him about the policies he should have preferred? If there were one or two key issues widely debated and universally understood, the election may tell him a great deal. But this is seldom the case. More likely there were many issues and it was difficult to separate out those that did or did not garner support for his opponent. Perhaps the election was decided on the basis of personal images or some events in the economic cycle or a military engagement—points that were not debated in the campaign and that may not have been within anyone's control. The losing candidate may always feel that if he continues to educate the public to favor the policies he prefers, he will eventually win out. Should he lose a series of elections, however, his party would undoubtedly try to change something—policies, candidates, organization, maybe all three—in an effort to improve its fortunes.

Let us suppose that a candidate wins an election. What does this event tell him and his party about the policies he should prefer when in office? He can take it on faith that the policies he proposed during the campaign are the popular ones. Some were undoubtedly rather vague, and specific applications of them may turn out quite differently than the campaign suggested. Others may founder on the rock of practicality; they sounded fine but they simply cannot be carried out. Conditions change and policies that seemed appropriate but a few months before turn out to be irrelevant. As the time for putting policies into practice draws near, the new officeholder may discover that they generate a lot more opposition than when they were merely campaign oratory. And those policies he pursues to the end may have to be compromised considerably in order to get the support of other participants in the policy-making process. Nevertheless, if he has even a minimal policy orientation, the newly elected candidate can try to carry out a few of his campaign proposals, seeking to maintain a general direction consonant with the approach that may—he cannot be entirely certain—have contributed measurably to his election.

The practical impossibility in our political system of ascertaining mandates is one important reason why it is so difficult for parties to emphasize their function as policy advocates. It is, however, entirely possible that by rearranging the rules of the game it will be possible for parties to adopt mandates that have little or no support in the general population. It is to the exploration of this trend that we now turn.

Parties of Advocacy versus Parties of Intermediation

The presidential election process in the United States is in transition. It was only a short time ago—1952—that a president of the United States could, and with good reason, dismiss Estes Kefauver's victory in the New Hampshire primary as "eyewash." Now primaries select most convention delegates, and it is widely believed that Eugene McCarthy's loss of the New Hampshire primary in 1968, interpreted by the media as a victory, drove President Lyndon Johnson into retirement.

Behind the shift in the role of primary elections lie shifts in the roles of political activists, both candidate enthusiasts and party regulars, and changes in the powers and the significance of the news media. We believe that these changes and other changes that we have discussed—the shift to public financing not only of the general election, for example, but also of primary elections, the vast increase in the number of primaries, and the new rules for converting votes into delegates—add up to a fundamental redefinition of the place of the national political parties in our public life. One way to characterize this redefinition is to say that the conception of parties as agents of policy government has begun to prevail, and the conception of parties as agents of consensus government has begun to fade.

Purists, likewise, are favored as never before by the rules of the game and politicians disfavored. In the early days of preprimary activity, the people who become most active are apt to be those who have the most spare time, the most ideological commitment, and the most enthusiasm for one candidate above all others. Since the rules are now written to encourage activity at an earlier and earlier date, as a basis for federal subsidies during the primaries, it follows that purists will have more to say about the eventual outcome of the nomination process. Party regulars, on the other hand, who tend to wait until they can see a majority forming and who dislike the wasted resources and effort of kamikaze candidacies, are systematically disfavored by the new rules of the game, because by the time their peculiar skills and interests in majority-building are desperately needed—notably at the convention—it is too late for them to get into the process: most of the seats will have been taken by the enthusiasts for particular candidates who won in the various primaries and state conventions.

Building upon these thoughts for a moment, we can ask how the emerging structure of presidential election politics helps and hinders political parties in performing the tasks customarily allotted to them in the complex scheme of American democracy. In essence, we would argue that the parties have been greatly strengthened in their capacities to provide advocacy and weakened in their abilities to provide intermediation in the political system.

Advocacy is strengthened because the rules of the game offer incentives to those party leaders able to attract personal followings on an ideological basis. This much is clear. What is lost, in our view, is a capacity to deliberate, to weigh competing demands and to compromise so that a variety of differing interests each gain a little. This loss would not be so great if the promise of policy government —to select efficacious programs and implement them successfully— were likely to be fulfilled in performance. But, on the record so far, this is doubly doubtful.

It is doubtful because for many of the problems that form the basis of political campaign discussion—crime, racism, hostility abroad—there are no known, surefire solutions. And secondly, even if we knew what to do about more of our problems, it is unclear that, given the ways in which various forces in our society are arranged, presidents alone could deliver on their promise.

This last dilemma is especially poignant in the case of a candidate like George McGovern, who spoke to a very wide spectrum of issues. Yet he could not prevent serious errors creeping into his discussion of defense spending, and there were contradictory implications in his social programs when they were considered in the light of total spending and hence inflation and taxation. These programs, as offered by McGovern, moreover, were apparently very unpopular. Yet gaining public acceptability is part of making policies work. Policy government might enhance the legitimacy of government by increasing the effectiveness of programs, but the insensitivity of its advocates to the needs for consensus makes that unlikely. Hence neither policy nor consensus, advocacy nor intermediation, is likely to be served.

Two factors account for the decline in the vital function of intermediation by parties. First, candidates have far fewer incentives than heretofore to deal with interest groups organized on traditional lines, or with state and local party leaders. These leaders and groups have in the past provided links between national politicians and the people and have focused the hopes and energies of countless citizens upon the party organizations as meaningful entities in the nomination process. Nowadays, as we have been told by politicians as varied as Eugene McCarthy and Richard Nixon, a candidate for the presidency need no longer build up a mosaic of alliances with interest groups and party leaders. Now, through the miracle of the mass media—especially television—and through mass mailings to appeal for money, and through federal subsidy if these mass mailings are successful, candidates for the presidency can reach every home and touch every heart and claim the allegiance of followers based on symbolic appeals rather than concrete bargains.

This is the first sense in which parties have been diminished in their capacity to mediate between the desires of ordinary citizens and the policies of government. In a second sense they have lost this capacity because the formal properties of plebiscitary decision-making, such as occurs in primary elections, leave so little room for the bargaining process. Contingent choices are impossible to express straightforwardly through the ballot box. Thus a candidate who is acceptable to a sizable majority but is the first choice of only a few systematically loses out under the new rules to candidates who are unacceptable to most but secure in their control over a middle-sized fraction (20 to 30 percent, depending on how many play the game) of first-choice votes.

It is in this powerful sense that we can say that "participatory" democracy, as the American party system has begun to practice it, is inimical to "deliberative" democracy. As more (and different) people have won the right to participate in the nomination process, the kinds of communication they have been able to send to one another have become impoverished. They can vote, but they cannot bargain. They can make speeches, but they cannot deliberate.

Let us see what happens when a free spirit like George McGovern breaks through the network of old politicians and gets nominated for president. A piece of bad luck afflicts his campaign: his vice-presidential candidate has concealed a medical history that may weaken the ticket. The *New York Times* writes, "Dump Eagleton." The *Washington Post* writes, "Dump Eagleton."

What does an "old" politics candidate do? Presumably he gets on the telephone and asks around among interest group leaders, state and local party bosses. Can we stand the flak? What do the party workers think? What do *you* think? Here's what *I* think.

What does a "new" politics candidate do? Well, what choice has he? To whom can he place a telephone call other than the far-flung members of his immediate family? There is no negotiating with the editorial board of the *New York Times* in a smoke-filled room. There is no give-and-take with the "moderator" of "Meet the Press." The "moderator" gives. Politicians take.

We have no certain way of knowing whether the paradox of participation swallowing up deliberation has had the net effect of turning citizens away from political parties. It is in any event the case that by a variety of measures—nonvoting, propensity of voters to decline to identify with a political party, direct expressions of disapproval of parties—political parties have, like so many other institutions of American society, suffered substantial losses in public confidence. In our view, the most promising way for them to regain public confidence is to avoid extremist candidates and to make an effort to become more deliberatively democratic in their internal processes.

What's wrong with policy government? What could be wrong with so intuitively attractive an idea? Governments must make policies. Candidates must be judged, in part at least, on their policy preferences as well as on indications of their ability to perform when in office. Has there not been, in the recent past, too much obfuscation of issues and too little candor in speaking one's mind? Obviously our society needs more rather than less discussion of issues, greater rather than less clarification of alternatives. Equally evident, mere lust for office, pandering to the popular whims of the moment, is no qualification. Getting people together may be worse than keeping them apart if they agree on the wrong thing or, as it turns out, on nothing substantial at all.

What is wrong is that the premises upon which policy government is based are false. Most people do not want parties that make extreme appeals by taking issue positions far from the desires of the bulk of the citizenry.[6] Perhaps people feel safer if their parties give them a choice but if losing is not a catastrophe. The idea that the American people are waiting in the wings for a consistent line of policy, much different from what they are getting, has now been conclusively refuted. The Goldwater election should have destroyed the myth of the "hidden" Republican vote, and if any Democrats neglected to vote in 1972, they were McGovern's opponents, not his supporters.

Untenable, also, is the assumption that when the parties focus on their issue differences there is more intelligent debate, thus helping citizens make wiser choices. What actually happens, as exemplified by the Goldwater-Johnson election of 1964 and the Nixon-McGovern election of 1972, is that the further apart the candidates are on the issues, the less discussion and the more emotion there will be. Apparently, when the distance is too large to be bridged, the candidates shout at (rather than speak to) each other. When one of them is quickly defined as outré by most people, his opponent need not reply to his arguments in a serious way. No one will ever know how much the country suffered by failing to have a serious debate on foreign policy in 1964. Charging that Goldwater would bring atomic war didn't answer the question of what the government should do in Vietnam. Discussing the unsuitability of George McGovern was not quite the same as endorsing the fitness of Richard Nixon.

Adherents of policy government have so far managed to control only one presidential nominating convention at a time; but suppose they manage in the future to face off a right-wing Republican against a left-wing Democrat? The trends now misperceived as a product of consensus government—alienation, nonvoting—will show an alarming increase as the vast majority of citizens discover that their preferences have been disregarded and that they have nowhere to turn.

It is one thing to say that policy options have been insufficiently articulated and quite another to create conflict and develop disagreements where these did not exist before. Political activists in the United States are now more ideological and polarized than they have been since studies were first conducted in the 1930s, and possibly since the Civil War. Should ordinary citizens be compelled to choose from policy alternatives that appeal to purists or are they entitled to select from a menu closer to their tastes? The question is not whether there will be issues, for inevitably there must be, but who will set the agenda for discussion and whether this agenda will primarily reflect differences in the population or among elites. Although a full range of experiences is lacking in the United States, modern French history shows that it is possible for a nation to be kept in turmoil by differences that, though real to certain elites, have little resonance in the population as a whole.

"What's wrong with policy government" is that it conceals a justification for rule by elites who act to impose preferences presently opposed by the great majority of people. Policy government does not lead to participatory democracy, because participation does not in fact increase uniformly. It decreases in the population as a whole and increases among certain selected elites, drawn from the upper middle and upper classes, who have the time and inclination to engage in bouts of intense activity.

Thus, the rationale behind parties of advocacy leads to plebiscitary democracy. If it is not only desirable for all citizens to vote in general elections but also for them to choose candidates through preelection primaries, it must be even more desirable for them to select directly governmental policies through referenda. Instead of rule by special interests or cliques of congressmen, the public's interest would supposedly be expressed by the public. Experience with referenda in California, however, suggests that this is not quite how things work in practice. Without measures for limiting the number of referenda, citizens are swamped by the necessity of voting on hundreds of items. Elites, not the people, participate in the selection and wording of referenda. Money to arrange for signing petitions to get on the ballot becomes more meaningful than ever. The public is faced with a bewildering array of proposals, all sponsored by special interests that want a way around the legislature. To learn what is involved in a single seemingly innocuous proposal to raise somebody's salary or issue bonds takes hours of study. To understand twenty or more is unduly onerous. Is the citizen better off guessing or following the advice of the local newspaper rather than trying to choose a legislator or a party to represent his interests?

After a decade of severe internal difficulty, when confidence in virtually all national institutions suffered repeated blows, the need for consensus-building parties seems clear. Political purism might be desirable for a people homogeneous in all ways except the economic; but can a multiracial, multiethnic, multireligious, multiregional, multiclass nation like the United States sustain itself when its main agents of political action—the parties—strive to exclude rather than include, to sharpen rather than dull the edge of controversy?

It is even doubtful that the rise of parties of advocacy leads to a more principled politics. If principles are precepts that must not be violated, when contrary principles are firmly embedded in the programs of opposing parties, one man's principles necessarily become another's fighting words. A few principles, such as those enshrined in the Bill of Rights, may be helpful in establishing boundaries beyond which governmental action may not go. A plethora of principles inevitably stakes out competing sovereignties whose jurisdictions can only be violated at great peril. The principle of having opposing principles is the worst of all hypocrisies: a declaration of war under protestations of peace, viciousness parading as virtue.

Compromise, of course, can also be a curse. If everything is bargainable, including basic liberties, no one would feel safe and, indeed, no one would be. Similarly, if candidates care everything about winning and nothing about how they win, if they are not restrained by internal norms or enforceable external expectations, elections would become outrages.

Without the desire to win elections, not at any cost but as a leading motive, however, there is no reason for politicians to pay attention to people. Winning, moreover, requires a widespread appeal that cannot be limited to just a narrow segment of the population. Thus the desire to win results in moderation in appeals to diverse groups in the electorate and in efforts to bring many varied interests together. This is why we prefer politicians to purists and parties of intermediation to parties of advocacy.

Despite significant changes in recent years leading to advocacy as a central activity of the most active participants in presidential election politics, it remains uncertain whether this tendency has as yet become firmly rooted in the orientations of ordinary citizens toward politics or in their voting habits. Politics is contingent; events that have every right to occur, as it were, may be forestalled by others no one can predict. Who, from the campaign and platform of 1932, could have foretold what Franklin D. Roosevelt would become? Who today can guess what the election of a popular president would do for the Democrats or four more years of Gerald Ford would do for the Republicans? By then, trends that appear irresistible to us now may fade away like the snows of yesteryear.

Because so many of the rules of presidential election politics are changing, it is impossible for us to say with a high degree of assurance how parties, candidates, and voters will adapt to the new incentives and disabilities that have been enacted into law. We are confident only in asserting that adaptations they—and we—make will be of enormous consequence in determining the ultimate capacity of the American political system to sustain the fascinating and noble experiment in self-government begun two hundred years ago.

Notes

1. This parallels in many respects an argument to be found in Robert A. Dahl, *A Preface to Democratic Theory* (Chicago, 1956).

2. Campbell, Converse, Miller, and Stokes, *The American Voter*, pp. 525–27.

3. Richard A. Brody and Benjamin I. Page, "Policy Voting and the Electoral Process: The Vietnam War Issue," *American Political Science Review* 66 (September 1972), p. 979.

4. An excellent popular treatment of this set of alternatives is contained in Richard Fryklund, *100 Million Lives* (New York, 1962).

5. See Dahl, *A Preface to Democratic Theory*, pp. 124–31.

6. See Jack Dennis, "Trends in Public Support for the American Political Party System," *British Journal of Political Science* 5 (April 1975), pp. 187–230.

Index

INDEX

329.00973
P778

100784

329.00973
P778

POLSBY & WILDAUSKY
STRATGIES OF AMERICAN

100784

DEMCO